"This book introduces an innovative method of integrating psychological type preferences into theory-driven case conceptualization. Gerrard and Shinefield's *Psychological Type Relationship Scale (PTRS)* and the *Psychological Type Relationship Inventory (PTRI)* are useful tools for facilitating meaningful conversations about how psychological type characteristics can be expressed differently within different relationships and settings. The authors also stress the importance of therapists being able to help clients identify not only the strengths of their psychological type characteristics, but also the challenges that each type may experience. I appreciate the examples of possible challenges and concrete suggestions for helping clients develop all of their psychological type characteristics. In addition, the authors' *Therapist Type Inventory* encourages therapists to examine how their own psychological types may impact how they work with clients, and is an excellent tool for stimulating therapists' self-reflection."

— **Carol E. Buchholz Holland, PhD,** *associate professor and school counseling coordinator, Counselor Education Program, North Dakota State University*

"This book is an excellent example of a well-written "How To" text on the exploration and utilization of Psychological Type in expanding the range of abilities and behaviors of all humans, regardless of type. Its inclusion of the importance of context in the development and expression of psychological type is a novel and useful way of integrating psychological type into diverse forms of therapeutic theory and technique. I especially appreciate the detailed description of its use in family therapy work in both theory and practice, and the case studies that are included are wonderful examples to learn from. This is a vital addition to any therapist's essential reading list, regardless of their theoretical orientation."

— **Michael J. Carter, PhD,** *coordinator, School-Based Family Counseling Graduate Program; director, School-Based Family Counseling Clinic, California State University, Los Angeles*

"An original and valuable contribution to applying psychological type theory in its MBTI sense. In particular, the authors treat type development as central and draw on their extensive experience of diverse approaches to counselling and psychotherapy."

— **Rowan Bayne,** *emeritus professor of Psychology and Counselling, University of East London, UK*

"The authors illuminate the keys to success with various forms of relationship therapy through the lens of psychological types. This is a guide for every therapist on how to match a particular therapeutic

course of action with the client's personality style. The authors use clinical examples to explain why a particular regimen is more likely to have success for a particular client. Additionally, the clinician is challenged to develop their own personality characteristics to better implement the therapy regimen. I highly recommend this book to enhance the quality of any therapeutic relationship."
— **Ernest Brown, PhD,** *senior case manager, Richmond Area Multi-Services, School Based/Juvenile Justice Involved Wellness, San Francisco, California*

"Much has been written about psychological type, however few books explore how this might be integrated into practice. In this book, the authors provide an overview of psychological type and assessment providing mental health practitioners a sound, evidence-based foundation to explore the use of psychological type in working with clients. The strength of this book is the focus on how we might use psychological type to help strengthen the development of personality qualities with our clients. The authors explore practice frameworks based on Cognitive-Behavioral Therapy, Humanistic Therapy, and Family therapy to provide methods for integrating psychological type into our work. This practice manual is essential reading for both beginning and advanced practitioners alike."
— **Robyne Le Brocque, PhD,** *honorary senior lecturer, School of Nursing, Midwifery, and Social Work, The University of Queensland, Brisbane, Queensland, Australia*

"*Psychological Type Therapy* is a gift to all therapists which surely can enrich our understanding of Jung's concept of psychological type and also provide us one more useful therapeutic intervention that can be applied to a wide range of potential users. What I like most is that this book provides a *Psychological Type Relationship Inventory* to help us collect information about our relationship with a specific person. Moreover, there are chapters elaborating strategies for developing the different dimensions of our personality type. This is a great tool for any person that would like to apply Psychological Type Theory in their clinical practice."
— **Dr. Yeung Ka Ching,** *principal lecturer, director of Solution-Focused Therapy Training Center, Department of Social Work and Social Administration, University of Hong Kong*

The stigma surrounding mental health has made it challenging to discuss personality traits and their ensuing impact on interpersonal relationships. Gerrard and Shinefield present evidence based strategies that demystify and destigmatize conversations on personality,

while providing tools to develop one's personality characteristics. This creates opportunities to enter into conversation about personality in a way that is non-pathological, by focusing on a strength-based model, which is in itself empowering, while still not ignoring possible challenges. I am excited to incorporate the lessons of Psychological Type Therapy in my daily clinical practice.
— **Daniel Emina, MD,** *child, adolescent, & adult psychiatrist, associate medical director, Amen Clinics Inc.*

Psychological Type Therapy

This book uses psychological type as a model for organizing mental health interventions, including assessing how a client's personality is affected within a specific relationship using the Psychological Type Relationship Inventory and the Psychological Type Relationship Scale.

By examining each psychological type characteristic, the book demonstrates how to help a client overcome a psychological type challenge by using techniques drawn from cognitive-behavioral, humanistic, and family therapy approaches. Over 20 techniques are described in explicit how-to format and chapters show the reader how to assess both positive personality characteristics as well as negative or challenging personality characteristics in developing therapy plans.

The interdisciplinary nature of the text benefits a wide spectrum of mental health practitioners who are interested in incorporating personality into their case conceptualizations to develop more effective interventions in relationship therapy.

Brian A. Gerrard, PhD, is chief academic officer, Western Institute for Social Research; chair, Institute for School-Based Family Counseling; emeritus faculty, Counseling Psychology Department, University of San Francisco.

Jacqueline M. Shinefield, EdD, is a licensed marriage and family therapist specializing in individual, couples, and family therapy with a private practice in New York City.

Psychological Type Therapy
A Practitioner's Guide to Strengthening Relationships

Brian A. Gerrard and
Jacqueline M. Shinefield

Cover image: © Getty Images

First published 2022
by Routledge
605 Third Avenue, New York, NY 10158

and by Routledge
2 Park Square, Milton Park, Abingdon, Oxon, OX14 4RN

Routledge is an imprint of the Taylor & Francis Group, an informa business

© 2022 Brian A. Gerrard and Jacqueline M. Shinefield

The right of Brian A. Gerrard and Jacqueline M. Shinefield to be identified as authors of this work has been asserted in accordance with sections 77 and 78 of the Copyright, Designs and Patents Act 1988.

All rights reserved. No part of this book may be reprinted or reproduced or utilized in any form or by any electronic, mechanical, or other means, now known or hereafter invented, including photocopying and recording, or in any information storage or retrieval system, without permission in writing from the publishers.

Trademark notice: Product or corporate names may be trademarks or registered trademarks, and are used only for identification and explanation without intent to infringe.

Library of Congress Cataloguing-in-Publication Data
A catalog record for this title has been requested

ISBN: 978-0-367-56289-2 (hbk)
ISBN: 978-0-367-56288-5 (pbk)
ISBN: 978-1-003-09716-7 (ebk)

DOI: 10.4324/9781003097167

Typeset in Times New Roman
by MPS Limited, Dehradun

To Emily S. Girault, PhD (INFP) who brought us the gift of Psychological Type

Contents

List of Illustrations — xv
About the Authors — xviii
Acknowledgments — xx
Foreword — xxi
How to Use This Book — xxv

1 An Overview of Psychological Type — 1
 Introduction to Psychological Type 1
 The Meaning of Balance on a Type Pair 3
 A Caution in Using Four Letter Type Descriptions 4
 The Four Temperaments 7
 Strengths of the Psychological Type Approach to Personality 8
 Resistance to Using Psychological Type 14
 Traditional Approaches to Assessing Psychological Type 15
 How to Develop Skill in Psychological Type Identification 16

2 Principles of Psychological Type Development — 22
 A Definition of Psychological Type Development 22
 The Challenge Side of Psychological Type 24
 The Identification of Type Strengths and Type Challenges 25
 Relationship-Specific Type Assessment: The Influence of Context on the Expression of Psychological Type 35
 Inventory Assessment of Psychological Type is Not Sufficient 38

xii Contents

3 Psychological Type Development Using Talking in Type   40
 A Six Step Approach to Teach Clients Talking in Type 40
  Step 1: Assess Client Motivation 40
  Step 2: Teach Psychological Type 41
  Step 3: Assess Relationship Type 41
  Step 4: Discuss Type Strengths and Challenges 44
  Step 5: Discuss Talking in Type 45
  Step 6: Obtain a Commitment 47
  Talking in Type with the Non-Psychologically Minded 47
  Overview of Strategies for Strengthening Psychological Type (Chapters 4–11) 50

4 Strategies for Strengthening Extraversion   53
 Challenges of Underdeveloped Extraversion 53
 Ways to Strengthen Extraversion 53
  Cognitive-Behavioral Therapy Strategies: Systematic Desensitization and In Vivo Desensitization 53
  Humanistic Therapy Strategies: Narrative Therapy 62
  Family Therapy Strategies: Staging an Enactment and Blocking Directives 68

5 Strategies for Strengthening Introversion   73
 Challenges of Underdeveloped Introversion 73
 Ways to Strengthen Introversion 73
  Cognitive-Behavioral Therapy Strategies: The Two-Question Rule and Group Social Skills Training 73
  Humanistic Therapy Strategies: Active Listening 77
  Family Therapy Strategies: Unbalancing and the Talking Stick Exercise 81

6 Strategies for Strengthening Sensing   87
 Challenges of Underdeveloped Sensing 87
 Ways to Strengthen Sensing 87
  Cognitive-Behavioral Therapy Strategies: Charting and Positive Reinforcement 87
  Humanistic Therapy Strategies: Multimodal Assessment 93
  Family Therapy Strategies: Caring Days 100

7 Strategies for Strengthening Intuition   104
 Challenges of Underdeveloped Intuition 104
 Ways to Strengthen Intuition 104
  Cognitive Behavioral Therapy Strategies: Cognitive Restructuring 104

*Humanistic Therapy Strategies: Imagery Meditation
and Guided Visualization 112
Family Therapy Strategies: Method III Problem
Solving 116*

8 Strategies for Developing Thinking 122
*Challenges of Underdeveloped Thinking 122
Ways to Strengthen Thinking 122
   Cognitive-Behavioral Therapy Strategies: Assertion
     Training and Behavior Rehearsal 122
   Humanistic Therapy Strategies: Empty Chair
     Technique 130
   Family Therapy Strategies: Unbalancing 134*

9 Strategies for Strengthening Feeling 138
*Challenges of Underdeveloped Feeling 138
Ways to Strengthen Feeling 138
   Cognitive Behavioral Therapy Strategies: Ordeal
     Therapy 138
   Humanistic Therapy Strategies: Doubling 143
   Family Therapy Strategies: Intentional Dialog 147*

10 Strategies for Strengthening Judging 154
*Challenges of Underdeveloped Judging 154
   Ways of Strengthening Judging 154
   Cognitive Behavioral Therapy Strategies: Decision
     Grid 154
   Humanistic Therapy Strategies: Paradoxical
     Intention 161
   Family Therapy Strategies: Contracting, Ignoring, and
     Positive Reinforcement 164*

11 Strategies for Strengthening Perceiving 170
*Challenges of Underdeveloped Perceiving 170
   Cognitive-Behavioral Therapy Strategies: Decision
     Grid 170
   Humanistic Therapy Strategies: The Miracle Question 175
   Family Therapy Strategies: Family Sculpting 179*

12 Strategies for Using Type Development With Children and Adolescents 187
*Introduction 187
   Assessment of Children's and Adolescents' Type 187*

Extraversion – Introversion in Children 188
Sensing – Intuition in Children 190
Thinking – Feeling in Children 191
Judging-Perceiving in Children 192
The Importance of Adult Type in Relating to Children 193
Recognizing Psychological Type in Children 194
Utilizing Personality Type in Clinical Practice With
  Children and Adolescents 194
Strategies for Strengthening the Type Characteristics 198
Stretching Personality Types in Children 198
Stretching the 16 Types 201
How to Help Educators Use Psychological Type
  With Students 201

13 Detailed Case Studies in Psychological Type Development — 209
The Boy in the Middle Trying to Grow Up 209
  Background 209
  Use of Psychological Type With a Cancer Patient 216
  The Concept of Challenge in Psychological Type 221
  Psychological Type and Discrimination 223
  Psychological Type and the Individual Discriminated
    Against 225
  Psychological Type and the Individual Who
    Discriminates 227
  Psychological Type and the Administrator's Role in
    Preventing Discrimination 227
  Case Study: The Professor Who Would Not See 228
  Discussion 231

14 The Importance of Therapist Type Development — 234
Evidence-Based Support for Therapist Psychological Type 234
  Consequences of Therapists Not Demonstrating Type
    Development 236
  The Therapist Type Inventory 238
  Strategies for Promoting Therapist Type Development 242

Appendix 1: Psychological Type Sorter — 245
Appendix 2: The Psychological Type Dictionary:
  A Computer Content Analysis Approach to
    Measuring Psychological Type Themes in Text — 249
Appendix 3: PTRI Case Example — 255
Appendix 4: Psychological Type Map — 264
Index — 265

Illustrations

Tables

1.1	The 16 Psychological Types	5
1.2	Example of How Preference for INFJ May Vary	6
1.3	Example of How ESTJ Preference May Vary	6
1.4	MBTI Scores for Psychotherapists (Levin, 1978)	7
1.5	The Four Temperaments	8
1.6	DSM Personality Disorders	8
1.7	Comparison of the DSM, Big Five, and Psychological Type Personality Systems	14
2.1	Common Type Strengths and Challenges	23
2.2	Examples of Psychological Type Development	23
2.3	PTRI Test-Retest Reliability (Pearson Correlation Coefficients)	25
3.1	The Client Readiness for Change Model	41
3.2	Suggestions for Talking in Type	48
4.1	In Vivo Desensitization Hierarchy of Homework Activities for Promoting Extraversion in Dealing with Parties	54
6.1	BASIC ID Assessment Questions	94
6.2	Caring Days List for Reji and Benjamin	102
7.1	Common Dysfunctional Beliefs	105
7.2	The ABCDE's of Behavior	106
7.3	Disputational Strategies	106
7.4	Step 2 Marcus' and Alain's Brainstormed Solutions	119
7.5	Step 3 Marcus' and Alain's Evaluation of Brainstormed Solutions	120
10.1	The Decision Grid	155
10.2	Example of a Completed Decision Grid	157
10.3	The Decision Grid for Kaycee	161
11.1	Decision Grid for Carlos (Car Situation)	173
11.2	Decision Grid for Carlos (Broken Window Situation)	174

xvi *Illustrations*

13.1	The Psychological Type Preferences with Examples of Strengths and Challenges	222
13.2	Examples of Psychological Type Strengths and Challenges Experienced by Administrators and Employees in Dealing with Discrimination	224
13.3	Examples of Type-Based Interventions by Administrators with Employees Who Discriminate	226
15.1	Psychological Type Sorter Headings	245
15.2	Psychological Type Sorter Words	246
16.1	Words and Phrases that Indicate Psychological Type Themes	250

Figures

1.1	The Eight Psychological Type Categories	2
2.1	Psychological Type Relationship Inventory (PTRI)	26
2.2	Psychological Type Relationship Inventory (PTRI) Self Rating	27
2.3	Psychological Type Relationship Inventory (PTRI) Other Rating	29
2.4	Scoring Sheets for Psychological Type Relationship Inventory	31
2.5	Psychological Type Relationship Inventory: Summary Scale	33
2.6	PTRI Bar Graphs for Strengths and Challenges	34
2.7	Comparison of PTRS Scores for Alexis with Three Different Persons	36
3.1	PTRI Bar Graphs for Strengths and Challenges	42
3.2	Overview of Strategies for Strengthening Underdeveloped Psychological Type Characteristics	50
6.1	Example of Form for Charting	90
6.2	Initial BASIC ID Sequence for Benjamin	97
6.3	Complete BASIC ID Sequence for Benjamin	99
7.1	The ABCDE Chart	107
7.2	The ABCDE Chart: Example	108
7.3	Marcus' ABCDE Chart	112
11.1	Current and Ideal Family Sculptures for Casey	183
12.1	Profiles of the 16 Psychological Types for Children and Adolescents	195
12.2	Strategies for Developing Children's Opposing Type	202
13.1	Psychological Type Map for Charlie's Family	214
13.2	Psychological Type Map for Patty's Family	219
13.3	Psychological Type Map for Beth and Nathan	232
16.1	Computer Content Analysis Flow Chart	251

16.2	Psychological Type Dictionary Analysis of an INFP Profile	252
16.3	Bar Chart for INFP Scores in Figure 16.2	253

Boxes

4.1	Steps for Implementing Systematic Desensitization	55
4.2	Interview Guide for Narrative Therapy	63
4.3	Five Additional Ways to Strengthen Extraversion	72
5.1	Five Additional Ways to Strengthen Introversion	85
6.1	Example of Charting for Benjamin	91
6.2	Five Additional Ways to Strengthen Sensing	103
7.1	Five Additional Ways to Strengthen Intuition	120
8.1	How to Make a DESC Confrontation	124
8.2	DESC Confrontation Form	125
8.3	DESC Confrontation Form for Camila	127
8.4	Five Additional Ways to Strengthen Thinking	137
9.1	Positive Ordeal Behavior Change Contract Between Vladimir and Thomba	142
9.2	Five Additional Ways to Strengthen Feeling	153
10.1	Behavior Modification Contract for Kaycee	167
10.2	Five Additional Ways to Develop Judging	169
11.1	Judy's Miracle Question Note for Carlos	178
11.2	Five Additional Ways to Strengthen Perceiving	186
12.1	Characteristics of Extraversion and Introversion in Children and Adolescents	190
12.2	Characteristics of Sensing and Intuition in Children and Adolescents	191
12.3	Characteristics of Thinking and Feeling in Children and Adolescents	192
12.4	Characteristics of Judging and Perceiving in Children and Adolescents	193
12.5	Suggestions for Parents for Talking in Type	197
12.6	Suggestions for Stretching Type to Opposites	203
12.7	Personality Type Reminders for Parents	204
12.8	Common Educator Temperaments and How It Affects Their Teaching	204
12.9	Suggestions for Teachers for Educating by Type	205
14.1	Research on Mental Health Practitioner Psychological Type	235

About the Authors

Brian A. Gerrard has a PhD in Sociology from the University of New South Wales, Sydney, Australia and a PhD in Counseling Psychology from the University of Toronto. He holds teaching awards from two universities. He has extensive experience teaching a wide variety of Master's and Doctoral level courses in counselor education. Dr. Gerrard is an emeritus faculty member of the University of San Francisco where he developed the masters MFT program and, for 14 years, served as MFT coordinator. His orientation emphasizes an integration of family systems and problem-solving approaches. He was formerly chair of the USF Counseling Psychology Department. Currently, he is the Chief Administrative Officer and a core faculty member for the Western Institute for Social Research in Berkeley, California. Dr. Gerrard is a member of the Board, Center for Child and Family Development, WISR. The Center, co-founded by Dr. Gerrard, has for years managed the largest longest-running School-Based Family Counseling program of its type in the USA. Its Mission Possible Program has served more than 20,000 children and families in over 70 Bay area schools. Dr. Gerrard is also chair of the Institute for School-Based Family Counseling and director for the Oxford Symposium in School-Based Family Counseling, an international association with members in 20 countries. His most recent book, for which he was senior editor, is School-Based Family Counseling: An Interdisciplinary Practitioner's Guide (Routledge Press, 2019). Dr. Gerrard has an active research project developing a computer content analysis program for measuring psychological type. In 2009 he received the Award for Best Application of Psychological Type from the Journal of Psychological Type for his article A Case Study Suggesting the Use of Psychological Type to Reduce Discrimination in Organizations. He has been teaching psychological type to graduate students for over 35 years.

Jacqueline Shinefield is a Licensed Marriage and Family Therapist specializing in individual, couples and family therapy and maintains a private practice in New York City after relocating from San Francisco. She holds a MA degree in Counseling Psychology with a specialization in

MFT, and an EdD in Counseling Psychology, from the University of San Francisco. In addition, she is a Registered Nurse, in New York State, and is a licensed MFT in New York as well as in California. Dr. Shinefield serves on the faculty of New York University School of Medicine, Department of Child and Adolescent Psychiatry as Clinical Instructor. In addition she has held positions as clinical supervisor for the University of San Francisco Center for Child and Family Development, adjunct faculty member at Mercy College in the Marriage and Family Therapy Master's program, and clinical supervisor at Pace University. Dr. Shinefield specializes in relationship counseling with a cognitive-behavioral and solution-focused approach and enjoys working with individuals, couples, families and children. She has presented at national conferences, and to general audiences, speaking on the topics of psychological type, professional burn-out, school-based family counseling, and stepparenting. She is a board member of the following organizations: The University of San Francisco Center for Child & Family Development (for which she is Chairperson), the Institute for School-Based Family Counseling, and the New York City chapter of the New York Association for Marriage and Family Therapy. She is also chair of the Metro Presentation and Training Committee, Metro Chapter of the New York Association for Marriage and Family Therapy. Dr. Shinefield is a fellow of the Oxford Symposium in School-Based Family Counseling and has given numerous lectures at Oxford Symposia held at Brasenose College, Oxford. In 2017 she gave a lecture on "The Use of Psychological Type in School-Based Family Counseling" at the 16th International Symposium in School-Based Family Counseling held at Venice International University. She has been teaching psychological type for over 20 years.

Acknowledgments

First, we want to acknowledge our debt to Dr. Emily S. Girault, Emerita faculty member in the Counseling Psychology Department at the University of San Francisco. It was Emily who taught us psychological type and it is to her this book is dedicated.

Second we want to thank our family members who supported us in our late night vigils writing and editing.

Brian: with deep appreciation to my wife Olive Powell who patiently reviewed my chapters.

Jackie: This has been a joyful adventure. I am grateful to my loving family, friends and colleagues for their binding ties of support and understanding. Seeing the positive relational results by including Personality Type into Family Therapy practice continues to be inspirational as it sees the best in human nature and the capacity for change and acceptance.

Foreword

Ralph S. Cohen

Why Look at Psychological Type?

I am pleased to be invited to write this forward with the rare privilege of having intimate exposure to the Myers Briggs Type Indicator (MBTI) years ago as a graduate student by one of the leading experts of the MBTI at the time (Allen Hammer). I was doing an internship at the Student Counseling Center at Washington University at Saint Louis in the mid-1980s, where Dr. Hammer was on the staff, conducting extensive research on the instrument. At that time, he was doing research on the use of the MBTI as a tool to teach dormitory personnel how to relate to their residents in regard to managing conflict, problem solving, and understanding differences among roommates. I was involved in the training program as well as scoring many hundreds of tests by hand with a physical template. Dr. Allen was also involved in studying the predictability of the MBTI in career counseling and development. For me, this exposure as a young clinical psychology graduate student to the MFTI and psychological type was formative – it brought into awareness the importance of understanding my clients through a dispositional preference lens. I was also in training as a family therapist at the time, and the implications for using this lens to examine how family members relate (or not) to each other was very clear.

Much of what I do in the therapy room is informed by my understanding of personality styles. In a recent family therapy session I conducted with a family consisting two parents and their two young adult daughters (aged 18 and 21) it was apparent that the older daughter's psychological type was very much different from the other three, who had more in common in how they perceived and operate in the world. The older daughter complained that her family did not understand nor appreciate her, and her parents complained that she was not communicating clearly to them and they could not "read" her. The younger sister took the "high road" and kept out of the middle of conflicts between her sister and her parents (although her "neutrality" was actually a tacit agreement with her parents). At one point, they talked about how in their family, they had two dogs and a cat and how they were very different – yet they seemed to develop a mutual understanding how to co-exist and even bond with each other. I asked the question, "How can a family of three "dogs" and one "cat" learn to understand each other's languages?" This analogy shifted the frame of polarization to one of becoming curious and interested in relating to each other in a different way.

In the 20th Century, there was much interest in a dispositional or "trait" approach in the study of personality. The MBTI is based on the work of Carl Jung and his theory of Archetypes. A major implication of his theory is that "personality" is not a unified construct, but rather, consists of a multiplicity of many dimensions that interplay to form a matrix of experience of thoughts, feelings, and behaviors that provides a unique signature of how we perceive ourselves and how others perceive us. There are many examples of dispositional multiplicity models to explain human behavior. For example, Robert Assagioli's Psychosynthesis model postulated that we contain many unique subpersonalities that carry various characteristics and dispositions (Assagioli, 1965). Harry Stack Sullivan advanced his Interpersonal Theory of Psychiatry (1953; Evans, 1996), further refined by Timothy Leary (1957). Based on Sullivan's work, Leary created a circumplex model of personality on two polar dimensions: Friendly-Hostile and Dominant-Submissive, leading to 16 combinations of characteristics based on a quadratic formula. Leary's development of Sullivan's ideas became one of the most widely-researched constructs at the time. A major development of this research was to be able to predict how family members would be expected to relate to one another based on their personality differences. Other such schemas that emerged during this time include R.D. Laing's theory of the Divided Self, Eric Berne's Transactional Analysis, and Fritz Perl's Gestalt therapy (1969). Most recently, Richard Schwartz developed the Internal Family Systems model, which subscribes to the multiplicity concept and applies family systems principles to understanding the interplay among a person's Self and subpersonalities. These models all pointed to implications of how personality plays a significant role in understanding interpersonal relationships.

Since the late 1970s, there has been a shift in Psychology toward an individual-oriented cognitive-behavioral approach to understanding thoughts, feelings and behavior, leading to techniques of re-conditioning people to change their beliefs from "irrational" to "rational" and to encourage new behaviors around which belief about experience could be modified (Beck, et. al., 1979). This has become the dominant model in psychotherapy due to the extensive laboratory research and available funding of such research in a world of "evidence-based practice." The authors of this book make a case for an alternative means of legitimizing methods of therapy (and other endeavors, such as in education) – "Practice-based Evidence," which allows for the demonstration of outcomes based on "local" factors, such as practice and experience of the practitioner and native knowledge of the population being served. This approach provides for flexibility and complexity of an approach while still demanding accountability of the outcomes. In this "evidence-based world," such an alternative approach reclaims space in the psychotherapy field to reconsider models that acknowledge a greater complexity in understanding the human mind and its connection to relationships.

The authors make a case for a relational approach to how Psychological Type can inform us as to how people organize their relationships – casual friendships, work relationships, family relationships and intimate relationships. The idea of relating from Psychological Type to find balance in relationships, as well as being attracted to like-minded types correspond to well-established patterns of attraction and liking described by social psychologists (i.e., "Opposites attract" and "Birds of a feather flock together").

The authors also offer a perspective of using Psychological Type in psychotherapy that elegantly "connects the dots" with dealing with relationship problems that often stem from a misunderstanding of differences. Their psychoeducational approach, coupled with a family systems perspective, helps people who are struggling with feeling disconnected and alienated from their significant others who hold psychological type preferences different from their own to be able to reframe such differences as non-malevolent and more positive, as the example above illustrates. Such reframes open up doors to viewing others' differences as strengths and even as opportunities to find more balance in their relationships.

An important premise of this book is that there is plasticity of type preferences – Psychological Type represents "preferences" and modes of relating based on idiosyncratic patterns, as opposed to fixed traits or characteristics of the personality. The authors demonstrate that people can learn to increase their range of functioning along the four dimensions of Psychological Type theory. The bulk of the book is spent describing therapeutic and educational techniques for strengthening the less exercised side of each of the four type categories (i.e., Introversion-Extroversion, Intuition-Sensing, Thinking-Feeling, and Perceiving-Judging). The authors systematically look at effective techniques to promote each of the eight preferences, utilizing a variety of techniques borrowed from the most widely-used therapeutic approaches (including both CBT and family systems approaches). They bring their descriptions to life with generous descriptions, case examples, and exercises. With this approach, "diagnosis" moves away from describing "psychopathology" to "normalizing differences" and understanding behavior in context.

In my estimation, Psychological Type Therapy: A Practitioner's Guide to Strengthening Relationships provides therapists with some important conceptual tools and skills that will enhance their understanding of how relational breeches occur through misunderstanding and how repair can be made on multiple levels of systems; Individuals can learn to recognize where their preferences can be expanded to make room for a greater range of relating to significant people in their lives and differences can be recognized as strengths that allow for greater mutuality and satisfaction in their relationships. With a combination of academic rigor and straightforward and practical clinical advice, this book is a great manual for bringing the "personality dimension" back into psychotherapy and family therapy in a contemporary and relevant way.

Ralph S. Cohen, PhD
professor of Marriage and Family Therapy
Central Connecticut State University

References

Assagioli, Robert (1965). *Psychosynthesis*. New York: Hobs & Dorman.

Beck, Aaron T., Bush, A. John, Shaw, Brian E., and Emory, Gary (1979). *Cognitive Therapy of Depression*. New York: The Guilford Press.

Berne, Eric (1964). *Games People Play: The Basic Handbook of Transactional Analysis*, New York: Ballantine Books.

Evans, F. Barton III (1996). *Harry Stack Sullivan: Interpersonal Theory and Psychotherapy*. New York: Routledge.

Laing, R. D. (1959). *The Divided Self*. London: The Tavistock Press.

Leary, Timothy (1957). *The Interpersonal Diagnosis of Personality*. New York: Ronald Press.

Perls, Frederick (1969). *Gestalt Therapy Verbatim*. Gouldsboro, ME: Gestalt Therapy Press.

Schwartz, Richard C. (1995). *Internal Family Systems Therapy*. New York: The Guilford Press.

Sullivan, Harry S. (1953). *The Interpersonal Theory of Psychiatry*. New York: W.W. Norton.

How to Use This Book

This book is intended as a guide for mental health practitioners who are interested in incorporating personality into their case conceptualizations in order to develop more effective interventions in relationship therapy. The case conceptualization includes an assessment of a client's symptoms, the precipitating factors, the interpersonal systems of which she/he is part (family, school, work organization, peer group, community), cultural variables, and the client's unique personality. The incorporation of personality into case planning and intervention is still relatively new and not routinely practiced by therapists.

Much of the evidence-based research in psychotherapy that emerged in the 1970s through to present day was stimulated by the "specificity question" posed by Gordon L. Paul in 1967:

> What treatment, by whom, is most effective for this individual, with that specific problem, and under which set of circumstances? (Paul, 1967, p. 114)

In Paul's statement, personality is covered in the reference to "this individual." In addition, a case can easily be made that Paul's reference to "which set of circumstances" includes circumstances involving different persons (i.e., different personalities).

Sperry, in the book *Highly Effective Therapy* makes the following statements describing the most effective approach to mental health assessment and intervention:

> The assessment is centered on the client's personality dynamics and patterns because therapists recognize that they treat persons with diagnoses and not just diagnoses (Sperry, 2021, p. 12).

> First-order change efforts can create stability, i.e., resolve symptoms or relational conflicts and/or return to baseline functioning, but does not address causes underlying the problem. In contrast, second-order change transforms the first-order solutions with sufficient personality

and pattern change that results in resolution of the cause of the presenting problem. (Sperry, 2021, p. 6)

In short, Sperry is making a case for personality assessment as a fundamental part of case conceptualization. In addition, he is making a case that personality change is essential for second-order change.

Personality comes to bear on the effectiveness of mental health intervention in a number of ways. For example, clients who are strongly introverted may decline participating in group therapy if they are particularly shy about dealing with groups. Such a client initially is likely to prefer attending individual counseling/therapy. Similarly, mental health practitioners who are introverts may have a strong preference for providing individual therapy because they feel less comfortable working with families or groups. Clients who are extraverts are more likely to talk a lot in therapy sessions and may enjoy being in group therapy. Therapists who are strongly extraverted may prefer to talk a lot when providing therapy and end up puzzled when an introverted client who wants to be listened to doesn't return for therapy.

Bayne (1997) describes type theory as having four advantages applied to counseling:

They are that type can:

1. help counselors understand, empathize with and accept clients whose personalities are very different from their own. This potential for quicker and deeper understanding and rapport is particularly important in brief counseling. Type can also encourage recognition and use of clients' strengths, easily overlooked when concentrating on problems, and, similarly, be useful as a framework for giving feedback to counselors on their counseling;
2. suggest which forms of counseling and which strategies are most likely to be effective with clients of a particular type and those that are less likely…
3. explain, in part, counsellors' choice of theoretical orientation;
4. be a useful perspective on change in clients and on how effective counseling is likely to be with which characteristics and problems (p. 109).

The focus of this book is on how to use psychological type to strengthen relationships. Although an understanding of psychological type will be helpful for clients who have non-relationship problems (e.g., fear of closed spaces, heights, spiders, recovering from addiction, etc.), an understanding of psychological type is particularly useful in relationship therapy where the client is having difficulties with others. Typical relationship therapy challenges include: couple problems, conflict between parents and children, sibling rivalry, difficulties with supervisors, family tensions, challenges with in-laws, disagreements between friends, difficulties making friends, difficulties keeping friends, anxieties about dealing with groups or strangers, etc.

In developing a case conceptualization for a client, we recommend therapists assess: (1) the personality of the client, (2) the personality of the person or persons the client is having difficulty with, (3) the personality demands of the therapy approach, and (4) the therapist's personality. Our belief is that personality matters, that it is important in all four of these domains, and that developing a comprehensive case conceptualization that includes personality assessment improves therapy.

The authors of this book have extensive experience, both in the clinical setting, and in academia, and have experience dealing with a wide variety of interpersonal challenges experienced by clients. We favor an Evidence-Based Practice (EBP) approach and a Practice-Based Evidence (PBE) approach to therapy. The PBE approach, whether used with teachers, physicians, or mental health professionals, may be described as:

> When collecting PBE, in-service and preservice teachers utilize a data-based decision making process to (a) investigate the degree to which a behavioral or pedagogical practice identified in the literature as an EBP produces desirable outcomes given the particular circumstances in the local educational context, or (b) collect data about an experientially-based practice that has little to no established record of validated evidence in the research literature. That is, when employing a PBE approach, data are collected and evaluated by practitioners in real-world settings to not only validate an EBP given the particular circumstances in an educator's classroom but also provide inquiry-based evidence related to an intervention grounded in their professional experience, intuition, or judgment. (Fink Chorzempa, Smith, & Sileo, 2018, p. 83)

In summary, we recommend that therapists use a data-driven approach to therapy and collect information that indicates whether a specific therapy approach is working. There is sufficient research on the effect of client personality in counseling and psychotherapy to justify including personality in case conceptualization. In the absence of extensive research into the use of specific "technique x" with specific "client personality y," it is important that therapists who wish to include client personality as a factor in case planning and intervention use a data-driven Practice-Based Evidence approach to monitor effectiveness.

Our premise, based on our collective 80 years of teaching and providing therapy, is that an understanding of personality as it affects clients and mental health practitioners can significantly improve case conceptualization and the matching of interventions to client situations.

References

Bayne, R. (1997). *The Myers-Briggs Type Indicator: A critical review and practical guide*. Nelson Thornes.

Fink Chorzempa, B., Smith, M. D., & Sileo, J. M. (2018). Practice-based evidence: A model for helping educators make evidence-based decisions. *Teacher Education and Special Education: The Journal of the Teacher Education Division of the Council for Exceptional Children*, 42(1), 82-92. https://doi.org/10.1177/0888406418767254

Paul, G. L. (1967). Strategy of outcome research in psychotherapy. *Journal of Consulting Psychology*, 31(2), 109–118.

Sperry, L. (2021). *Highly effective therapy*. 2nd edition. Routledge.

1 An Overview of Psychological Type

Introduction to Psychological Type

Psychological type is one of the most widely used personality approaches. It is used especially in conjunction with a popular inventory that measures psychological type – the Myers-Briggs Type Indicator (MBTI) – in mental health, educational, and organizational settings to promote insight into how people relate to each other. It is also used as a career development tool to help assess individuals' suitability for different professions.

Psychological type is the approach to personality developed by the psychiatrist Carl Jung. It was described in his 1921 book *Psychologische Typen* and published in English as *Psychological Types* in 1971. Jung described three pairs of core personality dimensions: Introversion-Extraversion, Sensing-Intuition, and Thinking-Feeling. A fourth pair: Judging-Perceiving was later added by Katharine Cook Briggs and her daughter Isabel Briggs Myers who developed a popular inventory for measuring psychological type: The Myers-Briggs Type Indicator (MBTI). These four pairs of personality dimensions are considered basic to psychological type personality assessment (see Figure 1.1). The abbreviation used to represent each personality characteristic is shown in parentheses.

The psychological type characteristics are arranged in pairs. Each pair represents opposite ways of dealing with the world. While each characteristic is present in everyone's personality, Jung believed that there is generally a preference for one personality characteristic over the other. But in dealing with everyday life, there are many situations where each of the psychological type characteristics is needed. We tend to be most effective when we use a personality characteristic that we have developed really well and prefer to use. Extraverts, for example, feel comfortable communicating with strangers and with groups. However, an Extravert who has not developed their Introversion may be challenged by situations in which listening at a deep level is called for. Similarly, an Introvert who is skilled at listening to others, may falter when dealing with a group if they haven't developed their Extraversion side. This speaks to the importance of type development which involves strengthening one's non-preferred personality characteristics.

DOI: 10.4324/9781003097167-1

2 An Overview of Psychological Type

Figure 1.1 The Eight Psychological Type Categories.

Extraversion – Introversion

Extraversion (E) and Introversion (I) are the two most well known personality characteristics. These are the parts of the personality that are used to deal with one's outer and inner worlds. They are referred to as the Attitudes because they reflect one's overall orientation to outer vs. inner world. Extraverts (persons with a strong preference for Extraversion) prefer to focus their attention on the outer world of persons and things. They tend to be outgoing, talkative, enjoy being in groups, and are comfortable in dealing with strangers. They are sometimes challenged when required to listen at a deeper level. Introverts (persons with a strong preference for Introversion) prefer to focus their attention on their inner world of thoughts and feelings. Introverts tend to be quiet, good listeners and thoughtful observers of what goes on around them. They are sometimes challenged when they have to interact with strangers or large groups.

Sensing – Intuition

Sensing (S) and Intuition (N) refer to what Jung described as two opposite ways of perceiving the world. Persons who score high on Sensing collect information about the world using their five physical senses: vision, hearing, smell, touch, and taste. Sensing types are skilled at noticing details and being specific when giving directions. They can be challenged when dealing with situations that require imagination. Persons who score high on Intuition collect information about the world around them by relying on small cues that they typically cannot describe. They often have a sense that something is so, or will happen, and to others it appears they have a "sixth sense." Intuitives are especially skilled at imagining future possibilities. They can be challenged when dealing with practical matters requiring detail. Sensing and Intuition are known as the Perceiving mental functions.

Thinking – Feeling

Jung's original terms for Thinking and Feeling were Thinking Judgment and Feeling Judgment. The word judgment here refers to making a judgment or decision. We have two different ways of judging (making a decision about) the information we have gathered using our perceiving functions. Persons who make decisions on the basis of Thinking make their decisions based on objectivity and rationality. Thinking types are logical, tough-minded and focused on facts. They can be challenged when dealing with other people's feelings. Feeling types make their decisions based on whether the result will be harmonious for all involved. Feeling types are warm, friendly and sensitive to the feelings of others. They can be challenged when people disagree sharply with each other and when conflict occurs in a relationship. Thinking and Feeling are known as the Judging mental functions.

Judging – Perceiving

The Judging-Perceiving pair refer to whether one has a preference for using the Perceiving mental functions or the Judging mental functions. The Perceiving mental functions refer to the Sensing-Intuition pair which are the mental functions used to collect information. The Judging mental functions refer to the Thinking-Feeling pair which are the mental functions used to make decisions. Perceiving types prefer to collect information, consider many alternatives, and avoid hasty decisions. Also, Perceiving types are flexible, good at seeing alternatives and are willing to modify a previously made decision to accommodate new information. They can be challenged when a situation demands an immediate decision. Judging types prefer to have things decided, often quickly, and without endless collection of information. Judging types are decisive, organized, and methodical. They can be challenged when a situation demands flexibility and the need to reverse a decision.

The Meaning of Balance on a Type Pair

In traditional psychological type assessment, individuals receive a four letter assessment that indicates the preferred type characteristic for each pair (E-I, S-N, T-F, J-P). Examples of this are: ESTJ (for Extraversion, Sensing, Thinking, Judging) or INFP (for Introversion, Intuition, Feeling, Perceiving). When a person receives a score of ESTJ this means that they scored higher on E than on I, higher on S than on N, higher on T than on F, and higher on J than on P. The letters are always shown in the same sequence: the Attitudes (E or I) first, the Perceiving mental functions (S or N) second, the Judging mental functions (J or P) third, and the preferred mental function (J or P) fourth. If an individual is balanced on a pair, this is shown as an X or as a split pair (E/I, S/N, T/F, J/P). The four letter classification with a balanced pair on T and F would look like this: ESXJ or INXP (EST/FJ or INT/FP). A client's balance on a type pair can have two possible meanings. The first is that balance represents a strength in that the client is equally good at using both type

4 *An Overview of Psychological Type*

characteristics effectively. The second alternative is that balance represents a challenge because both type characteristics are underdeveloped. In this case the client has difficulty managing when the type characteristics are required in a social situation. In assessing whether a client's balance on a type pair is a strength or a challenge, it is necessary to conduct a detailed invesitgation of the client's relationships and how each type characteristic is used. This is in line with Jung's belief that his psychological type system should not be used to pigeonhole people, but rather be used to develop a deeper understanding of someone's behavior.

A Caution in Using Four Letter Type Descriptions

Generally the four letter combination indicates one's overall preference for using the different parts of one's personality. However, the fact that one may prefer to use Extraversion generally does not mean that one is unskilled at using Introversion. An Extravert who is very talkative and comfortable dealing with strangers and groups may also be skilled at quietly listening when the situation demands it. However, it is also quite possible that if the Extravert has not done type development (developing one's less preferred personality characteristics), they may not be very skilled at listening. To summarize, the four letter type assessment only indicates preference. The opposite type characteristics may or may not be well developed. In determining preference the therapist should conduct a thorough interview and client history and develop a rapport with the client to establish openness, trust and sharing in their relationship.

The letters of the eight psychological type characteristics can be combined into 16 different types. Table 1.1 lists the 16 types along with a brief description of each type.

A common error in using Psychological Type, as measured by the MBTI and other assessment approaches that provide a four letter "diagnosis," is to treat the four letter pattern as an "always." That is, the four letter classification is regarded as the manner that a person responds in *all* situations. There is a situational component to the expression of personality. Even though we may prefer to use certain personality functions most of the time, in reality we will modify the parts of our personality in different contexts. For example, I (BG) score consistently as INFJ on a variety of different type measures. However, in different social situations I show different parts of my personality. For example, when I am teaching a class for the first time and encounter students I have not previously met, I often appear as ESTJ to the class. That is because when in a leader role as a teacher the role demands that I take charge (E), describe in detail the course requirements (SJ) to the course material, and withhold my sense of humor (F) until I know my audience better. After teaching these same students many classes, and becoming more familiar

Table 1.1 The 16 Psychological Types

ESTJ	**ISTJ**	**ENTJ**	**INTJ**
Outgoing	Contemplative	Outgoing	Contemplative
Realistic	Realistic	Imaginative	Imaginative
Logical	Personal	Logical	Logical
Organized	Flexible	Organized	Organized
ESTP	**ISTP**	**ENTP**	**INTP**
Outgoing	Contemplative	Outgoing	Contemplative
Realistic	Realistic	Imaginative	Imaginative
Logical	Logical	Logical	Logical
Flexible	Flexible	Flexible	Flexible
ESFJ	**ISFJ**	**ENFJ**	**INFJ**
Outgoing	Contemplative	Outgoing	Contemplative
Realistic	Realistic	Imaginative	Imaginative
Personal	Personal	Personal	Personal
Organized	Organized	Organized	Organized
ESFP	**ISFP**	**ENFP**	**INFP**
Outgoing	Contemplative	Outgoing	Contemplative
Realistic	Realistic	Imaginative	Imaginative
Personal	Personal	Personal	Personal
Flexible	Flexible	Flexible	Flexible

with them and feeling that I am valued by them as an instructor, I will show my feeling side typically through humor (and appear ESFJ to the class). With a close friend I will appear INFJ, speaking only as much and perhaps less than they (especially if their preference is E). Being very relaxed with a friend I will often show my N side by making imaginative suggestions. When meeting a stranger I generally appear as ISTJ as I say very little and often appear reserved. With my wife I frequently appear as INFP as I am often somewhat disorganized (P) in my relaxed home environment. To summarize, different contexts draw out different parts of our personality. As Jung noted, we need and use all the personality functions at different times. In addition, it is common to score high on three type dimensions, but be balanced on one dimension. I (BG) score consistently high on I, N, and F. I strongly prefer to relate to others using these functions. However, I am basically balanced on J and P and only score slightly higher on J. My type scores generally look like this: I (81%), N (40%), F (60%), J (15 %). This means I have a strong preference for I, a moderate preference for N and F, and a slight preference for J.

Table 1.2 shows the sort of variation in personality expression that someone with a preference for INFJ might have when they only have a slight preference for J.

Table 1.3 shows the sort of variation in personality expression that someone with a preference for ESTJ might have when they only have a slight preference for E and N.

6 An Overview of Psychological Type

Table 1.2 Example of How Preference for INFJ May Vary

ESTJ	**ISTJ**	**ENTJ**	**INTJ**
Outgoing	Contemplative	Outgoing	Contemplative
Realistic	Realistic	Imaginative	Imaginative
Logical	Personal	Logical	Logical
Organized	Flexible	Organized	Organized
ESTP	**ISTP**	**ENTP**	**INTP**
Outgoing	Contemplative	Outgoing	Contemplative
Realistic	Realistic	Imaginative	Imaginative
Logical	Logical	Logical	Logical
Flexible	Flexible	Flexible	Flexible
ESFJ	**ISFJ**	**ENFJ**	**INFJ**
Outgoing	Contemplative	Outgoing	Contemplative
Realistic	Realistic	Imaginative	Imaginative
Personal	Personal	Personal	Personal
Organized	Organized	Organized	Organized
ESFP	**ISFP**	**ENFP**	**INFP**
Outgoing	Contemplative	Outgoing	Contemplative
Realistic	Realistic	Imaginative	Imaginative
Personal	Personal	Personal	Personal
Flexible	Flexible	Flexible	Flexible

Table 1.3 Example of How ESTJ Preference May Vary

ESTJ	**ISTJ**	**ENTJ**	**INTJ**
Outgoing	Contemplative	Outgoing	Contemplative
Realistic	Realistic	Imaginative	Imaginative
Logical	Personal	Logical	Logical
Organized	Flexible	Organized	Organized
ESTP	**ISTP**	**ENTP**	**INTP**
Outgoing	Contemplative	Outgoing	Contemplative
Realistic	Realistic	Imaginative	Imaginative
Logical	Logical	Logical	Logical
Flexible	Flexible	Flexible	Flexible
ESFJ	**ISFJ**	**ENFJ**	**INFJ**
Outgoing	Contemplative	Outgoing	Contemplative
Realistic	Realistic	Imaginative	Imaginative
Personal	Personal	Personal	Personal
Organized	Organized	Organized	Organized
ESFP	**ISFP**	**ENFP**	**INFP**
Outgoing	Contemplative	Outgoing	Contemplative
Realistic	Realistic	Imaginative	Imaginative
Personal	Personal	Personal	Personal
Flexible	Flexible	Flexible	Flexible

Table 1.4 MBTI Scores for Psychotherapists (Levin, 1978)

	N	EI	SN	TF	JP	Comments
Psychotherapists	91	E52	N91	F61	J56	INFP modal
Psychoanalytic	15	I67	N93	F67	J80	INFJ Modal
Rational Emotive	24	E62	N83	T58	J71	ENTJ modal
Gestalt	12	E/I 50	N92	F75	P75	E/INFP modal
Behavioral	15	I53	N87	T60	J53	ENTJ modal
Experiential	25	E56	N96	F84	P56	ENFP modal

Note: Modal = the most frequently occurring type.
E/I = balanced on E and I.

The four letter classification is only a starting point for exploring someone's personality. As Jung said: "My typology is far rather a critical apparatus serving to sort out and organize the welter of empirical material, but not in any sense to stick labels on people at first sight." (p. xiv). Failure of some MBTI researchers to appreciate this point has lead to them using the four letter 16 personality types to calculate reliability. Because most people are balanced on at least one type dimension, when test-retest reliability is calculated the INFJ at pretest becomes an INFP at post-test. This has resulted in low reliability scores and has lead some to describe the MBTI as unreliable and therefore lacking validity.

The correct way to calculate MBTI reliability is to use the continuous scores for each pair: E-I, S-N, T-F, J-P. This produces inter-rater reliability coefficients of .80 overall (see Evidence-Based Support section below). This more appropriate way of calculating type reliability is illustrated by Table 1.4 from Levin's (1978) study of therapist types.

As can be seen in the table, the scores for specific type pairs are more informative than the four letter classification. For example, for psychoanalytic therapists their modal type is INFJ but the percentage scores for N and J are significantly higher than the scores for I and F. This information is missing from the four letter rating. The fact that there is significantly more information in the scores for the type pairs is why test-retest reliability for type assessment instruments (like the MBTI) should be conducted using the type pairs and not the four letter classification.

The Four Temperaments

Persons new to psychological type may find it difficult to discriminate between the 16 types. David Keirsey (1998) developed a description of what he calls the four temperaments which represent four distinct easily recognizable personality types. These are the Artisan (SP), the Idealist (NF), the Guardian (SJ), and the Rational (NT). A brief description of each temperament is shown in Table 1.5.

Table 1.5 The Four Temperaments

Type Combination	Keirsey Label	Values and Characteristics
Sensing-Perceiving (SP)	Artisan	Adventure-seeking, freedom to act, enjoying life, athletic, artistic, easygoing, tolerant, skilled with machines and tools
Sensing-Judging (SJ)	Guardian	Responsible, protective, organized, sensible, dependable, hard-working, conservative, factual, persevering
Intuition-Feeling (NF)	Idealist	Compassionate, friendly, sensitive, harmonious, valuing love and mercy, caring for others, avoiding conflict
Intuition-Thinking (NT)	Rational	Objective, logical, rational, tough-minded, abstract, theoretical, curious, scientific, competent, independent, intellectual

Strengths of the Psychological Type Approach to Personality

The Psychological type approach to personality has several strengths.

Strength-Based

Psychological type is a strength-based model of personality. Jung took the view that all the type characteristics were valuable and needed in different situations. The title of the classic book on psychological type: *Gifts Differing*, Briggs Meyers & B. Myers (1995) reflects this positive view. The type categories are not derogatory and are in stark contrast to the American Psychiatric Association DSM personality labels (see Table 1.6).

Table 1.6 DSM Personality Disorders

Paranoid
Schizoid
Schizotypal
Antisocial
Borderline
Histrionic
Narcissistic
Avoidant
Dependent
Obsessive-Compulsive

The Diagnostic and Statistical Manual of Mental Disorders (DSM) is the most widely used mental health diagnostic system in the world. Consequently its personality classification system is widely used by mental health practitioners. The main problem with the DSM personality classification system is that it is stigmatizing. Few clients would welcome being labeled as Borderline, Antisocial, or Histrionic. Fear of being negatively labeled is a reason why many persons who could benefit from mental health counseling/therapy do not seek it.

Ben-Zeev et al. (2010) state:

> Stigma associated with mental illness has been shown to have devastating effects on the lives of people with psychiatric disorders, their families, and those who care for them ...
>
> Psychiatric disorders have catastrophic effect on the lives of people with these disorders because of their associated distress and disability. Many advocates and scientists also believe the stigma of these disorders wreaks havoc on many lives. Goffman (1963) originally adopted the term stigma from the Greeks who used it to represent bodily signs indicating something bad about the moral character of the bearer marked with the stigma. When applied to individuals with mental illness, this kind of moral imputation has egregious effects on a number of levels, what we have called public stigma, self-stigma, and label avoidance (Corrigan et al., 2004; Corrigan & Watson, 2002) (p. 318).

The advantage of using positive labels for clients' behaviors is that clients become more interested in learning about their personality characteristics and how these characteristics serve them well (or not). For example, consider a client who on the DSM is labeled as having a Dependent Personality Disorder and who is fearful of making decisions on their own. By using a Psychological Type Development (PTD) approach you would first introduce this client to type concepts. Then you would discuss with them the advantages of strengthening their Thinking Judgment in order to become more tough-minded, and thus make firm decisions that others might occasionally disapprove of. DSM deficiency labels can disempower clients and lead them to feel they have a permanent deficiency. The PTD approach emphasizes that challenges can be overcome by working to strengthen different parts of one's personality.

Multiculturally Sensitive

Psychological type is a multiculturally sensitive approach precisely because it avoids the use of deficiency labels. There is research that indicates that clients from minority groups are often more likely to be given a stigmatizing DSM label. Loring and Powell (1988), in a study of 488 psychiatrists applying DSM diagnoses to identical case studies differing only in the client's race and gender, found disproportionate assignment of paranoid schizophrenic disorder to black males and paranoid personality disorder to black females. Loring and Powell (1988) concluded: "Clinicians appear to ascribe violence, suspiciousness, and dangerousness to Black clients even though the case studies are the same as the case studies for the white clients" (p. 20). Neighbors et al. (2003), in their study of the DSM, found "The results are consistent with previous sociological research showing that patient race is related to diagnosis even when standardized diagnostic criteria are used" (p. 237).

The relevance of Psychological type across different cultures is indicated by research summarized in the MBTI® Manual (Myers & McCaulley, 2003):

> While type has not been assessed in all cultural societies, it has been surveyed in about 30 countries on all continents, some with more than one culture. So far, the studies have suggested the following:
>
> - All type preferences (E-I, S-N, T-F, and J-P) appear in all cultures studied to date.
> - People in different cultures report that the descriptions of the individual.
> - Preferences make sense to them. They find value and usefulness in using type concepts in various ways, for example, to improve interactions and communication between diverse individuals and within groups.
> - People in different cultures report that Isabel Myers' original whole type descriptions, or more recent versions, are appropriate and applicable. They react with, "This is me!"
> - Distributions of the sixteen types differ across different cultures.
> - Distribution patterns are similar across all the cultures studied.

In summary, studies to date provide support for the theory that psychological type is universal across cultures.

Evidence-Based Support

Capraro and Capraro (2002) summarize the reliability of the MBTI based on research prior to 1989 as follows:

> Cronbach's alpha was computed for large sample studies collected from the Center for Applications of Psychological Type (CAPT) databank. These scores exhibited reliability coefficients averaging EI = .79, SN = .84, TF = .74, and JP = .82 on more than 32,000 participants and a range of EI = .74 to .83, SN = .74 to .85, TF = .64 to .82, and JP = .78 to .84 on more than 10,000 participants (Myers & McCaulley, 1985). Harvey (1996) conducted a meta-analysis on the studies summarized in the MBTI Manual (Myers & McCaulley, 1985) for which data are given by gender on a sample of 12,174 respondents. This meta-analysis gave corrected split-half estimates on men and women, respectively: EI, .82 and .83; SN, .83 and .85; TF, .82 and .80; JP, .87 and .86. Test-retest reliabilities for MBTI scores suggest score consistency over time. Test-retest coefficients from 1 week to 2.5 year intervals ranged from .93 to .69 on the SN scale, .93 to .75 on the EI scale, .89 to .64 on the JP scale, and .89 to .48 on the TF scale (Myers & McCaulley, 1989). When respondents do show a change in type, it is usually only in one preference and then in scales where they were originally not strongly differentiated (Myers & McCaulley, 1985, p. 594). Overall, the lowest reliabilities were found in the TF scales.

In their Reliability Generalization study based on 70 studies conducted between 1998 and 2001, Capraro and Capraro (2002) provide the following table summarizing test-retest and split-half reliability for the MBTI.

Myers-Briggs Type Indicator (MBTI) Score Reliability Estimates Across Studies

Reliability	M	SD	Min.	Max.	n
Overall	.815	.086	.480	.970	70
α	.816	.082	.550	.970	50
Test-retest	.813	.098	.480	.910	20
EI	.838	.052	.740	.950	17
SN	.843	.052	.780	.970	17
TF	.764	.122	.480	.970	19
JP	.822	.073	.630	.970	17

Note. EI = Extravert-Introvert, SN = Sensing-Intuitive, TF = Thinking-Feeling, and JP = Judgement-Perception.

To summarize, the MBTI shows moderate to strong reliability for the four psychological type pairs (E-I, S-N, T-F, J-P) which is an important prerequisite for validity. Capraro and Capraro (2002) summarize the evidence for the validity of the MBTI as follows:

> Several researchers have studied the construct validity of the MBTI scores. Carlyn (1977) found evidence indicating that "a wealth of circumstantial evidence has been gathered, and results appear to be quite consistent with Jungian Theory" (p. 469). Validity of MBTI scores is typically established by correlating the scores with findings from various personality instruments and inventories of interest. Statistically significant correlations have been found between MBTI scores, behaviors reflective of MBTI constructs, and persons' self-assessment of their own MBTI type (De Vito, 1985; Myers & McCaulley, 1989). Using factor analysis, Thompson and Borrello (1986) reported that the factors were largely discrete in their sample, and all items had factor pattern coefficients higher than .30. These results supported the structure of the MBTI. More recently, Tischler (1994) noted that "factor analysis provided unusually strong evidence that the MBTI items are correlated with their intended scales: the scales are almost factorially pure" (pp. 30, 594).

Arain (1968) and Carskadon (1979) found that individuals whose preferance was Feeling preferred humanistic and emotionally expressive therapies, whereas individuals who preferred Thinking preferred cognitive or cognitive-behavioral therapies. Levin (1978) administered the MBTI to therapists of different orientations and found significant differences in type preference. The modal type for each therapy approach was: Psychoanalytic (INFJ), Rational Emotive (ENTJ), Gestalt (E/I NFP), Behavioral (ENTJ), Experiential (ENFP). The Project MATCH Research Group (1998) compared therapists trained in twelve-step facilitation, cognitive-behavioral skills training, and motivational enhancement therapy on the MBTI. They found that twelve step facilitation therapists scored significantly higher on Feeling than therapists in the other approaches. The cognitive-behavioral skills therapists scored significantly higher on Thinking than the therapists in the other approaches. Nelson and Stake (1994) examined the relationship between therapist-client match using the MBTI. They concluded that when therapists and clients had more similar type profiles, especially in Thinking-Feeling and Judging-Perceiving, clients rated the quality of the therapy relationship significantly higher. Both clients and therapists rated the therapy relationship very positive when the therapists scored high on Extraversion and Feeling.

There are several studies that suggest psychological type preference influences therapy outcome. Di Loreto (1971) compared the effects of

Client-Centered Therapy, Rational Emotive Therapy, and systematic desensitization on Introverts and Extraverts (based on the MBTI) who were assigned to each treatment condition. Standardized anxiety scales were used to measure outcome. He found that Extraverts showed the most improvement with Client-Centered Therapy. Introverts improved the most with Rational Emotive Therapy. Introverts and Extraverts improved equally well with systematic desensitization. Graff (1976) found that the behavior therapy technique systematic desensitization was more effective for male Thinking types and female Feeling types. Fairbanks (1987) found that relaxation therapy with imagery rehearsal had superior outcomes for clients who preferred Intuition. This is consistent with the preference of Intuitive types to use imagination and be comfortable with unstructured situations. Fairbanks also found relaxation therapy combined with cognitive restructuring had superior outcomes for Sensing types. Cognitive restructuring is a cognitive therapy technique that is very structured. Jinkerson et al. (2015) found that individuals who preferred the Thinking function showed greater benefit from cognitive therapy than individuals who preferred Feeling.

Positive Reframing

An important strength of the psychological type approach is that it can easily be taught to clients. It can also be used to positively reframe negative attributions clients have about others and themselves. For example, the client who complains that a family member is insensitive may be helped to look at the relationship differently by a therapist who explains that the client is a Feeling type and the family member they feel challenged by is a Thinking type. It is in the nature of Thinking types to be direct and sometimes blunt in speech and Feeling types often take the bluntness as rejection which is not the intent of the Thinking type family member. Type language is well suited to reframe negative or pejorative labels which often arise in work and family relationships.

Extensive Self-Help Literature

There are more than 75 books that have been written on psychological type as it applies to adults, children, work, family, school, love relationships, and marriage. The size and variety of PT self help books provides a valuable bibliotherapy resource for clients who are psychologically minded and want to learn more about themselves and how to relate more effectively to others. Information provided by randomized control group studies on the effectiveness of bibliotherapy indicate that self-help books dealing with mental health can often be as effective in promoting change as seeing a therapist.

14 An Overview of Psychological Type

Table 1.7 Comparison of the DSM, Big Five, and Psychological Type Personality Systems

Attribute	DSM	Big Five	Psychological Type
Strength-Based	L	M	H
Multiculturally Sensitive	L	M	H
Evidence-Based Support	L	H	H
Positive Reframing	L	L	H
Self-help Literature	L	L	H

Notes
H = personality system scores High on this attribute.
M = personality system scores Moderate on this attribute.
L = personality system scores Low on this attribute.

Table 1.7 shows a comparison of the three most widely used personality systems: The Diagnostic and Statistical Manual of Mental Disorders (DSM) personality disorders (see Table 1.6 above), the Big Five (Openness to Experience, Conscientiousness, Extraversion, Agreeableness, Neuroticism) and Psychological Type.

Resistance to Using Psychological Type

Despite the many advantages to using psychological type there are mental health professionals who are reluctant to learn or use psychological type. We think there are two main reasons for this:

1. The association with Jungian therapy. Because psychological type was developed by Carl Jung, it is associated with Jungian therapy which is a humanistic approach to psychotherapy and counseling. Many of Jung's ideas about archetypes, dreams, alchemy, astrology, gnosticism, metaphysics, myth, and the paranormal are a definite "turn-off" for 21st century therapists. To the uninitiated, type tables showing the 16 types (using four letter identifiers), look suspiciously like an astrology table.

    However, psychological type, as measured by the MBTI, is one of the most rigorously investigated personality theories with 60 years of research investigating its reliability and validity. In addition, what Jung called the mental functions – Perceiving and Judging – are best described in terms of a problem solving cognitive model. The Perceiving mental function relates to how one collects information (data in) and the Judging mental function relates to how one makes decisions (data out). We contend that this aspect of Jung's work was very much "before its time" and fits in with modern approaches to cognition and problem-solving.

The authors of this book are not Jungian therapists. Actually, we have a leaning towards family systems and Cognitive-Behavioral Therapy (CBT) approaches, which we integrate with a variety of humanistic therapy techniques.

2. Unrefined Use of the four letter Types. This refers to the mistaken use of a type "diagnosis" as an absolute. That is, if one is diagnosed as an ISFJ, this means you always behave as an Introverted Sensing Feeling Judging type in all situations. That, of course, is untrue. Jung was clear on this point when he emphasized that psychological type is about one's preference, and that while we may prefer to act a certain way, social context affects how psychological type is expressed (Jung, 1976, p. 287). The extensive self-help literature on psychological type generally does not present what we call a relationship-specific type assessment approach, which is the approach taken in this book, and is congruent with Jung's writings on psychological type.

To summarize, the two abovementioned reasons for mental health professionals being reluctant to learn or use psychological type are common, but mistaken.

Traditional Approaches to Assessing Psychological Type

Fee Based Assessments

The Myers-Briggs Type Indicator (MBTI)

The MBTI is the most widely used self-report instrument for assessing psychological type. It is available for purchase from The Myers-Briggs Company by: (a) persons who have completed the MBTI® Certification Program or (b) professionals with a master's degree, or higher, in psychology, counseling, organizational development or a related field. Persons not meeting these requirements who wish to take the MBTI can do so online for a fee. The MBTI has been extensively researched and a useful resource summarizing this research is the *Manual: A Guide to the Development and Use of the Myers-Briggs Type Indicator 3rd Edition* (Myers & McCaulley, 2003).

The Murphy-Meisgeier Type Indicator for Children (MMTIC)

The Murphy-Meisgeier Type Indicator for Children is a self-report instrument for assessing the psychological type of children and adolescents. The MMTIC instrument is available for use only by adults who are 21 years of age or older, have a four-year degree from an accredited college or university, and have successfully completed the MMTIC® Certification Program (which may be taken for a fee).

Free Psychological Type Assessments

The Keirsey Temperament Sorter II

The Keirsey Temperament Sorter II (KTS II) is a self report inventory that assesses psychological type and is available in David Keirsey's book: *Please Understand Me* II: *Temperament, Character, Intelligence.* This inventory may be taken online for free (https://profile.keirsey.com/#/b2c/assessment/start). A study that compared the KTS II with the MBTI found moderate to strong positive correlations between the two instruments (Kelly & Jugovic, 2001) which suggests that the KTS II has moderate to strong concurrent validity.

Humanmetrics Jung Typology Test

The Humanmetrics Jung Typology Test is a free self report online inventory that measures the eight psychological type categories and provides a four letter result (http://www.humanmetrics.com/cgi-win/jtypes2.asp).

How to Develop Skill in Psychological Type Identification

We recommend that you develop your skill in identifying psychological type by beginning with:

1. Take one or more of the traditional type measures and see if your scores compare.
2. Examine the 16 types in Table 1.1 and circle the ones that seem to describe you. In addition, what are the types that you consider very opposite to you?
3. Examine the values and characteristics typical of the four Temperaments. Which temperament do you identify with? How does that temperament match up with the type categories you selected in #2 above?
4. Read one or more books on psychological type that have detailed descriptions of the 16 types (see Resources below).

Additionally, it will be helpful in the beginning to try a simple approach to assessing psychological type: The *Psychological Type Relationship Scale* (PTRS). The PTRS was designed for educational purposes. To get a feel for the application of psychological type in relationships try completing it for yourself and someone you get along really well with, and then someone you get along less well with.

An Overview of Psychological Type 17

Psychological Type Relationship Scale

Name_____ Other Person_____ Date_____

Instructions: This inventory is used to examine how you express your personality in relationship to another person. Please show your assessment of how you and the other person generally relate to each other in terms of the 4 pairs of personality characteristics shown below. Brief definitions for each characteristic are shown in italics. Characteristics that are viewed as strengths are shown with a + sign. Characteristics that may be a challenge in the relationship are shown as a - . Using the letter S for yourself, and O for the other person, place these letters on the line joining the characteristics to show your assessment of how you and the other person generally express the characteristic in your relationship with each other.

For example, if you are very extraverted and the other person is very introverted in terms of how you relate to each other, then your ratings might look like this:

EXTRAVERSION   S _____ O   **INTROVERSION**
                   1 2 3 4 5 6 7 8 9 10

Alternatively, if you are slightly introverted, and the other person is slightly extraverted, in terms of how you relate to each other, your rating might look like this:

EXTRAVERSION _____ O _____ S _____ **INTROVERSION**
                  1 2 3 4 5 6 7 8 9 10

Remember, you are not rating how you or the other person relate generally to other persons: you are only rating how the two of you behave in your relationship with each other.

Note: + = Type Characteristic as a strength in the relationship.
      - = Type characteristic as a challenge in the relationship.

+ TALKATIVE + OUTGOING + INITIATING ACTIVITIES **EXTRAVERSION**											+ SEEKING TIME ALONE + THINKING THINGS OVER + CONTEMPLATIVE **INTROVERSION**
- MONOPOLIZING - TALKING LOUDLY - DOMINATING	1	2	3	4	5	6	7	8	9	10	- WITHHOLDING FEELINGS - APPEARING SHY - NOT PARTICIPATING
+ COLLECTING DETAILS + REALISTIC + PRACTICAL **SENSING**											+ SEING THE UNDERLYING ISSUE + SEEING FUTURE POSSIBILITIES + USING IMAGINATION **INTUITION**
-NITPICKING -BEING OVERCAUTIOUS -MISSING UNDERLYING ISSUE	1	2	3	4	5	6	7	8	9	10	- ABSENT-MINDED - MISSING IMPORTANT DETAILS - BEING IMPRACTICAL
+BEING RATIONAL +BEING OBJECTIVE +TOUGHMINDED **THINKING**											+BEING SUPPORTIVE +BEING SYMPATHETIC +HARMONIOUS **FEELING**
-BEING CRITICAL -BEING INSENSITIVE -BEING ARGUMENTATIVE	1	2	3	4	5	6	7	8	9	10	- EASILY HURT - AVOIDING CONFRONTATION - BEING IRRATIONAL
+STICKING WITH A DECISION +METHODICAL +WELL- ORGANIZED **JUDGING**											+OPEN TO ALTERNATIVES +SPONTANEOUS +FLEXIBLE **PERCEIVING**
- BEING RIGID - CLOSED TO ALTERNATIVES - PREMATURE DECISIONS	1	2	3	4	5	6	7	8	9	10	- INDECISIVE - DISORGANIZED - NOT STICKING TO PLANS

Handout 1.1

18   *An Overview of Psychological Type*

A preliminary review of test-retest reliability for the PTRS based on a sample of 24 ratings made two weeks apart showed the following Pearson correlation coefficients: Extraversion/Introversion: r = .74, Sensing/Intuition: r = .57, Thinking/Feeling: r = .65, Judging/Perceiving: r = .75. This suggests moderate reliability. The lower rating for Sensing/Intuition possibly has to do with the fact that Intuition is less observable than the other type characteristics.

This chapter is intended as a basic overview of psychological type. In the next chapter we will present basic principles of type development and how to assess type strengths and challenges within relationships.

Resources

YouTube videos
Gifted Leaders LLC (Nov. 6, 2012). *Extraversion/introversion vignette: Who's who?*
https://www.youtube.com/watch?v=z5JgGTc6tfU
Gifted Leaders LLC (Nov. 6, 2012). *Sensing/intuition vignette: Who's who?*
https://www.youtube.com/watch?v=fbUzpqrqBJc
Gifted Leaders LLC (Nov. 6, 2012). *Thinking/feeling vignette: Who's who?*
https://www.youtube.com/watch?v=zWGXhnlUW_Y
Gifted Leaders LLC (Nov. 6, 2012). *Judging/perceiving vignette: Who's who?*
https://www.youtube.com/watch?v=b_pL-Us_0nA
These four vignettes give a clear picture of the differences between each pair of the eight psychological type characteristics.

Psychological Type Therapy Videos
https://www.youtube.com/channel/UCmKTWZ9ZGR9HezPe7waAoXQ
This Youtube channel contains videos made by Gerrard and Shinefield that complement this Psychological Type Therapy book.

Additional Psychological Type Assessments
The following Psychological Type assessments are new and under development and may be found in the Appendices of this book.

Psychological Type Sorter (Appendix 1)
This instrument uses Q sort methodology to assess an individual's Psychological Type. Briefly, the person taking the PT Sorter places words (typed on individual strips of paper) under categories labelled Very Like Me, Moderately Like Me, Slightly Like me, Slightly Unlike Me, etc. There are four word descriptions for each of the eight Psychological type categories (E-I, S-N, T-F, J-P). The resulting distribution of type words can then be scored to determine the individual's dominant type preference. Research is currently being conducted into the validity and reliability of this instrument.

An Overview of Psychological Type 19

Psychological Type Dictionary (Appendix 2)
The Psychological Type Dictionary (PTD) is a 2000 word computer content analysis dictionary designed for analyzing text for psychological type themes. The PTD is a research tool meant to be used with WORDSTAT and QDA-MINER software which apply the dictionary to relevant text. Research is currently being conducted into the validity of this instrument. A video explaining the PTD may be found on YouTube under the heading: Psychological Type Dictionary Computer Content Analysis https://youtu.be/k4iIm1EJcBE

Bayne, R. (1997). *The Myers-Briggs Type Indicator: A critical review and practical guide*. Nelson Thornes.
Chapter 7: "Type and Counselling" provides a valuable overview of the role of psychological type in facilitating counseling and therapy.
Bayne, R. (2012). *The Counsellor's Guide to Personality: Understanding Preferences, Motives and Life Stories* (Professional Handbooks in Counselling and Psychotherapy). Red Globe Press.
This book provides a comprehensive approach to utilizing psychological type in counseling within the framework of an integrative therapy approach. It contains very practical examples of how to help clients with love, health and work challenges.
Jung, C. (1976). *Psychological types (The collected works of C. G. Jung, vol. 6) (Bollingen series XX)*. Princeton, NJ: Princeton University Press.
This is the book that started it all. In Jung's words: "This work sprang originally from my need to define the ways in which my outlook differed from Freud's and Adler's. In attempting to answer this question, I came across the problem of types; for it is one's psychological type which from the outset determines and limits a person's judgment. My book, therefore, was an effort to deal with the relationship of the individual to the world, to people and things. It discussed the various aspects of consciousness, the various attitudes the conscious mind might take toward the world, and thus constitutes a psychology of consciousness regarded from what might be called a clinical angle."
Myers, I. B. & Myers, P. B. (1995). *Gifts differing*. Palo Alto, CA: Consulting Psychologists Press.
This is the basic text on psychological type. The senior author is one of the developers of the MBTI. The book gives an excellent overview of the type characteristics and includes detailed descriptions of the 16 types and their application in marriage, work, and with children.
Keirsey, D. (1998). *Please understand me II: Temperament, character, intelligence*. Del Mar, CA: Prometheus Nemesis Book Company.
This book contains the Keirsey Temperament Sorter II with scoring instructions. In addition there is an excellent chapter on the 16 types.
Drenth, A. J. (2017). *The 16 personality types: Profiles, theory, & type development*. Bakersfield, CA: A.J. Drenth.
This book provides a detailed examination of the 16 types over the lifespan.
Hass, L. & Hunziker, M. (2014). *Building blocks of personality type: A guide to discovering the hidden secrets of the personality type code*. Pacific Grove, CA: Eltanin Publishing.
The book uses an 8 process model of type and describes in detail Extraverted Sensing, Introverted Sensing, Extraverted Intuiting, Introverted Intuiting, Extraverted Thinking, Introverted Thinking, Extraverted Feeling, Introverted Feeling.

Tieger, P. & Barron-Tieger, B. (1997). *Nurture by nature: Understand your child's personality type - and become a better parent*. New York, NY: Little, Brown, Spark.

If you are a parent this is the book to read. It contains many useful suggestions on how parents can understand and help their children as they progress through each of the three stages of development - preschool, school age and adolescence.

References

Arain, A. A. (1968). *Relationships among counseling clients' personalities, expectations, and problems*. (Doctoral dissertation). Rutgers University.

Ben-Zeev, D., Young, M. & Corrigan, P. (2010). DSM-V and the stigma of mental illness. *Journal of Mental Health, 19*, 318–327. doi: 10.3109/09638237.2010.492484.

Capraro, R. & Capraro, M. (2002). Myers-Briggs Type Indicator score reliability across studies: A meta-analytic reliability generalization study. *Educational and Psychological Measurement, 62*, 590–602.

Carskadon, T. R. (1979). Behavioral differences between Extraverts and Introverts as measured by the Myers-Briggs Type Indicator: An experimental demonstration. *Research in Psychological Type, 2*, 78–82.

Di Loreto, A. (1971). *Comparative psychotherapy: An experimental analysis*. Chicago: Aldine Atherton, Inc.

Fairbanks, W. D. (1978). *A comparison study of two cognitive treatment modalities crossed with selected Myers-Briggs personality typologies in the reduction of anxiety*. (Master's thesis). University of Wyoming.

Frances, A. (2017). Newsflash from APA meeting: DSM-5 has flunked its reliability tests. *Huffpost* 05/08/2012 01:24 pm ET Updated Dec 06, 2017.

Graff, W. S. (1976). The effectiveness of systematic desensitization in the reduction of test anxiety in Jungian thinking versus feeling personality types. *Dissertation Abstracts International, 5944* 36(09).

Jinkerson, J., Masilla, A. & Hawkins II, R. (2015). Can Myers-Briggs dimensions predict therapy outcome? Differences in the Thinking-Feeling function pair in cognitive therapy for depression/anxiety. *Research in Psychotherapy: Psychopathology, Process and Outcome, 18* (1), 21–31.

Jung, C. (1976). *Psychological types (The collected works of C. G. Jung, vol. 6) (Bollingen series XX)*. Princeton University Press.

Kelly, K. R., & Jugovic, H. J. (2001). Concurrent validity of the online version of the Keirsey Temperament Sorter II. *Journal of Career Assessment, 9*(1), 49–59.

Keirsey, D. (1998). *Please understand me II: Temperament, character, intelligence*. Prometheus Nemesis Book Company.

Levin, L. S. (1978). Jungian personality variables of psychotherapists of five different theoretical orientations. (Doctoral dissertation, Georgia State University). *Dissertation Abstracts International, 39*, 4042B–4043-B.

Loring, M. & Powell, B. (1988). Gender race and DSM-III: A study of the objectivity of psychiatric diagnostic behavior. *Journal of Health and Social Behavior, 29* (1), 1–22.

Myers, I. B. & McCaulley, M. (2003). *Manual: A guide to the development and use of the Myers-Briggs Type Indicator* 3rd Edition. Consulting Psychologists Press.

Neighbors, H., Trierweiler, S., Ford, B. & Muroff, J. (2003). Racial differences in DSM diagnosis using a semi-structured instrument: The importance of clinical judgment in the diagnosis of African Americans. *Journal of Health and Social Behavior*, (43), 237–256.

Nelson, B. A., & Stake, J. E. (1994). The Myers-Briggs Type Indicator personality dimensions and perceptions of quality of therapy relationships. *Psychotherapy: Theory, Research, Practice, Training*, *31*(3), 449–455. 10.1037/0033-3204.31.3.449.

Project MATCH Research Group (1998). Therapist effects in three treatments for alcohol problems. *Psychotherapy Research*, *8* (4), 455–474, doi: 10.1080/10503309812331332527.

2 Principles of Psychological Type Development

A DEFINITION OF PSYCHOLOGICAL TYPE DEVELOPMENT

Psychological type development (PTD), also known as type development, refers to strengthening both one's preferred, and non-preferred (sometimes referred to as auxilliary), type characteristics. For example, the fact that a client prefers Extraversion over Introversion may mean that the client expresses their Extraversion as a strength. This would be expressed in behaviors like being talkative, comfortable in groups, actively reaching out to others, being venturesome, and enjoying socializing. However, a client might also express their Extraversion in challenging ways that others find upsetting: By being over-talkative, dominating the conversation, monopolizing conversations, frequently interrupting others, not listening and not giving others an opportunity to speak. In extreme examples, the Extravert can appear domineering, rude and anti-social. When Extraverts lack a balance of Introversion, their Extraversion becomes a challenge. This is an indication that type development is needed. In this situation the client's non-preferred Introversion side is typically undeveloped and the client is exhibiting negative Extraversion behaviors. From a PTD point of view the goal is to help this client strengthen their Introversion (especially listening skills) and reduce their "negative" Extraversion behaviors that others find upsetting.

Conversely, the fact that a client prefers Introversion may mean that their Introversion is present as a strength. This would be expressed in behaviors like: quietly listening to others, making skilled observations as to what is going on in a group, and being able to reflect on the inner meaning of conversations. However, a client who has not developed their non-preferred Extraversion side, may express their Introversion in ways that others find troubling: for example being non-talkative to the point of appearing reclusive, avoiding situations that involve large groups, avoiding dealing with strangers, not sharing thoughts and feelings with others, and acting extremely shy. In extreme situations, the Introvert can appear fearful, socially avoidant, and uncommunicative. If you are

DOI: 10.4324/9781003097167-2

working with a client who is using their Introversion in a challenging way, the PTD approach would be to help them strengthen their Extraversion (e.g., developing conversational skills) and reduce the "negative" Introversion behaviors that other find alienating.

A basic assumption of PTD is that one's non-preferred type characteristics can be strengthened and that one's preferred type characteristics that are being expressed negatively can be moderated in a positive direction. Table 2.1 shows some common strengths and challenges for the eight type characteristics. Table 2.2 shows examples of PTD directions that could be taken with each type challenge.

A person who demonstrates psychological type development is able to use their non-preferred type characteristic when the situation requires it. For example, the Extravert who can listen quietly to a friend's concerns. Or, the Introvert who is able to effectively lead a meeting and do most of the talking when extraverted behavior is needed from a leader. Jung was quite clear that a person needs all the psychological type characteristics to lead an effective life. There are moments when Feeling types need to take an assertive stand and confront injustice. Similarly, there are times that

Table 2.1 Common Type Strengths and Challenges

Type Characteristic	Strength (+)	Challenge (−)
Extraversion (E)	Socializing (E+)	Monopolizing (E−)
Introversion (I)	Listening (I+)	Isolating (I−)
Sensing (S)	Being practical (S+)	Nitpicking (S−)
Intuition (N)	Being imaginative (N+)	Being absent-minded (N−)
Thinking (T)	Being rational (T+)	Acting indifferent (T−)
Feeling (F)	Being caring (F+)	Avoiding conflict (F−)
Judging (J)	Being organized (J+)	Being rigid (J−)
Perceiving (P)	Being flexible (P+)	Being indecisive (P−)

Table 2.2 Examples of Psychological Type Development

Type Characteristic	Challenge	Example of PTD
Extraversion (E)	Monopolizing	Practising active listening
Introversion (I)	Isolating	Anxiety management in groups
Sensing (S)	Nitpicking	Tolerating ambiguity
Intuition (N)	Being absent-minded	Improving memory re tasks
Thinking (T)	Acting indifferent	Expressing appreciation
Feeling (F)	Avoiding conflict	Developing assertion skills
Judging (J)	Being rigid	Being willing to reverse a decision
Perceiving (P)	Being indecisive	Being willing to risk making mistakes

Thinking types need to show affection and warmth. Judging types need to be able to reverse a decision when circumstances change; Perceiving types need to be able to make a quick decision in a crisis where immediate action is required. In the life of every Sensing type there will be a moment when their intuition that something is wrong will help keep them out of trouble. Every Intuitive type knows that being able to focus on small details is a valuable skill that can be helpful (especially when doing one's taxes). What we are talking about here is the ability to lead a balanced, productive life by using the existing strengths in our preferred type characteristics and strengthening our non-preferred type characteristics so that we can rely on them when they are needed.

The Challenge Side of Psychological Type

The psychological type literature is very strength based. Typical of this is the classic book "Gifts Differing." It is rare for psychological type authors to talk about negative or pathological type behaviors. Nevertheless there is a literature on this and it is important for understanding type development. Jung frequently described how the non-preferred type characteristics could produce very destructive behaviors if sufficiently undeveloped. For example, Jung (1971) comments about what can happen when an Extraverted Feeling type has not developed their non-preferred or inferior Thinking:

> A classic example of this is the extraverted feeling type, who enjoys an excellent feeling rapport with the people around him, yet occasionally "happens" to express opinions of unsurpassable tactlessness. These opinions spring from his inferior and half-conscious thinking, which, being only partly under his control and insufficiently related to the object, can be quite ruthless in its effects." (p. 341)

In describing the Introverted Thinking type who has not developed their Feeling side Jung (1971) describes the following possible outcome:

> Although he will not try to press his convictions on anyone personally, he will bust out with vicious, personal retorts against every criticism, however just. Thus his isolation gradually increases. His originally fertilizing ideas become destructive, poisoned by the sediment of bitterness. His struggle against the influences emanating from the unconscious increases with his external isolation, until finally they begin to cripple him. He thinks that his withdrawal into ever-increasing solitude will protect him from the unconscious influences, but as a rule it only plunges him deeper into the conflict that is destroying him from within.

... The counterbalancing functions of feeling, intuition, and sensation are comparatively unconscious and inferior, and therefore have a primitive extraverted character that accounts for all the troublesome influences from outside to which the introverted thinker is prone. (p. 386–387)

What Jung is saying here is that all the psychological type characteristics are essential for everyday life and that while we may have a preference for a particular type characteristic and develop it as a strength, we frequently have to deal with situations that require use of our non-preferred type characteristics. If we fail to develop and use our non-preferred or inferior type characteristics, we do so at our peril. However, by engaging in type development, we can strengthen our inferior functions and turn them into strengths. In order to do that we must first be able to identify both strengths and challenges in psychological type.

The Identification of Type Strengths and Type Challenges

When using Psychological Type in counseling and psychotherapy, it is essential that the therapist be able to identify a client's strengths and challenges. Because the psychological type literature is very strength-focused this poses an assessment challenge. For example the *MBTI* and *Keirsey Type Sorter II* measure only the strength side of the type characteristics. We have developed two inventories that measure *both* type strengths and challenges: the *Psychological Type Relationship Scale (PTRS)* introduced in Chapter 1, and the *Psychological Type Relationship Inventory (PTRI)* shown on the next pages. The PTRS is probably better to use if a client has already become familiar with psychological type. This is because the four pairs of type characteristics are anchored at each end of the scale by a limited number of positive descriptions and challenging descriptions.

Preliminary data on the test-retest reliability of the PTRI (calculated over a 2 week interval) is shown in Table 2.3. The combined reliability scores for self and other ratings range from r = .62–.87 for the eight psychological type categories.

Table 2.3 PTRI Test-Retest Reliability (Pearson Correlation Coefficients)

Type Category	Self Rating (n = 45)	Other Rating (n = 45)	Combined (n = 90)
Extraversion	.82	.62	.72
Introversion	.73	.63	.68
Sensing	.74	.66	.70
Intuition	.79	.79	.79
Thinking	.50	.75	.62
Feeling	.83	.90	.87
Judging	.63	.74	.68
Perceiving	.67	.88	.78

Psychological Type Relationship Inventory (PTRI)

Name of Rater:_____

Name of Person Rated:_____

Name of the Other Person:_____

Date:_____

Instructions: This inventory is designed to collect information on how you perceive your relationship with a specific person. On the next two pages are lists of adjectives/phrases that describe different ways a person can behave in a relationship.

In Part 1 you rate your behavior towards the Other Person in the relationship.

In Part 2 you rate the Other Person's behavior towards you in the relationship.

Part 1 and Part 2 together provide a picture of how you perceive the Other Person and yourself behaving towards each other in the relationship. This information can be used to get a better idea of the areas of strength in your relationship and any areas in which you would like to see an improvement.

Part 1: As you read down the lists, check any adjectives/phrases that describe how **you** typically behave towards the Other Person.

Part 2: As you read down the lists, check any adjectives/phrases that describe how the **Other Person** typically behaves towards you.

Figure 2.1 Psychological Type Relationship Inventory (PTRI).

PART 1. SELF RATING: Rate **yourself** as you currently behave with _____ (the Other Person).

A	B	C	D
___ intruding	___ initiating	___ receptive	___ withdrawn
___ monopolizing	___ outgoing	___ reflective	___ reclusive
___ domineering	___ assertive	___ observing	___ submissive
___ overinvolved	___ company-seeking	___ privacy-seeking	___ uninvolved
___ over-talkative	___ talkative	___ quiet	___ close-mouthed
___ over-expressive	___ expressive	___ reserved	___ inhibited
___ impetuous	___ passionate	___ tranquil	___ unresponsive
___ excitable	___ enthusiastic	___ calm	___ detached
___ overbold	___ bold	___ contemplative	___ timid
___ impulsive	___ venturesome	___ introspective	___ shy
Total	Total	Total	Total

E	F	G	H
___ unimaginative	___ realistic	___ imaginative	___ unrealistic
___ trite	___ practical	___ inventive	___ impractical
___ obsessive	___ precise	___ abstract	___ vague
___ nitpicking	___ focused on details	___ focused on ideas	___ absent-minded
___ hairsplitting	___ factual	___ creative	___ forgetful
___ unoriginal	___ traditional	___ original	___ eccentric
___ banal	___ conventional	___ ingenious	___ odd
___ trite	___ conservative	___ novel	___ peculiar
___ fails to see future possibilities	___ deals with present reality	___ sees future possibilities	___ fails to deal with present reality
Total	Total	Total	Total

Figure 2.2 Psychological Type Relationship Inventory (PTRI) Self Rating.

28 Principles of Psychological Type Development

PART 1. SELF RATING: Rate **yourself** as you currently behave with _____ (the Other Person).

I	J	K	L
___ impersonal	___ logical	___ personal	___ illogical
___ deciding without compassion	___ deciding with objectivity	___ deciding with compassion	___ deciding without objectivity
___ unfeeling	___ rational	___ emotional	___ irrational
___ indifferent	___ objective	___ sympathetic	___ unreasonable
___ insensitive	___ tough	___ sensitive	___ oversensitive
___ hard-hearted	___ tough-minded	___ tender-hearted	___ overly soft-hearted
___ argumentative	___ disagreeing	___ agreeing	___ placating
___ intolerant	___ critical	___ tolerant	___ glossing over
___ rebuking	___ criticizing	___ praising	___ whitewashing
___ punishing	___ confronting	___ forgiving	___ avoiding
___ Total	___ Total	___ Total	___ Total

M	N	O	P
___ inflexible	___ organized	___ flexible	___ disorganized
___ rigid	___ focused	___ spontaneous	___ unfocused
___ unbending	___ systematic	___ improvising	___ unsystematic
___ has difficulty modifying plans	___ sticks to plans	___ open to changing plans	___ has difficulty sticking to plans
___ unmovable	___ prepared	___ impromptu	___ unprepared
___ closed to alternatives	___ decisive	___ open to alternatives	___ indecisive
___ unchangeable	___ certain	___ changeable	___ uncertain
___ stubborn	___ determined	___ adaptable	___ hesitant
___ unmodifiable	___ decided	___ searching	___ unsure
___ uncompromising	___ methodical	___ seeking	___ wavering
___ Total	___ Total	___ Total	___ Total

Figure 2.2 Continued

Principles of Psychological Type Development 29

PART 2. OTHER RATING: Rate _____ **(the Other Person)** as she/he currently behaves with you.

A	B	C	D
___ intruding	___ initiating	___ receptive	___ withdrawn
___ monopolizing	___ outgoing	___ reflective	___ reclusive
___ domineering	___ assertive	___ observing	___ submissive
___ overinvolved	___ company-seeking	___ privacy-seeking	___ uninvolved
___ over-talkative	___ talkative	___ quiet	___ close-mouthed
___ over-expressive	___ expressive	___ reserved	___ inhibited
___ impetuous	___ passionate	___ tranquil	___ unresponsive
___ excitable	___ enthusiastic	___ calm	___ detached
___ overbold	___ bold	___ contemplative	___ timid
___ impulsive	___ venturesome	___ introspective	___ shy
$\overline{\text{Total}}$	$\overline{\text{Total}}$	$\overline{\text{Total}}$	$\overline{\text{Total}}$

E	F	G	H
___ unimaginative	___ realistic	___ imaginative	___ unrealistic
___ trite	___ practical	___ inventive	___ impractical
___ obsessive	___ precise	___ abstract	___ vague
___ nitpicking	___ focused on details	___ focused on ideas	___ absent-minded
___ hairsplitting	___ factual	___ creative	___ forgetful
___ unoriginal	___ traditional	___ original	___ eccentric
___ banal	___ conventional	___ ingenious	___ odd
___ trite	___ conservative	___ novel	___ peculiar
___ fails to see future possibilities	___ deals with present reality	___ sees future possibilities	___ fails to deal with present reality
$\overline{\text{Total}}$	$\overline{\text{Total}}$	$\overline{\text{Total}}$	$\overline{\text{Total}}$

Figure 2.3 Psychological Type Relationship Inventory (PTRI) Other Rating.

30 Principles of Psychological Type Development

PART 2. OTHER RATING: Rate _____ (**the Other Person**) as she/he currently behaves with you.

I	J	K	L
___ impersonal	___ logical	___ personal	___ illogical
___ deciding without compassion	___ deciding with objectivity	___ deciding with compassion	___ deciding without objectivity
___ unfeeling	___ rational	___ emotional	___ irrational
___ indifferent	___ objective	___ sympathetic	___ unreasonable
___ insensitive	___ tough	___ sensitive	___ oversensitive
___ hard-hearted	___ tough-minded	___ tender-hearted	___ overly soft-hearted
___ argumentative	___ disagreeing	___ agreeing	___ placating
___ intolerant	___ critical	___ tolerant	___ glossing over
___ rebuking	___ criticizing	___ praising	___ whitewashing
___ punishing	___ confronting	___ forgiving	___ avoiding
___ Total	___ Total	___ Total	___ Total

M	N	O	P
___ inflexible	___ organized	___ flexible	___ disorganized
___ rigid	___ focused	___ spontaneous	___ unfocused
___ unbending	___ systematic	___ improvising	___ unsystematic
___ has difficulty modifying plans	___ sticks to plans	___ open to changing plans	___ has difficulty sticking to plans
___ unmovable	___ prepared	___ impromptu	___ unprepared
___ closed to alternatives	___ decisive	___ open to alternatives	___ indecisive
___ unchangeable	___ certain	___ changeable	___ uncertain
___ stubborn	___ determined	___ adaptable	___ hesitant
___ unmodifiable	___ decided	___ searching	___ unsure
___ uncompromising	___ methodical	___ seeking	___ wavering
___ Total	___ Total	___ Total	___ Total

Figure 2.3 Continued

Scoring Sheets for Psychological Type Relationship Inventory

Scoring Instructions Part 1:
Step 1: On pages 2A, 2B, 3A and 3B total up the number of words/phrases you checked in each column.

Step 2: Transfer these totals to the sheet below.

Score Category	Score for: Self	Score for: Other	Type Symbol	Type Category	Colloquial Name
A	____	____	E-	Extraversion Challenge	Monopolizing
B	____	____	E+	Extraversion Strength	Socializing
C	____	____	I+	Introversion Strength	Contemplating
D	____	____	I-	Introversion Challenge	Withdrawing
E	____	____	S-	Sensing Challenge	Nitpicking
F	____	____	S+	Sensing Strength	Being Realistic
G	____	____	N+	Intuition Strength	Being Visionary
H	____	____	N-	Intuition Challenge	Being Absent-Minded
I	____	____	T-	Thinking Challenge	Being Critical
J	____	____	T+	Thinking Strength	Being Objective
K	____	____	F+	Feeling Strength	Being Harmonious
L	____	____	F-	Feeling Challenge	Abdicating
M	____	____	J-	Judging Challenge	Being Autocratic
N	____	____	J+	Judging Strength	Organizing
O	____	____	P+	Perceiving Strength	Being Flexible
P	____	____	P-	Perceiving Challenge	Hesitating

Figure 2.4 Scoring Sheets for Psychological Type Relationship Inventory.

32   *Principles of Psychological Type Development*

Scoring Instructions Part 2: Transfer the scores from Part 1 to this page. To calculate overall E/I, S/N, T/F, and J/P scores within each pair making up a type continuum subtract the smaller score from the larger. For example, if Total Extraversion = 8 and Total Introversion = 2, the E/I score is 8 – 2 = 6 (on Extraversion). If Total Extraversion = 2 and Total Introversion = 8, then the E/I score is 8 – 2 = 6 (on Introversion).
* Note preference direction (e.g., E or I).

Score Category	Score for: Self	Type Other	Symbol	Type Category
A + B	____	____	E	Total Extraversion
C + D	____	____	I	Total Introversion
Subtract	____ ____*	____ ____*	E/I	**Extraversion/Introversion score**
E + F	____	____	S	Total Sensing
G + H	____	____	N	Total Intuition
Subtract	____ ____*	____ ____*	S/N	**Sensing/Intuition score**
I + J	____	____	T	Total Thinking
K + L	____	____	F	Total Feeling
Subtract	____ ____*	____ ____*	T/F	**Thinking/Feeling score**
M + N	____	____	J	Total Judging
O + P	____	____	P	Total Perceiving
Subtract	____ ____*	____ ____*	J/P	**Judging/Perceiving score**

Summary: Psychological Type expressed in this relationship

Self: ___ ___ ___ ___

Other: ___ ___ ___ ___

Figure 2.4 Continued

PSYCHOLOGICAL TYPE RELATIONSHIP INVENTORY: SUMMARY SCALE

Names:
SELF (**S**):_____   OTHER (**O**):_____

Instructions: Using the scores from Part 2 and **S** for Self and **O** for Other Person, label where each of you is on the scale below.

EXTRAVERSION _____ INTROVERSION
                20 18 16 14 12 10 8 6 4 2 0 2 4 6 8 10 12 14 16 18 20

SENSING _____ INTUITION
            20 18 16 14 12 10 8 6 4 2 0 2 4 6 8 10 12 14 16 18 20

THINKING _____ FEELING
             20 18 16 14 12 10 8 6 4 2 0 2 4 6 8 10 12 14 16 18 20

JUDGING _____ PERCEIVING
            20 18 16 14 12 10 8 6 4 2 0 2 4 6 8 10 12 14 16 18 20

Psychological Type: * SELF ___ ___ ___ ___

                       ** Score: ___ ___ ___ ___

                       * OTHER ___ ___ ___ ___

                       **Score: ___ ___ ___ ___

*Show letters here, e.g., E, I, etc.
** Show actual score here.

Figure 2.5 Psychological Type Relationship Inventory: Summary Scale.

34 *Principles of Psychological Type Development*

PTRI Bar Graphs for Strengths and Challenges

Instructions: Use this page to develop bar graphs for comparing strengths and challenges.

Score	SELF TYPE STRENGTHS	SELF TYPE CHALLENGES
10		
9		
8		
7		
6		
5		
4		
3		
2		
1		
	E+ I+ S+ N+ T+ F+ J+ P+	E- I- S- N- T- F- J- P-

Self Strength: ___ ___ ___ ___   Self Challenge: ___ ___ ___ ___

Score	OTHER TYPE STRENGTHS	OTHER TYPE CHALLENGES
10		
9		
8		
7		
6		
5		
4		
3		
2		
1		
	E+ I+ S+ N+ T+ F+ J+ P+	E- I- S- N- T- F- J- P-

Other Strength: ___ ___ ___ ___   Other Challenge: ___ ___ ___ ___

Figure 2.6 PTRI Bar Graphs for Strengths and Challenges.

Illustrated Use of the Psychological Type Relationship Inventory: Alexis and Blair

An example of how the PTRI is completed is shown in Appendix 3. A hypothetical client Alexis, age 30, is experiencing challenges in the relationship with Blair. Alexis describes the relationship with Blair as basically positive but that there are times the two don't get along because "Blair is critical of me." When Alexis is asked if Blair has any complaints about Alexis, Alexis says: "Blair complains that I am incapable of making a decision and that I avoid dealing with Blair when either of us feels angry with the other." This case example is generic and lacking in detail as the purpose is only to illustrate how the PRTI can be completed. In Chapters 11 and 12 we will provide detailed case presentations.

What the PTRS demonstrates with Alexis is that there are many strengths in the relationship between Alexis and Blair. Alexis scores high on INFP in the relationship with Blair and Blair (as seen by Alexis) scores high on ESTJ. Blair and Alexis relate positively to each other in terms of Extraversion/Introversion and Sensing/Intuition. However, Alexis frequently experiences Blair as blunt and critical, behavior often typical of Thinking types who place a higher value on being rational than on being sensitive to others. In turn, Alexis shows a common challenge of Feeling types which is that they are often conflict avoidant and don't deal effectively with tension in a relationship. In addition, Blair appears to be challenged by Alexis's "inability to make a decision" which is a challenge experienced by Perceiving types like Alexis who have not developed their Judging side.

Relationship-Specific Type Assessment: The Influence of Context on the Expression of Psychological Type

The assumption behind the development of the PTRS and the PTRI is that there is a situational context to one's expression of their personality. We may have a preferred way of expressing our type characteristics, but this can change depending on who one is with. Jung (1971) expressed it this way:

> A tense attitude is in general characteristic of the introvert, while a relaxed, easy attitude distinguishes the extravert. Exceptions, however, are frequent, even in one and the same individual. Give an introvert a thoroughly congenial, harmonious milieu, and he relaxes into complete extraversion, so that one begins to wonder whether one may not be dealing with an extravert. But put an extravert in a dark and silent room, where all his repressed complexes can gnaw at him, and he will get into such a state of tension that he will jump at the slightest stimulus. The changing situations of life can have the same

36 *Principles of Psychological Type Development*

effect of momentarily reversing the type, but the basic attitude is not as a rule permanently altered. (p. 287)

Jung is referring to what we call relationship-specific type assessment: the need to assess psychological type taking into context specific relationships. We express our personalities in different ways depending on whom we are with. Using Alexis as our example, consider her relationship with three very different persons: Blair (friend), Jan (younger sister), and Brad (supervisor at work). The PTRS scores for Alexis for each relationship is shown as Figure 2.7.

PTRS Scores for Alexis (S) and Blair (friend) (O)

EXTRAVERSION	O........S	INTROVERSION
	20 18 16 14 12 10 8 6 4 2 0 2 4 6 8 10 12 14 16 18 20	
SENSING	O........S	INTUITION
	20 18 16 14 12 10 8 6 4 2 0 2 4 6 8 10 12 14 16 18 20	
THINKING	O........S	FEELING
	20 18 16 14 12 10 8 6 4 2 0 2 4 6 8 10 12 14 16 18 20	
JUDGING	O........S	PERCEIVING
	20 18 16 14 12 10 8 6 4 2 0 2 4 6 8 10 12 14 16 18 20	

PTRS Scores for Alexis (S) and Jan (Sister) (O)

EXTRAVERSION	S........O	INTROVERSION
	20 18 16 14 12 10 8 6 4 2 0 2 4 6 8 10 12 14 16 18 20	
SENSING	S........O	INTUITION
	20 18 16 14 12 10 8 6 4 2 0 2 4 6 8 10 12 14 16 18 20	
THINKING	S O	FEELING
	20 18 16 14 12 10 8 6 4 2 0 2 4 6 8 10 12 14 16 18 20	
JUDGING	S........O	PERCEIVING
	20 18 16 14 12 10 8 6 4 2 0 2 4 6 8 10 12 14 16 18 20	

PTRS Scores for Alexis (S) and Brad (Supervisor) (O)

EXTRAVERSION	S........O	INTROVERSION
	20 18 16 14 12 10 8 6 4 2 0 2 4 6 8 10 12 14 16 18 20	
SENSING	O........S	INTUITION
	20 18 16 14 12 10 8 6 4 2 0 2 4 6 8 10 12 14 16 18 20	
THINKING	O........S	FEELING
	20 18 16 14 12 10 8 6 4 2 0 2 4 6 8 10 12 14 16 18 20	
JUDGING	O........S	PERCEIVING
	20 18 16 14 12 10 8 6 4 2 0 2 4 6 8 10 12 14 16 18 20	

Figure 2.7 Comparison of PTRS Scores for Alexis with Three Different Persons.

What do we notice about Alexis' expression of her type characteristics in these different relationships? First we see that Alexis who scores consistently as INFP on type measures like the MBTI and the KTS II, scores as INFP with Blair and her sister Jan, but scores as ISFJ with her supervisor Brad. Furthermore, Alexis's scores for INFP are not the same with Blair as they are for Jan.

Alexis' PTRS scores with: Blair Alexis = I 11 N 7 F 14 P 15
Jan Alexis = I 4 N 8 F 14 P 8
Brad Alexis = I 11 S 2 F 2 J 4

In Alexis' relationship with Blair, there is tension experienced by Alexis because Brair is frequently blunt in communication (T-). Alexis avoids confronting Blair (F-) and frequently upsets Blair by being indecisive (P-). In Alexis' relationship with Jan, Jan is so introverted that Alexis responds by being more outgoing (extraverted) in relationship to Jan. Alexis still scores on the Introverted side, but less so. Jan and Alexis both score on Introversion, but Jan will experience her older sister as more extraverted. This is the concept of *relationship-specific type*.

Relationship-Specific Type: How we experience another person is always in relationship to their personality. When Jan and Alexis are at home together and the doorbell rings, it is more likely that Alexis will go to the door. In this relationship Alexis functions like an Extravert *in relation to* Jan. Alexis often complains that Jan is so indecisive (P-) that Alexis has to decide for both of them. Jan's extreme score on Perceiving has "pushed" Alexis to act more Judging *in relation to* Jan. Jan's complaint about Alexis is that her older sister occasionally acts rigid and will not be flexible. Both sisters are INFPs but their behavior towards each other is different. We observe here the fundamental difficulty of unitary measures of psychological type that only provide a global type score across all relationships. Too much data is lost because we do not behave exactly the same with all persons. Furthermore, this illustrates the importance of knowing not only our type in relation to another's type, but knowing the extent to which we are expressing each type characteristic. That is, knowing whether someone is slightly, moderately, or very introverted (or extraverted, etc.) is critical to understanding relationship dynamics.

In examining Alexis' relationship with her supervisor Brad, who scores ISTJ with extreme scores on S, T, and J, we see Alexis' behaving like an ISFJ. This is because Alexis' job as a phlebotomist taking blood samples at a medical clinic involves a great deal of detail and exactitude. Brad has written Alexis up for being careless about her case files and as a result Alexis is vigilant about not making further mistakes that can jeopardize her job. Brad, who is a very competent hospital administrator, has a brusque manner and frequently makes surprise visits to the room where

Alexis draws blood from patients. As a result, Alexis focuses on being efficient and detail focused in case Brad enters the room. Alexis' natural inclination is to joke with patients, but she has suppressed this side of her self because Brad considers it "not professional behavior." Here we see how context in the form of a strict supervisor can exert a "press" on one's personality.

In summary, relationship-specific type refers to how we express our psychological type characteristics in a specific relationship. The personality (psychological type) of the other person affects how we express our personality (psychological type) and vice versa.

Inventory Assessment of Psychological Type is Not Sufficient

The essential question in using psychological type in counseling and psychotherapy is not "What is this client's type?" Rather it is: "In this specific relationship how is the client using their psychological type characteristics for better or worse?" The former question leads to a concern with classification; the latter question leads to a detailed exploration of the client's relationship with other persons and the complex ways their personalities intersect. Therefore, it is suggested to use type inventories with clients *only* as a starting point. Remember to continue on with interviewing and observing your clients as you construct a detailed picture of how type fits into their presenting problem and specific relationships.

This chapter has presented the rationale for assessing both type strengths and challenges. In the next chapter we will discuss a generic approach for teaching clients type development using "Talking in Type."

Resources

Bayne, R. (1997). *The Myers-Briggs Type Indicator: A critical review and practical guide*. Nelson Thornes.

Chapter 7: "Type and Counselling" provides a valuable overview of the role of psychological type in facilitating counseling and therapy.

Harkey, N. & Jourgensen, T. (2012). *Parenting by temperament*. San Luis Obispo, CA: Nancy Harkney.

This book describes how parents can identify the 8 psychological type characteristics in their children and it contains useful descriptions of children's strengths and weaknesses for each type.

Jung, C. G. (1971). *Psychological types. v. 6*. Princeton, NJ: Princeton University Press.

The book that started it all. Jung's descriptions of the type characteristics clearly indicate that he was not as interested in labelling people as he was in providing a useful tool for understanding personality.

Myers, I., McCaulley, M., Quenk, N, & Hammer, A. (2003). *MBTI manual: A guide to the development and use of the Myers-Briggs Type Indicator,* Third Edition. CPP, Inc.

Chapter 10: "Uses of type in counseling and psychotherapy" contains valuable information of psychological type development in counseling and psychotherapy, and the use of type with different age groups, couples and families.

Proust, J. A. (1993). *Applications of the Myers-Briggs Type Indicator in counseling: A casebook.* Gainsville, FL: Center for Applications of Psychological Type.

This book presents 18 case histories of college students representing the 16 types. The book is valuable for its demonstration of how mental health professionals can use a knowledge of psychological type to help clients overcome challenges.

Quenk, A. (1985). *Psychological types and psychotherapy.* Center for Applications of Psychological Type.

This early, classic work on the use of psychological type in psychotherapy provides examples of how the auxiliary function affects the conduct of therapy as well as the choice of therapy approach.

Reference

Jung, C. G. (1971). *Psychological types. v. 6.* Princeton, NJ: Princeton University Press.

3 Psychological Type Development Using Talking in Type

A SIX STEP APPROACH TO TEACH CLIENTS TALKING IN TYPE

If you are working with an adult client who is psychologically minded, consider teaching them about Psychological Type as a way to help them engage in type development and strengthen their relationships.

Step 1: Assess Client Motivation

A client who is psychologically minded is one who is interested in understanding their personality and the personalities of others. This type of client can be encouraged to learn about Psychological Type and take steps to engage in type development. One way to recognize this type of client is that they are already reading psychological self-help books. Another way to identify them is to use the Client Readiness for Change Model developed by Proshaska et al. (1992). Table 3.1 lists the five stages of client readiness.

If your client is at the Preparation stage and is interested in reading psychology self-help books, tell them about Psychological Type and see if they have any interest in learning more. Explain that if the client learns more about their personality and the personality of the person they are having difficulty with, they will be in a stronger position to make changes that improve the relationship.

Therapist: *Something that might be helpful to you in dealing with _____ (Name of person) is to develop an understanding of how your personality is affected by their personality. One way to do this is to learn a popular approach to understanding how different people behave called Psychological Type. Many clients who learn this approach develop a deeper understanding of how they get along, or don't get along, with others, and this helps them to make changes to improve the relationship. Would you be interested in hearing more?" If they say yes, go to step 2.*

DOI: 10.4324/9781003097167-3

Table 3.1 The Client Readiness for Change Model

Readiness for Change Stage	Description
Precontemplation	Individual does not see the need for counseling
Contemplation	Client is open to seeing the need for counseling
Preparation	Client is open to planning for change
Action	Client implements change
Maintenance	Client takes steps to maintain change

Keep in mind that not every client will be at the Preparation stage and if this is the case – irrespective of the counseling and psychotherapy approach you use – you are not likely to get anywhere. If your client is at the Precontemplation or Contemplation stages you will first need to spend more time developing rapport with the client and this may take many sessions.

Step 2: Teach Psychological Type

Show the *Psychological Type Relationship Scale* (PTRS) to the client and explain the strengths and challenges of the four pairs of type characteristics to the client. If the client continues to show interest, recommend some of the YouTube videos on Psychological Type mentioned in the Resources in Chapter 1. In addition, you may suggest to the client that they take one of the general type tests such as the *MBTI*, the *Keirsey Type Sorter II*, the *Humanmetrics Jung Typology Test*, or the *Psychological Type Relationship Inventory (PTRI)* that measures type strengths and challenges. The *Psychological Type Strengths and Challenges Checklist* (Figure 3.1) can be used as well.

If the client returns to the next session having explored some of the type videos, tests, or literature, and/or expresses a clear interest in learning more about psychological type, go to Step 3.

Step 3: Assess Relationship Type

This is illustrated with the hypothetical case of Alexis and Blair introduced in the previous chapter.

Therapist: For our session today would you be interested in exploring how you and Blair express your Psychological Type in your relationship with each other?
Alexis: Yes I think that would be good to do. I know that we are very different.

42 *Psychological Type Development*

Type Strengths and Challenges Checklist

Instructions: Below are listed common strengths and challenges of each of the 8 psychological type characteristics. Check all that you think apply to yourself.

EXTRAVERSION STRENGTH	**EXTRAVERSION CHALLENGE**
___OUTGOING	___MONOPOLIZES
___TALKATIVE	___INTERRUPTS
___MULTI-TASKING	___NOT LISTENING
___TAKES CHARGE	___TAKES OVER

INTROVERSION STRENGTH	**INTROVERSION CHALLENGE**
___CONTEMPLATIVE	___WITHDRAWN
___LISTENS	___RECLUSIVE
___OBSERVES	___SILENT
___INNER MEANING	___PASSIVE

SENSING STRENGTH	**SENSING CHALLENGE**
___DETAILED	___NIT-PICKS
___PRECISE	___MISSES BIG PICTURE
___PRACTICAL	___LACKS VISION
___REALIST	___RELUCTANT TO TRY NEW THINGS

INTUITION STRENGTH	**INTUITION CHALLENGE**
___VISIONARY	___ABSENT-MINDED
___SEES POSSIBILITIES	___FORGETFUL
___INSIGHTFUL	___IMPRACTICAL
___SEES BIG PICTURE	___UNFOCUSED

THINKING STRENGTH	**THINKING CHALLENGE**
___TOUGH-MINDED	___OVERLY BLUNT
___ASSERTIVE	___INSENSITIVE
___RATIONAL	___ARGUMENTATIVE
___OBJECTIVE	___COLD

FEELING STRENGTH	**FEELING CHALLENGE**
___HARMONIOUS	___CONFLICT-AVOIDANT
___FRIENDLY	___UNASSERTIVE
___WARM	___LACKS OBJECTIVITY
___FORGIVING	___FAILS TO SEE WEAKNESS IN OTHERS

JUDGING STRENGTH	**JUDGING CHALLENGE**
___ORGANIZED	___AUTOCRATIC
___PLANFUL	___RIGID
___DECISIVE	___INFLEXIBLE
___FOLLOWS A SCHEDULE	___CONTROLLING

PERCEIVING STRENGTH	**PERCEIVING CHALLENGE**
___FLEXIBLE	___INDECISIVE
___OPEN TO CHANGE	___DISORGANIZED
___SEEKS ALTERNATIVES	___PROCRASTINATES
___INVITES SUGGESTIONS	___HESITATES

Figure 3.1 Type Strengths and Challenges Checklist.

Therapist:	Ok, lets look at this scale showing the four pairs of Psychological Type characteristics and see if we can figure out where you and Blair are with each other. *(Therapist places PTRS where they can both view it).*
Therapist:	Let's begin with Extraversion and Introversion on this scale which goes from zero in the middle up to 20 on each dimension. The higher the number the more you show that characteristic in the relationship. Remember you are only rating how you and Blair relate to each other. So, in your relationship with Blair, where would you put yourself on the Extraversion/Introversion line.
Alexis:	Definitely on the Introversion end. I am not very talkative!
Therapist:	Ok, so what number would you pick on the Introversion side?
Alexis:	About an 11.
Therapist:	Ok so you are about in the middle of the Introversion scale which means you behave in a moderately Introverted way with Blair.
Alexis:	Yes, that's correct.
Therapist:	OK, now where would you place Blair in terms of how Blair relates to you on Extraversion/Introversion?
Alexis:	Oh Blair would be on the Extraversion side about an 11.
Therapist:	So Blair relates to you in a moderately Extraverted way. Can you give me an example of that?
Alexis:	Yes, She usually phones me rather than me phoning her. And she does most of the talking. She usually will end up asking me: "So how's your day?" but it's always after she has told me all about her day.
Therapist:	Let's look at Sensing and Intuition now. Where would you place each of you?
Alexis:	I would be at the Intuition end at 7 and she would be at the Sensing end at 11.
Therapist:	Can you give me an example of how this looks in your relationship?
Alexis:	I can tell when she is upset, sometimes before she realizes it herself.
Therapist:	That's a real strength of Intuitive types.
Alexis:	She is really good at remembering small details. Like once I forgot where I parked my car. That would never happen with Blair. And she always remembers birthdays and things like that whereas I am quite forgetful.
Therapist:	Tell me now where you see yourself and Blair on Thinking/Feeling.
Alexis:	We are really different on this one. Blair is 14 on Thinking and I am 14 on Feeling. Night and Day!
Therapist:	Can you give me an example of that difference?

Alexis:	Well, when a friend makes a mistake Blair thinks the friend should be punished. Me, I'm a softie. I think they should be forgiven. I also have a friend who doesn't like Blair because they think she is rude. I have talked to her about this and she says she is just being honest and people can't take the truth. My philosophy is live and let live, why rock the boat?
Therapist:	So you two are quite different on this type dimension.
Alexis:	Yes I think so.
Therapist:	Let's examine the last pair: Judging/Perceiving. Where would you place yourself?
Alexis:	We are pretty different here as well. Blair is an 11 on Judging and I am a 15 on Perceiving.
Therapist:	Can you give me an example of how this comes up in your relationship?
Alexis:	Well I like to keep things open and not get rigid about what things to do on the weekend, but Blair wants to nail down on Monday exactly what we are going to do on the weekend and I would rather not decide until Saturday morning.
Therapist:	Ok, that's really helpful in helping me to understand your relationship with Blair. If we look at how each of you is relating to each other you are INFP overall and Blair is ESTJ. The two of you have opposite preferences generally.
Alexis:	Yes it really stands out on the scale.

Step 4: Discuss Type Strengths and Challenges

Therapist:	Looking at where you have positioned yourself and Blair on the Psychological Type Relationship Scale, in which type pair do the two of you get along best.
Alexis:	We get along really well on Extraversion and Introversion.
Therapist:	Can you give me an example of that?
Alexis:	Yes. I am not a very outgoing person and I am very shy around groups. So I appreciate that when I am with Blair she connects with others quickly and then draws me into the conversation. I am not good at "breaking the ice" in a conversation and I appreciate that she is very good at it. In addition, she encourages me to get out of my apartment and do things with her. I always enjoy the activities we do, but if it were up to me to initiate them I'd probably would just stay at home reading or watching TV.
Therapist:	So Blair's extraverted behavior helps you by connecting you more to others and getting you to be more active?
Alexis:	That's right.
Therapist:	How do you think your Introversion affects Blair?

Alexis: Well she is always telling me what a great listener I am!
Therapist: I can see how her Extraversion and your Introversion complement each other in your relationship. In what type pair do you think you and Blair experience challenges?
Alexis: I think in Thinking/Feeling.
Therapist: Can you give me a recent example of that?
Alexis: Yes, last Saturday when we were having dinner, Blair suddenly said: "When we were talking with Barbara this morning she was saying outrageous things and you didn't say a thing. You really need to stop acting like a marshmallow!" I was furious with her but didn't say anything.
Therapist: How do you see that as relating to her and your Psychological Type?
Alexis: Well, as it describes for Thinking on the Psychological type Relationship Scale, Blair is being critical and I guess like a typical Feeling type I am feeling easily hurt. I felt really hurt that she called me a marshmallow.
Therapist: Yes that must have hurt your feelings. And I note that you didn't confront her with that which is very typical of Feeling types who find it challenging to deal with anger and conflict. This pattern of Blair being blunt and critical towards you and your feeling upset and saying nothing seems to be the main source of tension between the two of you.
Alexis: It is. About every three weeks she will say something that really upsets me and I say nothing. I would like to tell her that I don't like it when she criticizes me, but I say nothing.
Therapist: The saying nothing is also very typical of Introverts.
Alexis: Yeah, I just go into my "cave" and hide.

Step 5: Discuss Talking in Type

Therapist: On a scale from 1 to 10 with 10 meaning you strongly want to solve this challenge in your relationship and 1 you really don't want to do anything about it right now, what rating would you give?
Alexis: A 10. It's hurting our friendship and I often like awake at night feeling upset with her.
Therapist: I can see that you are really motivated to improve your relationship. Would you be interested in our exploring some ways you could take steps to improve things with Blair?
Alexis: Yes.
Therapist: You said that you would really like to be able to tell Blair that you don't like it when she criticizes you, especially when she

	calls you names, like "marshmallow." Is that something you would be interested in working on?
Alexis:	Very much.
Therapist:	What would you ideally like to say to Blair? Pretend I am Blair and say it to me.
Alexis:	You are so mean to me calling me marshmallow. It is really insensitive of you and hurtful. It really hurts my feelings.
Therapist:	OK that's a good start because you are using your Extraversion to speak out and express yourself. Here is one additional thing you could do if you wanted: it's called "Talking in Type." What this means is that you modify what you are saying so that Blair can hear you better. Blair is clearly a Thinking type, but you are confronting her with your feelings of hurt which is typical of a Feeling type. Thinking types look at the world in a very rational and objective manner and you will likely influence Blair more if you can give her a more logical reason she should not call you marshmallow. For example, you could say something like: "When you call me names like marshmallow it has a very negative effect on me and I withdraw from conversation with you. If you refrain from making comments like that I will be more likely to want to keep talking to you." Do you see how this is a way of connecting with Blair than would make it more likely she would be more sympathetic to your confrontation?
Alexis:	Yes, I do. She thinks I am "too emotional" and would probably dismiss me as being irrational if you talk too much about my feelings.
Therapist:	That is very typical of how Thinking types respond when Feeling types get upset with them. The way to get a Thinking type's attention is to talk type with them, that is to use Thinking language which means to present them with facts and details that appear logical. This process is called type development because it involves you strengthening two of your type characteristics: Thinking and Extraversion. Extraverts appreciate it when folks talk to them so by using your Extraversion and making the effort to explain to Blair why you object to her using the term "marshmallow" you will be connecting with her Extraversion as well as her Thinking. That is you will be communicating with her in the type language she understands best. Does this make sense?
Alexis:	Yes, I believe so. I need to develop my Extraversion by speaking out and my Thinking function by confronting Blair in a rational not emotional manner.

Therapist: That's right. In order to get her to change, you need to change first and you can do that by talking to her in a way that connects with her personality.

Suggestions for ways of Talking in Type may be found in Table 3.2. Ways that parents can talk in type to communicate more effectively with their children are shown in Chapter 12.

Step 6: Obtain a Commitment

Therapist: Do you feel ready to talk with Blair about how you want her to not call you names?
Alexis: It's scary but I'd like to do it.
Therapist: One way to prepare yourself is to practice what you would like to say to Blair. You could do that with me during our sessions or you could practice at home and tape record yourself as you practice to monitor whether you are remembering to Talk in Type.
Alexis: I would like to do both so I can build my confidence before I try it with Blair.

Talking in Type With the Non-Psychologically Minded

If your client is not psychologically minded, they are likely to have no interest in learning about psychological type. With these clients, assuming they are at the Preparation stage of counseling readiness, you can still introduce the idea of Talking in Type: you just use colloquial language rather than type terms. If, for example, Alexis was not interested in learning Psychological Type, the therapist could proceed in this fashion:

Therapist: On a scale from 1 to 10 with 10 meaning you strongly want to solve this challenge in your relationship and 1 you really don't want to do anything about it right now, what rating would you give?
Alexis: A 10. It's hurting our friendship and I often like awake at night feeling upset with her.
Therapist: I can see that you are really motivated to improve your relationship. Would you be interested in our exploring some ways you could take steps to improve things with Blair?
Alexis: Yes.
Therapist: You said that you would really like to be able to tell Blair that you don't like it when she criticizes you, especially when she calls you names, like "marshmallow." Is that something you would be interested in working on?

Table 3.2 Suggestions for Talking in Type

When the Other Person's Preference is:	And Your Preference is:	Consider Talking in Type By:
Extraversion	Introversion	Let them talk at length. If they monopolize the conversation, don't take it personally.
Introversion	Extraversion	Don't interrupt them. Invite them to express their opinion. Remember being quiet does not mean one is shy.
Sensing	Intuition	Respect their need to be neat and precise. Give them detailed information when you want them to do something. Explain why what you want to do has a practical value
Intuition	Sensing	Remember that they are good at seeing "beyond the surface." Allow them to be imaginative. Do not confuse their being absent-minded with being careless or uncaring.
Thinking	Feeling	The fact that they appear unfeeling does not mean they don't care. Remember they value truth over harmony. When you want them to do something, emphasize logical and rational reasons for doing so
Feeling	Thinking	Understand that being caring is a core value for them. When criticizing them, first let them know you value them. When making a decision that affects them, consider how their feelings will be impacted.
Judging	Perceiving	When you make a plan with them don't change it unless absolutely necessary. Understand that they like to make decisions quickly. Invite them to come up with alternatives.
Perceiving	Judging	If they want to change a plan be flexible with them. If they have trouble making a decision, allow them more time. Be aware that allowing more time for brainstorming solutions often comes up with a better solution.

Alexis:	Very much.
Therapist:	What would you ideally like to say to Blair? Pretend I am Blair and say it to me.
Alexis:	You are so mean to me calling me marshmallow. It is really insensitive of you and hurtful. It really hurts my feelings.
Therapist:	OK that's a good start because you are being more assertive. Here is one additional thing you could do if you wanted: you modify what you are saying so that Blair can hear you better. As I understand it when you told Blair once before that you feel hurt when she criticizes you, it didn't go so well. Is that correct?
Alexis:	Yes, she responded by saying: "You are way too emotional. You need to get a grip on yourself!" So I gave up. She really didn't hear me.
Therapist:	Blair does not seem to be a person who considers feelings as good reasons for doing anything.
Alexis:	Yes, she often says to me that the best way to solve a problem is to analyze it and make rational decisions.
Therapist:	That is very different from your point of view.
Alexis:	Absolutely! Peoples' feelings are important and you should always consider them.
Therapist:	Here is my suggestion: because Blair does not value feeling and instead values logic and rationality, when you talk to Blair about her criticizing you use language that she will accept. For example instead of you saying "I feel hurt" you could say something that appears more rational: "Blair when you criticize me and call me names like "marshmallow" it distracts me completely and has the negative effect of causing me to want to withdraw from conversation. If you will refrain from calling me names like that our relationship will be more productive." What do you think?
Alexis:	Yes, I see your point. I keep quiet because I feel she doesn't hear me when I share my feelings. But if I share my thoughts instead I will be talking a language she understands.
Therapist:	Yes, and since Blair values being talkative, she will likely value your speaking out more and not retiring into your "cave."
Alexis:	That's hard for me, speaking out, but I really want to change that part of myself.

In summary, you do not need to teach clients psychological type language in order to help them "talk in type."

Overview of Strategies for Strengthening Psychological Type (Chapters 4–11)

In the next eight chapters we will present counseling and psychotherapy strategies that we believe are very useful in strengthening the eight psychological type characteristics. Figure 3.2 gives an overview of the strategies we will use.

The reader will see that we have used a wide range of therapy techniques – 22 in fact – to illustrate how different therapy techniques can be used to strengthen psychological type. We used a wide range of techniques in order to show that there are many ways to effect change. However, the reader should be aware that most of the techniques that are shown as applied to only a single psychological type characteristic, can in fact be used with most, if not all, of the other psychological type characteristics. To illustrate, positive reinforcement can be used to strengthen

	Therapy Modality		
Type Category	Cognitive Behavior therapy	Humanistic Therapy	Family Therapy
Extraversion	Systematic Desensitization In Vivo Desensitization	Narrative Therapy	Staging an Enactment
Introversion	Two Question Rule Group Social Skills Training	Active Listening	Talking Stick Exercise Unbalancing
Sensing	Charting Positive Reinforcement	Multimodal Assessment	Caring Days
Intuition	Cognitive Restructuring Disputing	Imagery Meditation Guided Visualization	Method III Problem-Solving Brainstorming
Thinking	Assertion Training Behavior Rehearsal	Empty Chair Technique	Unbalancing
Feeling	Ordeal Therapy	Active Listening	Reverse Role Play
Judging	Decision Grid	Paradoxical Intention	Contracting, Ignoring, Positive Reinforcement
Perceiving	Decision Grid	The Miracle Question	Family Sculpting

Figure 3.2 Overview of Strategies for Strengthening Underdeveloped Psychological Type Characteristics.

all eight psychological type characteristics. So can The Miracle Question, as well as Cognitive Restructuring. Our purpose in writing this book is to introduce the idea that just as "there are many roads to Rome," there are many therapy approaches that can be used to strengthen a client's psychological type.

The strategies are divided into three broad categories of theoretical approaches: Cognitive-Behavioral Therapy, Humanistic Therapy, and Family Therapy. Our goal is to show how techniques from very different theoretical approaches can be used to strengthen a particular psychological type characteristic.

Each therapy technique is described under seven sub-headings:

Definition: This is a brief description of the technique and its origins.

Procedure: This section is a step by step description of how to implement the technique.

How This Approach Strengthens Psychological Type: This section explains how this particular technique is well suited to effect change in a particular psychological type.

Type Demand of this Approach: Type demand refers to the fact that most therapy techniques favor, even require, that the therapist use particular type characteristics if the technique is to be effective. For example, group therapy typically requires that the therapist must use Extraversion in order to be active in leading the group. Behavior therapy requires that the therapist must use Sensing in order to focus on specific client behaviors and Judging to follow the specific steps in proper sequence so often required of behavioral techniques such as systematic desensitization. The use of family sculpting, as Virginia Satir practiced it, requires the therapist to have a highly developed Intuition as well as Extraversion. This section describes both the Therapist Type Demand of the technique as well as the Type Demand of the technique for the client. An example of client Type Demand would be that systematic desensitization requires that the client visualize challenging scenes (Introversion) in great detail (Sensing) and be willing to follow a very structured exercise guided by the therapist (Judging).

Case Study: The case study illustrates how to implement the procedure for the technique The case studies are hypothetical, but based on our experience of using these techniques with actual clients. Only the barest case histories are provided because the goal here is to show how a single psychological type characteristic can be strengthened. In Chapters 11 and 12, we will present more detailed case examples and demonstrate how one can work with more complex type situations.

Additional Strategies: Five additional strategies are listed that could be used to strengthen the undeveloped psychological type characteristic.

Resources: The resources section lists further reading about a particular technique.

Reference

Proshaska, J., DiClemente, C., & Norcross, J. (1992). In search of how people change: Applications to addictive behaviors. *American Psychologist*, 47, 1102–1114.

4 Strategies for Strengthening Extraversion

CHALLENGES OF UNDERDEVELOPED EXTRAVERSION

Clients who score high on Introversion, but have not developed their Extraversion often experience challenging behaviors like: avoiding groups; feeling very uncomfortable when in a group, especially if there are present people they don't know; appearing very shy to others; being reluctant to initiate conversations; having difficulty breaking into on-going conversations; going out of their way to avoid dealing with strangers; feeling lonely because they find it hard to develop new relationships.

This, and subsequent chapters, will present a sampling of different counseling/psychotherapy strategies from Cognitive-Behavioral Therapy, Humanistic Therapy, and Family Therapy that illustrate different ways that underdeveloped psychological type characteristics can be strengthened.

WAYS TO STRENGTHEN EXTRAVERSION

Cognitive-Behavioral Therapy Strategies: Systematic Desensitization and In Vivo Desensitization

Systematic Desensitization is a Cognitive-Behavioral Therapy technique that can be used to help strengthen Extraversion.

Definition: Systematic Desensitization is the technique of having your client visualize the situation they fear for short, and later progressively longer, periods of time, while in the safety of the therapist's office. The visualization of stressful scenes is alternated with a relaxation exercise based on muscle relaxation or visualization of a relaxing scene. The goal is to build up the client's ability to visualize the situation that in real life makes them anxious without the visualization having as much potency. Systematic desensitization has a long history of evidence-based support in reducing anxiety for a wide range of anxiety provoking situations varying from fear of flying, snakes, spiders, etc., to dealing with strangers, public speaking, dealing with difficult persons, and other interpersonal problems.

DOI: 10.4324/9781003097167-4

Table 4.1 In Vivo Desensitization Hierarchy of Homework Activities for Promoting Extraversion in Dealing with Parties

Activity	Description
1	Attend a party for 3 minutes, keep to oneself, speak to no one.
2	Attend a party for 6 minutes, keep to onesself, speak to no one.
3	Attend a party for 15 minutes, keep to oneself, speak to no one.
4	Attend a party for 30 minutes, speak to one person for 1 minute.
5	Attend a party for 30 minutes, speak to one person for 3 minutes.
6	Attend a party for 45 minutes, speak to two persons for 3 minutes each.
7	Attend a party for 45 minutes, speak to three persons for 3 minutes each.
8	Attend a party for 45 minutes, join the center of the party and speak for 1 minute to each of three persons.

Definition: In Vivo Desensitization is desensitization based on exposing the client to the actual thing they fear in small doses. For a person who feels very anxious dealing with group situations where they have trouble speaking, the therapist would construct with the client a hierarchy of homework activities for the client to practice between sessions. The group activities would vary from those that produce low anxiety in the client to those that are more challenging.

This is illustrated in Table 4.1 which shows an *in vivo desensitization* hierarchy for someone like James who wishes to become more comfortable and Extraverted at parties and other groups. This type of hierarchy is constructed with the client and always progresses from easy to more difficult situations. Typically, as clients build a tolerance for easy situations they feel ready to try the next level. With clients who are very anxious about dealing with others (e.g. groups) you should begin with Systematic Desensitization based on imagery. If a client is only moderately anxious dealing with others (e.g. groups), in vivo desensitization should be attempted.

Procedure: There are 12 basic steps in implementing Systematic Desensitization (see Box 4.1). These steps are adapted from a desensitization procedure developed by Christensen and Pass (1983).

How This Approach Strengthens Extraversion: Images of unresponsive or rejecting persons are a common block to Introverts developing Extraverted behaviors such as speaking to strangers, or expressing opinions in a group setting. Introverts often experience these images in a potent form: the anticipated rejection, for example, is severe not mild. Systematic Desensitization introduces the feared images in a significantly reduced, "watered down" way so that the client can habituate, that is – become desensitized – to the image and begin to associate the image with the sense of relaxation that immediately follows exposure to the "feared" image. This process of becoming less

Box 4.1 Steps for Implementing Systematic Desensitization

Step	Description
1	*Determine motivation to change*
	Ask client to rate their motivation to change on a 1 to 10 scale (10 = very motivated to change).
2	*Explain the procedure and the rationale for doing it*
	Explain the procedure as one of exposing the client to the thing they fear in small doses. Use "the strange noise at night" story to illustrate how a child might have difficulty getting to sleep because of a strange noise (e.g., tree branch tapping on window) but on getting used to the sound is able to relax and fall asleep. Have client share a similar story.
3	*Invite the client to try the procedure*
	Use more neutral words like "exercise" or "approach" to describe the procedure rather than a more technical word like "technique."
4	*Select a challenging scene to have the client visualize*
	Discuss with the client what would be a good scene for them to visualize. The scene should be one that they experience as challenging and which gets a high rating on the 1-10 tension scale. However, the scene should not be so intense that the client cannot tolerate visualizing it.
5	*Have client visualize challenging scene*
	Ask the client whether they prefer to visualize the scene with their eyes open or closed. Tell the client you are going to have them visualize the scene "up close" as if they were there for 30 seconds. Ask the client to notice in detail what is going on in the scene, particularly how other persons are looking and behaving. Emphasize the importance of the client not modifying the scene in any way.
6	*Debrief the impact of the visualization*
	Always debrief challenging or relaxing scenes the same way. Ask: (1) "Were you able to focus on the scene." (If the client says no, have them visualize the scene a second time). (2) "How tense did you feel on the 1-10 tension scale while visualizing the scene?" (This is to give you feedback on the effect of the scene on the client and to permit you to track improved tolerance to the scene). (3) "Did you have an urge to do anything while visualizing the scene?" (This is for tracking behavioral urges of the client to fight, flee, or change the scene). Client tension ratings for the initial 30 seconds. presentation of the scene should typically be at the high end of the scale: 8, 9,10. If the client's rating is low (1,2,3) check to see if they were able to focus clearly on the scene or if they became distracted while focusing. If the scene is not that potent, search with the client for a more potent scene to work with.
7	*Visualize a relaxing scene*
	Ask the client to visualize the most relaxing scene they can think of (e.g., lying on a tropical beach, etc.). Ask the client to breathe slowly and deeply while visualizing their relaxing scene.
8	*Debrief the relaxing scene*

Use the three debriefing questions described in Step 6.

9 *Have the client visualize a "distanced" scene*
Distancing a scene means reducing its tension by altering the size of the scene and/or the length of time the scene is visualized. For example, you can ask the client to visualize the scene on a TV screen that is 100 feet away, then 75 feet away, then 25 feet away, and so forth.

10 *Alternate between "distanced" scenes and relaxed scenes*
When the client is able to tolerate visualizing the scene from (say) 100 feet away, you would then bring the scene closer (to say 75 feet). As their tension level lowers with repeated presentations at a particular distance, you progressively move the scene closer. Another way to distance the scene is to have the client visualize it for very short time periods that are lengthened as the client demonstrates scene tolerance at a particular length of exposure (e.g., 5 seconds, then 10 seconds, then 20 seconds, etc.).

11 *Alternate between "up close" scene and relaxed scene*
This step involves having the client visualize the "up close" or "full" scene for short (e.g., 5 seconds) then progressively longer periods of time. When the client can tolerate the scene for 25 seconds go to Step 12.

12 *Test for degree of desensitization by repeating Step 5 (30 seconds)*
If you have spent an adequate amount of time in Steps 10 and 11 and the client's tension rating is lower (e.g., four or less) and the client has no urges for flight, fight, or desires to change the scene, have the client repeat Step 5. Point out to client any reduced tension between Step 5 and Step 12. Give the client credit for the reduced tension rating and indicate that the client is now becoming desensitized to the formerly challenging scene. Point out that when the client is next in a situation similar to the challenging scene they will not be as tense and this will free them up to act differently.

"sensitized" to images that inhibit Extraverted behavior, frees the Introvert to be more talkative, socialize more, and take risks in speaking to strangers or expressing opinions in groups.

Type Demand of This Approach:

For the Therapist: Extraversion Sensing Thinking Judging. To use this therapy approach, the therapist has to take charge of the session (E), get the client to focus on detailed imagery and have the client report stress levels on a rating scale (S), expose the client to stressful images (T), and follow clearly delineated steps (J) to implement the technique.

For the Client: Introversion Intuition/Sensing Feeling Judging. To experience this therapy approach the client must follow directions (I), be able to image interpersonal scenes (N) in great detail (S), tolerate strong emotion in response to visualizing challenging scenes (F), and be able to follow a structured exercise (J).

An example of how to implement this procedure to strengthen Extraversion is shown in the case study below.

Case Study: James

James, age 22, comes to therapy because of feelings of depression associated with social isolation. James is strongly introverted and spends a lot of time in his room at his parents' home reading and watching TV. He has no close friends and has the therapy goal of making close friends and overcoming his anxiety about attending parties and other social gatherings that he is occasionally invited to attend. James recognizes that his anxiety about being in groups where he doesn't know others is impairing his ability to meet new persons and develop friendships. James' therapist Indira decides to use Systematic Desensitization to help James strengthen his Extraversion.

Indira: *In our last session you told me that you believe that if you were more comfortable attending parties and other groups where there are new persons you don't know that this would significantly improve your chances of making friends. Is that correct? (Step 1: Determine motivation to change)*

James: *Yes, I want to get over this fear of groups.*

Indira: *I have an exercise we can do that I think could help you: it's called systematic desensitization. Can you remember a time when you were a child and you had difficulty getting to sleep because there was a tree branch the wind was scraping against the side of your house and it frightened you? But after hearing it 100 more times you got used to it and fell asleep?*

James: *Yes, but it wasn't a tree, it was the furnace making weird clunking noises at night. It was spooky, but when I realized what it was and heard it over and over I got used to it and fell asleep.*

Indira: *That is basically how systematic desensitization works. It involves having you visualize here in the room with me the sort of group settings that make you anxious. Initially I would have you visualize a scene that makes you feels very anxious, like being at the large party you told me about last week. I would have you do that for a short amount of time and then we would have you think of a relaxing scene to calm you. Then we would alternate the stressful scene with the relaxing scene as we progressively lengthen the amount of time you visualize the stressful scene until we reach a point where you can visualize the formerly stressful scene*

	without experiencing much stress. Research shows that when clients can visualize challenging scenes but remain relatively relaxed, that sense of relaxation transfers into everyday life so that they can experience the real life situation that caused the original stress without experiencing the stress to the same degree. I think this exercise could help you overcome your fear of groups. Would you like to try it? (Step 2: Explain the procedure and the rationale for doing it. Step 3: Invite the client to try the procedure).
James:	Yes I would.
Indira:	OK, let's begin. Is there a scene from the part last week that you can visualize and that represents a moment when you felt pretty tense?
James:	It was when Barbara asked me to join her and a group she was talking with. They were all talking loudly about politics and I felt really uncomfortable.
Indira:	Let's use that scene. *(Step 4: Select a challenging scene to have the client visualize).* Do you visualize better with your eyes open or closed?
James:	Closed.
Indira:	Ok in a moment I will ask you to close your eyes and for 20 seconds visualize that scene. I want you to imagine you are right there with Barbara and the group. I want you to notice their faces and what they are saying and doing. As you do that don't try to modify the scene in any way: just let yourself experience it. OK, go ahead and visualize the scene *(Step 5: Have client visualize the challenging scene).*
Indira:	*(After 20 seconds).* Alright, I'd like you to stop visualizing the scene and return your awareness to this room. Were you able to visualize the scene?
James:	Yes, it was awful.
Indira:	On a scale from one to ten, with ten the most stressful and one not at all stressful, what was you rating?
James:	A 10+!
Indira:	Did you have an urge to do anything during the scene?
James:	I wanted to do what I actually did at the time. Pretend I had a phone call and leave the room.
Indira:	So the scene was pretty powerful and really brought up your anxious feelings? *(Step 6: Debriefing the impact of the visualization).*
James:	Yes I could feel my breathing get faster.
Indira:	That means this is a good scene for us to work with. Now I want you to take some slow deep breaths and for 1 minute visualize the most peaceful scene you can think of. Ok go ahead. *(Step 7: Visualize a relaxing scene).*

Strategies for Strengthening Extraversion

Indira: *(After 1 minute).* OK, please return your awareness to the room. Were you able to visualize a relaxing scene?
James: Yes, I imagined I was at the beach on a warm day.
Indira: Excellent! What was your tension rating on the one to ten scale? *(Step 8: Debriefing).*
James: Definitely a 1!
Indira: Very good. Now we are going to visualize the party scene again but this time we are going to reduce its strength by having you imagine you are watching it on a TV 100 feet away from you.
James: Am I in the scene?
Indira: No, you are 100 feet away but you can see Barbara and the group on the TV screen.
James: OK.
Indira: As you visualize the scene on the TV I want you to again notice how their faces look and what they are saying and doing. But don't try to alter the scene in any way. OK, go ahead and visualize the scene for 10 seconds. *(Step 9: Have client visualize a "distanced" scene).*
Indira: *(After 10 seconds).* Ok please return your awareness to this room. Were you able to visualize the scene?
James: Yes, I could see it on the TV.
Indira: What was your tension rating?
James: About a five, not so strong.
Indira: Did you have an urge to do anything?
James: Yes, I wanted to turn the TV off.
Indira: OK so the scene was still strong, but not as strong as before. *(Debriefing).* Indira then had James repeat the relaxing visualization for 1 minute and checked to make sure that he was indeed feeling very relaxed. *(Relaxation scene and Debriefing).*
Indira: Now I want you to imagine the TV is only 50 feet away and you can see the picture more easily. Go ahead and imagine that for 10 seconds. *(Step 10: Alternate between "distanced" scenes and relaxed scenes).*

Indira then determined that James' tension rating remained a five even though the TV was closer. She then had James visualize the TV only 10 feet away several times (repeatedly alternating with the relaxing scene for 1 minute) until James was able to visualize the TV party scene and only experience a tension rating of two or three. Had James' tension on visualizing the TV scene the first time been very strong (say a nine or ten), Indira would not have brought the TV closer, but might have had James visualize it 150 feet away. The goal here is to reduce the anxiety "dosage" of the scene to a tolerable level and once James' tension rating comes down to then slowly increase the potency of the scene by (a) bringing the scene closer and/or (b) extending the length of time the client visualizes the scene. Use this "distancing" technique to avoid overstressing the client. When James is able to visualize the TV scene up close (10 feet away) for 30 seconds with only a tension rating of two to three, James is ready to visualize the "undistanced" scene.

Indira: Now I would like you to visualize the scene again, but imagine you are right there with Barbara and the group. Again, focus on noticing in detail everything that is happening and don't try to change the scene. *(Step 11: Alternate between "up close" scene and relaxed scene).*

Indira: (After 10 seconds). Ok, please bring your awareness back to the room. Were you able to visualize the scene?

James: Yes but my tension was only a four.

Indira: Did you have an urge to do anything?*(Debriefing).*

James: Yes I wanted to keep very still and say nothing.*Indira then had James visualize the relaxing scene.*

Indira: Now I want you to visualize the party scene for 20 seconds. Go ahead.

Indira: (after 20 seconds). Please return your awareness to the room. Were you able to visualize the scene?

James: Yes.

Indira: What was your tension rating?

James: A four.

Indira: So even though we increased from 10 to 20 seconds you still got the same lower rating.

James: Yeah, it seems to be losing its grip.*Indira repeats the relaxation visualization and debriefing.*

Indira: Now go ahead and visualize the scene for 30 seconds. *(Step 12: Test for degree of desensitization by repeating Step 5).*

Indira: (After 30 seconds). Were you able to focus on the scene?

James: Yes, and my tension rating was only a three. It was like no big deal! It was strange. I wanted to ask Barbara if she agreed with what one of the guys was saying!

Indira: So you are beginning to experience the scene a little differently.

James: Yes. It's different that it was before.

Indira: That is because you are becoming desensitized to the scene. You began with a rating of 10+ at the beginning of our session and now you are down to a 3. This means that you are experiencing the scene differently. The next time you are at a party it is likely that it will not have the same "grip" on you.

James: I'd like that!

This brief case example illustrates the basic desensitization process. You have the client visualize the thing they fear in small doses by "distancing" the scene (using the TV and shorter presentation times) and as they build up their tolerance for the scene, you then start to bring the scene "closer" and for longer periods of time. Depending on the intensity of the client's anxiety it may be necessary to repeat the desensitization exercise over several sessions. When the client can visualize a formerly stressful scene, but give it a low tension rating and experience no urge to flee or alter the scene, it is time to switch to In vivo (live) desensitization.

In vivo Desensitization is illustrated in our continuing example with James.

Indira: (*At a following session*) Now that the party scene you visualized no longer has a strong grip on you, there is a next step we can take to help you build up your Extraversion side and have you be able to relax more in a group setting. This would involve you exposing yourself to being actually in a party or group in small doses initially.

James: What do you mean?

Indira: Well you would for homework take a small step. For example you would go to a party, but only stay 3 minutes and not talk to anyone. Then the next week you would go to a party and remain 6 minutes, but not talk to anyone. The third week you would go for 10 minutes and talk to one person, but only for 1 minute. Each week a little bit more, but only as much as you can handle. This is called in vivo desensitization. In vivo is Latin for "in real life." What you are doing is building up your tolerance for parties and groups by exposing yourself not to a visualized scene, but to the actual thing. Does that make any sense?

James: Yes, absolutely. I'd like to try it.

Indira: Here is what I recommend. This week if you go to a party, start small by standing in a corner where you can observe everyone and stay for a limited length of time, say 3 minutes, and you don't need to talk to anyone. Then, the next time you go, increase the length of time you are there and stand closer to people, again a little at a time.

Several weeks later James reported that he was at a party and was about to leave after 10 minutes when a young woman spoke to him and he ended up talking to her for an hour.

Summary: By using Systematic Desensitization and In Vivo Desensitization, Indira helped James increase his Extraversion by reducing his fears about being in groups with strangers. By proceeding in a step-by-step fashion, only exposing James to small

> increases in challenging situations (in imagery and in real life), she desensitized James to the anxiety associated with strangers and groups and helped strengthen his Extraversion.

Resources

McKay, M., Davis, M., & Fanning, P. (2021). *Thoughts and feelings: Taking control of your moods and your life.* Oakland, CA: New Harbinger Publications. *In this book Chapter 14: Brief Exposure and Chapter 15: Prolonged Exposure describe different ways to use desensitization with cognitive therapy techniques.*

Reference

Christensen, C. & Pass, L. (1983). *A social interactional approach to counseling/psychotherapy.* Monograph Series/16, Toronto, Ont.: OISE Press.

Humanistic Therapy Strategies: Narrative Therapy

Narrative Therapy is a humanistic therapy approach that promotes client change by helping clients to change the narrative (story) of their life from a negative narrative to a positive one. Narrative Therapy employs two central techniques: *Externalizing the Problem* and *Identifying Unique Outcomes.*

Definition: Externalizing the Problem is the technique of defining the client's problem as external to themselves rather than as a deficient part of their self. This is done by the therapist asking the client to give a name to their problem. Then the therapist investigates the problem continuously referring to it by the Name as though it were outside of the client. A classic example of this is a family with a child with encopresis that was treated by Michael White, a founder of the narrative therapy approach. The family experienced a lot of shame around the child's symptom. White handled this by asking the family to give a name to the problem. They came up with "Sneaky Poo." White then asked externalizing questions like: "How has Sneaky Poo been affecting your lives?" The goal of externalizing the problem is to reduce self blame and empower clients.

Definition: Identifying Unique Outcomes refers to the therapist looking for and emphasizing instances where the client's problem was not present or was effectively handled. Clients tend to present their lives with what White calls a "problem-saturated account" that focuses on negatives and overlooks positives. In Narrative Therapy this is handled by the therapist being more interested in talking about the client's strengths and instances where the problem was not dominant. This focus on client strengths has a powerful reframing effect on clients and builds their sense of self-efficacy – the belief that they can change their behavior.

Procedure: Examples of questions that can be used to externalize the problem and identify a client's unique outcomes (positive behaviors) are shown in Box 4.2.

Box 4.2   Interview Guide for Narrative Therapy

STEP 1
INVITATION TO TALK "What are you most interested in talking about today?"
"As you talk I'm going to just take some brief notes in order to…"
STEPS 2–5 EXTERNALIZING THE PROBLEM

STEP 2
GIVE THE PROBLEM A NAME (Dominant Plot Name)
"If you were to give this problem a name, what would it be?"

STEP 3
EXPLORE THE EFFECTS OF THE PROBLEM ON THEIR LIVES
"How has _____ (Insert "the Name" e.g. CONFLICT) been affecting you?"
"When does CONFLICT seem to show up?"
"What has _____ (e.g. CONFLICT) got you into believing about yourself?"
"What has _____ (e.g. CONFLICT) got you doing that gets you into trouble?"
"How has _____ (e.g. CONFLICT) got you into acting in ways you don't want?"
If client gives example: "Give me an example of what you rather would have happened.")

STEP 4
ASK CLIENT TO EVALUATE AND JUSTIFY THE EFFECTS OF THE PROBLEM
"What about _____ (e.g. CONFLICT) is most upsetting to you?"
"Why is this upsetting? Does it have any positive effects?"
(Have client justify their position.)

STEP 5
ASK RECRUITMENT QUESTIONS
(Establishing the Context of the Problem)
"How did _____(CONFLICT) trick you into a relationship?"
"Have you witnessed_____(CONFLICT) in your family or other families?"

64 *Strategies for Strengthening Extraversion*

> If so: "Tell me about how observing_____ (CONFLICT) affected you."
>
> *STEPS 6-9 IDENTIFYING NEW PATTERNS (UNIQUE OUTCOMES)*
>
> STEP 6
> IDENTIFY AN INSTANCE OF POSITIVE INTERACTION
> "Have there been any times that _____ (e.g. CONFLICT)
> didn't get the better of you?"
> "Was that positive or negative?"
> If positive: "Why do you regard that as positive?"
>
> STEP 7
> GIVE THE POSITIVE BEHAVIOR A NAME (Alternative Plot Name)
> "What Name might you give this Positive Behavior?"(e.g. COURAGE)
>
> STEP 8
> EXPLORE THE EFFECTS OF THE POSITIVE BEHAVIOR_____
> (e.g. COURAGE)
> "What did you do that facilitated the presence of _____ (e.g. COURAGE)?"
> "How has _____ (e.g. COURAGE) helped you?"
> "What do you like best about_____(COURAGE)?
>
> STEP 9
> EXPLORE THE CLIENT'S POSSIBLE FUTURE WITH _____ (e.g. COURAGE)
> "If _____ (e.g. COURAGE) were to become stronger in your life, how would that affect you?"
> "If you wanted to do one thing to increase to presence of _____
> (e.g. COURAGE) in your life, what might you try?"
> "Who do you know who would not be surprised at all to learn that you took this step?"

How This Approach Strengthens Extraversion: The use of Externalizing the Problem helps the Introvert who blames themself for having the deficit of shyness in social situations to instead think of their underdeveloped Extraversion as not a core or permanent part of their self. This reduces self-blame and facilitates problem solving. The use of Identifying Unique Outcomes reinforces in the client the belief that they already have developed some competency in Extraversion and that their growing skill in this area is legitimate and praiseworthy.

Type Demand of This Approach:

For the Therapist: Extraversion Thinking Judging. To use this technique the therapist must be very active in asking narrative therapy questions (E), conduct a detailed inquiry (T), and follow a structured sequence beginning with Externalizing questions, then moving to Unique Outcome questions (J).

For the Client: Extraversion Thinking Perceiving. To use this technique the client needs to be talkative in response to the therapist's questions (E), consider rationally the questions posed (T), and be open to the therapist's reframing (P).

Case Study: **James**

We will use the same case with James and illustrate how his therapist Indira could use Narrative Therapy to help strengthen his Extraversion.

Indira: *What are you most interested in talking about today? (Step 1: Invitation to Talk).*

James: *I spend a lot of my time alone and I would like to be more outgoing and make friends but I am very shy and I just find it hard to talk to anyone I don't already know. Like last Saturday I was invited to a party. I left after about 10 minutes because I only knew one person there, Barbara, and she was busy talking to a group I didn't know. I stood in a corner for a while and then I couldn't take it anymore and I left. I am just too shy and I don't like being this way. I have always been like this even as a child.*

Indira: *If you were to give this problem a name, what would it be? (Step 2: Give the Problem a Name).*

James: *That's interesting...I would call it FROZEN. I freeze up completely in a group.*

Indira: *How has FROZEN been affecting you? (Step 3: Explore the Effects of the Problem).*

James: *It keeps me from making friends, dating, going to parties. It's destroying my social life!*

Indira: *When does FROZEN seem to show up?*

James: *Usually on the weekends when I know people are going out and doing things or I get invited to a party.*

Indira: *What has FROZEN got you into believing about yourself?*

James: Well, basically that I am a hopeless loser.
Indira: How has Frozen got you into acting in ways you don't want?
James: It prevents me from meeting new people and it prevents me from asking persons I am interested in on a date. For example, I like Barbara, but I could not bring myself to speak to her at the party last Saturday.
Indira: Give me an example of what you would rather have happened.
James: Well, I would have joined the group she was talking to and then at some point have spoken to her.
Indira: What about FROZEN is most upsetting to you? (Step 4: Ask Client to Evaluate and Justify the Effects of the Problem).
James: It isolates me and makes me lonely.
Indira: Does FROZEN have any positive effects.
James: I don't think so. Maybe it protects me from being rejected if I reach out to others and they don't respond.
Indira: How did FROZEN trick you into a relationship? (Step 5: Ask Recruitment Questions).
James: (Laughs) It lied to me by saying it would protect me from being rejected.
Indira: Have you witnessed FROZEN in your family or other families?
James: Yes, my father is a very shy man. He lets my mother deal with strangers who come to the door and she's the one who likes to go to parties with friends and Dad just hates doing that.
Indira: Tell me about how observing your father affected you?
James: Well, I've always been told that I was "just like Dad."
Indira: So maybe you learned about FROZEN from him?
James: Yes, it's possible.
Indira: Have there been any times that FROZEN didn't get the better of you? (Step 6: Identify an Instance of Positive Interaction).
James: Yes, in my class on Sociology I missed a class. And so I asked a student I like, Janice, if I could borrow her notes. She said yes and we talked about what we liked about the class for 5 minutes, even though there were lots of other people standing nearby.
Indira: What name might you give this positive behavior? (Step 7: Give the Positive Behavior a Name).
James: WARMTH!
Indira: That's a great name because WARMTH melts FROZEN. What did you do that facilitated the presence of

	WARMTH? (Step 8: Explore the Effects of the Positive Behavior).
James:	I'm not sure. I think I was genuinely interested in what she had to say, so I wasn't focused on myself.
Indira:	How has WARMTH helped you generally?
James:	It makes me forget myself and my feelings and whether or not I am going to be rejected.
Indira:	How has WARMTH helped you?
James:	Well, it got me those notes I needed and I enjoyed talking to Janice. It helps me connect with others.
Indira:	What do you like best about WARMTH?
James:	When I experience WARMTH I am able to take risks and I don't worry about what others think of me.
Indira:	If WARMTH were to become stronger in your life, how would that affect you? (Step 9: Explore the Client's Possible Future with the Positive Behavior).
James:	Well, I'd go to parties and feel more relaxed and I would talk to different people there and maybe make friends.
Indira:	That sounds really great. If you wanted to do one thing to increase the presence of WARMTH in your life, what might you try?
James:	Well, the next time I get invited to a party I would go and then I would look for some people talking about something I was interested in and join that group. Then I would focus on listening to what they were saying rather than tuning into my feelings.
Indira:	That sounds like a good plan to defeat FROZEN. Who do you know who would not be surprised at all to learn that you took this step?
James:	My grandmother. She is always telling me that I tell entertaining stories and that others would enjoy hearing me tell them.

At James' next session he reported that he had attended a party and that while he had said very little to anyone there, he stayed for 2 hours and enjoyed listening to others. His plan now is to practice expressing his views more on different topics when in a group. This case illustrates how James' Extraversion can be strengthened through the Narrative Therapy techniques Externalizing the Problem and Identifying Unique Outcomes. By Externalizing James' lack of Extraversion (being anxious in large groups and being reluctant to talk to strangers) Indira succeeded in reducing James' tendency to blame himself and feel deficient. By using

> Identifying Unique Outcomes Indira encouraged James to focus on the times he was successful at using Extraversion and helped James to think of himself as beginning to strengthen his Extravert side.

Resources

White, M., Wijaya, M., White, M. K., & Epston, D. (1990). *Narrative means to therapeutic ends.* New York, NY: W. W. Norton & Company.
This is the classic book on Narrative Therapy and contains the "must read" Sneaky Poo case.

White, M. K. (2007). *Maps of narrative practice.* New York, NY: W. W. Norton & Company.
This is a more advanced book on Narrative Therapy and covers re-authoring conversations, remembering conversations, scaffolding conversations, definitional ceremony, externalizing conversations, and rite of passage maps.

Winslade, J., & Monk, G. D. (2006). *Narrative counseling in schools: Powerful & brief.* New York, NY: Corwin Press.
This book describes how school mental health professionals can help students successful re-author their lives in a positive direction.

Family Therapy Strategies: Staging an Enactment and Blocking Directives

Staging an Enactment is a Structural Family Therapy technique that can be used to strengthen a client's Extraversion in a family situation.

Definition: Staging an Enactment involves the therapist asking a family member to engage in a new or underused behavior. This typically involves the therapist asking the family member to share their thoughts and feelings with other family members in speaking about something important. In the case of an Introverted family member who wants to develop their Extraversion, *Staging an Enactment* could be used to facilitate the Extraverted behavior. The technique of *Blocking Directive* (a therapist request that someone wait their turn to speak) is frequently used with *Staging an Enactment* to prevent other family members from preventing a client from speaking.

Procedure: Because this procedure involves asking a family member to do something the other family members will likely not be used to, it is important that the therapist use their Extraversion to both encourage the Introvert to speak out and to gently block family members who may try to interrupt this process. Before using this approach making friends with the family, especially members who are influential, is essential. Taking charge of the session requires that the therapist have developed his/her Extraversion, Thinking, and Judging functions. That is, the therapist needs to be active (Extraversion), firm (Thinking), and organized (Judging) to successfully use this technique.

How This Approach Strengthens Extraversion: Often the reason Introverts don't speak or express their opinions is because they find it difficult to break into the rapid moving conversation of Extraverts or because they are sometimes interrupted by Extraverts. By the therapist (a) blocking interruptions and (b) encouraging the Introvert to speak in a family session, a safe space is created where clients can practice expressing their opinions in a climate of support.

Type Demand of This Approach

For the Therapist: Extraversion Thinking Judging. To use this technique the therapist must take charge of the session (E), be willing to block interruptions firmly (T), and stay focused on getting the Introverted family member to speak up and share their concerns (J).

For the Client: Extraversion Thinking. To use this technique the client must be willing to speak up (E) and often say things that other family members will find it hard to hear (T).

Case Study: James

The client James, previously discussed, also reported to his therapist Indira that he was living at home with his parents and was experiencing a problem with them.

James: *I need to get out more and meet people but my parents insist I be home by 10 o'clock every night. This makes it difficult to attend parties on the weekend. I try to explain this to them, but they keep talking and I just sit there in silence.*

Indira: *We have been talking in our sessions about how you want to learn to be more outgoing and talkative, especially in groups and at parties. It sounds like you want to express yourself more with your parents, but it's hard for you to get a word in edgewise.*

James: *Yes, I have lots of opinions about politics and social problems that I would like to be able to talk with my parents about, but I find it difficult to share my opinions with them.*

Indira: *Is this something you would like us to work on?*

James: *Very much!*

[With James' consent Indira invited James parents Vera and Mike Smith to come for a family session]

Indira: *Thank you Mr. and Mrs. Smith for coming to this meeting with James.*

Mrs. Smith:	We are so happy James is seeing someone like you. He is a very moody boy and we have been very worried about him. Isn't that right Mike?
Mr. Smith:	Yes.
Mrs. Smith:	We are always telling James to go out and make friends, but he just spends all his time in his room. We think that he is very moody just like Uncle Jack who also was very shy. Shyness seems to run in Mike's side of the family, it certainly doesn't run in my side.
Indira:	James is there something you would like to tell your parents?
James:	Yes. I am trying to be more outgoing ...
Mrs. Smith:	(interrupting) We know dear, but you have been trying for a long time and getting nowhere. It so distresses us to see you locked in your room hour after hour. Isn't that right Mike?
Mike:	Yes.
Indira:	Your point of view is important Mrs. Smith, but I would like to ask you to listen for a few minutes while James is talking (Blocking Directive). Please continue James. (Staging an Enactment).
James:	I am trying to be more outgoing, but the 10 o'clock curfew you insist I follow prevents me from attending parties. Most parties on the weekend don't start until dark and then last until midnight. I'm 22 and none of my friends have such an early curfew.
Mrs. Smith:	(becoming angry) While you are in our horse these are our rules! You really need to ...
Indira:	(Interrupting) Mrs. Smith, I realize you have strong feeling about this, but it is still James' turn to speak. You will get your turn later. James, can you tell your parents why this is so important to you?
James:	This is how young people like me meet other young people and make friends. I am not asking to stay out until 2 am! But I would like to have the opportunity to stay out late at least one night a week so that I can mix with other young people and make new friends. You both are always telling me that you want me to get out more and make friends, but making me have the curfew of a 16 year old is preventing me from having a social life. I care about you both a lot, but I need the freedom to be myself. I feel like I am a prisoner at home!
Indira:	What I hear James saying is that he agrees with you Mr. and Mrs. Smith that he needs to get out more and

Strategies for Strengthening Extraversion 71

	make friends. But that an important way young people make friends is by going to parties on the weekend and James feels he is unable to do this because of your 10 o'clock curfew (*Restates James' point of view*).
Mrs. Smith:	(*To James*) I didn't know you felt that way! We only want what's best for you.
Indira:	James, can you tell your parents what you would like from them?
James:	The parties I would like to go to are every Saturday at the Community Center where there is dancing and soft drinks (with no alcohol). The dance runs from 8 to 11 pm and all the people there are in my age group and there are Community Center staff there to supervise. I would like you both to support me in doing this. I know I can make friends there if I really try.
Mrs. Smith:	Why can't you make friends at our church? There's that nice girl Ella there and lots of other young persons to talk to.
James:	I really don't ….
Mrs. Smith:	(*Interrupting*) And there's that nice Bible study group for young people. I think you just need …
Indira:	(*Interrupting*) Mrs. Smith, let's hear what James has to say (*Blocking Directive*).
James:	The problem with that is that I already know all the young people there. Most are quite a bit younger than me and don't share my interests in politics and social issues. I know that you and Dad met at church and that worked for you. It's not working for me and I need to do things differently.

Although this is only part of the family session, it illustrates how Indira creates space for James to express himself to his parents by being more talkative than he would normally be at home. That is, Indira is using Staging an Enactment to facilitate James enacting Extraverted behavior. In order to use this technique the therapist must use her/his own Extraversion to interrupt using Blocking Directives and encourage the client to express thoughts and feelings that normally would go unheard.

Additional Strategies: Box 4.3 lists five additional strategies for strengthening Extraversion.

Box 4.3 Five Additional Ways to Strengthen Extraversion

Approach	Example
Positive Reinforcement	Using the Premack Principle have the client reward themself with a favorite activity only when they act more Extraverted.
Cognitive Restructuring	Dispute dysfunctional beliefs blocking Extraverted behavior (e.g., "If I Express my opinion and others don't like it, it will be terrible.")
Narrative Therapy	Ask the client for an instance when they once acted outgoing and explore this positive behavior in depth.
Empty Chair Technique	Have the client have a discussion between their Introverted Self and their Extraverted Self.
The Miracle Question	Ask the client if a miracle occurred and they became more Extraverted, what would be the smallest behavior that would indicate they had changed.

Resources

Nichols, M. P. (1997). The art of enactment. *Family Therapy Networker*, *21*(6), 23.

Nichols, M. P., & Fellenberg, S. (2000). The effective use of enactments in family therapy: A discovery-oriented process study. *Journal of Marital and Family Therapy*, *26*, 143–152.

Youtube Video

BC428 Unfolding the Laundry Session 2
https://www.youtube.com/watch?v=9DXghgwr_DI

In this video family therapist Salvador Minuchin effectively demonstrates Staging an Enactment to help a family member become more outspoken with her husband.

5 Strategies for Strengthening Introversion

CHALLENGES OF UNDERDEVELOPED INTROVERSION

Clients who score high on Extraversion, but have not developed their Introversion often experience challenging behaviors: e.g., monopolizing conversations, failing to listen when others are speaking, interrupting others when they try to speak, not noticing when others feel left out of the conversation, upsetting others by encroaching on their personal space, and feeling anxious when having to spend time alone.

WAYS TO STRENGTHEN INTROVERSION

Cognitive-Behavioral Therapy Strategies: The Two-Question Rule and Group Social Skills Training

The *Two Question Rule* is a technique developed by couples behavior therapist Richard Stuart.

Definition: The *Two Question Rule* states that before expressing your opinion you first have to ask the person who is talking two questions related to what they are talking about. This keeps the focus in the conversation on the other person and has the effect of inhibiting any tendency to dominate the conversation. This technique can be combined with *Group Social Skills Training.*

Definition: Group Social Skills Training involves the explicit practice of constructive social skills (such as listening, sharing feelings, and being more assertive) in a group counseling setting where people can receive feedback from group members in a safe environment.

Procedure: This involves three steps.

Step 1　Determine the client's motivation to change and willingness to participate in group therapy.
Step 2　Introduce the Two Question Rule to the group and use Blocking Directives (see Chapter 4) to prevent interruptions.

74   *Strategies for Strengthening Introversion*

Step 3 Encourage positive feedback from the group for clients who demonstrate better listening skills.

How This Approach Strengthens Introversion: The Two Question Rule interrupts the Extravert's tendency to talk by requiring the Extravert to ask for an opinion, rather than giving one. This "interruption" step facilitates the Other Person talking and the Extravert listening. Instead of the Extravert only passive listening, the Two Question Rule keeps the Extravert active in the conversation, but in a way that promotes more equal talk time with the Other Person. Group Social Skills Training helps promote Introversion by providing the Extravert with constructive peer feedback when the Extravert listens and doesn't listen.

Type Demand of This Approach:

For the Therapist: Extraversion Thinking. To use this approach the therapist must be comfortable working with groups (E) and actively block interruptions (T).

For the Client: Introversion Feeling. To use this approach the client must be willing to listen more (I) and develop an interest in what others have to say (F).

Case Study: **Alice**

Alice, age 42, is in counseling with Jacques because of difficulties she is having with friends and family members. The following conversation takes place during the first session.

Jacques: *What would you like us to talk about today?*
Alice: *I am having trouble with my sister Gwen who won't talk to me. Last Saturday she yelled at me on the phone and said not to call anymore. She lives in a another city. We usually talk every week and this week she just blew up and hung up on me.*
Jacques: *Can you tell me more about what she said to you?*
Alice: *Well, she said I don't listen to her and that when I call her all I do is talk about myself. I mean she is my sister so she should be glad to hear me talk about my life and what is going on with me. Always at the end of our phone call I ask how she is doing!*
Jacques: *How long are your phone calls usually?*
Alice: *Oh, at least an hour. I have so much to report, especially about some problems I am having at work, such as last week a nasty cold I had, plus a crazy TV show I watched,*

Strategies for Strengthening Introversion 75

	it was awful. And my car, you would not believe the problems I have been having with the engine light that keeps coming on. I don't understand why my mechanic can't fix it properly. He is always talking about his daughter who I think is involved with drugs.
Jacques:	I understand that you have a lot you want to share with your sister. So during a typical 1 hour phone call how much time do you usually spend talking about Gwen's concerns?
Alice:	Well, let's see. Maybe 10 minutes but she says no minutes!
Jacques:	And what sort of things does Gwen want to talk to you about?
Alice:	Lately it's about this guy she is seeing, Robert. I think he's a jerk and not good for her. I've told her she should dump him.
Jacques:	It sounds like Gwen feels that she doesn't get enough talk time during your phone calls.
Alice:	Yeah, she actually said that just before she said she didn't want me to call her.
Jacques:	Would it be fair to say that you are an outgoing, talkative sort of person and Gwen is a more introverted, less talkative person?
Alice:	Yeah, I've always been a good talker and Gwen is not that talkative. My father once told me I talk so much I should have been a politician giving speeches.
Jacques:	It sounds like Gwen is upset with you because she feels she doesn't get enough time to talk during your phone calls.
Alice:	Yes, she said "You never listen to me!"
Jacques:	What do you think of that?
Alice:	She is right. I've been told before that I am not a good listener.
Jacques:	Who told you that?
Alice:	My friend Betty.
Jacques:	Is this something you want to change?
Alice:	I have to. I don't want to lose my relationship with Gwen. And she is right: I tend to talk about myself too much.

During the remainder of the session Jacques invited Alice to join a weekly group meeting that focuses on developing social skills. At this meeting all the members are asked to use the Two Questions Rule during the meeting and to take turns sharing. During the meeting the following exchange takes place:

Jan:	I was upset when the doctor said to me that there was nothing wrong with me because ...

76 *Strategies for Strengthening Introversion*

Alice:	(*Interrupting*) That is so like doctors. They think they are gods and answerable to no one. I remember once I saw a physician and ...
Jacques:	(*Interrupting Alice*) Alice, I don't think Jan has finished what she was saying. Jan could you give some feedback to Alice on how her talking about herself affected you.
Jan:	I didn't like the way she interrupted me.
Jacques:	Could you please talk directly with Alice.
Jan:	Oh, sorry. Alice, I didn't like it when you interrupted me. I had not finished speaking.
Jacques:	Can you also tell Alice how you felt about that and why you felt that way?
Jan:	I felt angry because I thought you didn't care about what I was saying.
Alice:	I'm sorry. This is something I am working on.
Jacques:	Alice could you use the Two Question Rule with Jan?
Alice:	OK, Jan could you say more about what you felt about this doctor? (*Two Question Rule*)
Jan:	Thank you. I was upset because she once told me that a pain I had would go away on its own, but it didn't. So I have learned ever since that sometimes they make mistakes, so you have to be vigilant and always be on guard.
Alice:	So how did you handle this situation? (*Two Question Rule*)
Jan:	I insisted that she take my blood and get it tested. She did and contacted me the following week and it appears I was right. I do have something wrong with me. I have low blood sugar which means I have to eat at regular intervals and avoid sugar as much as possible.
Alice:	I am impressed at how well you stuck up for yourself!
Jacques:	Jan can you give Alice some feedback on how Alice has been responding to you now?
Jan:	I feel like you are really making an effort to listen to me and understand my point of view. Thank you.
Sarah:	(*group member*): You did a great job Alice!

This case study illustrates the advantages of social skills training in a group setting. The therapist and group members are able to give positive feedback to a member like Alice in a constructive manner. Alice is able to try out her listening skills in a safe setting and is able to receive "positive reinforcement" when she demonstrates good listening. The good listening skills that Alice is practicing in group can be user later with her sister Gwen.

Resources

Zastrow, C. (2014). *Brooks/Cole empowerment series: Social work with groups: A comprehensive Worktext.* Cengage Learning.
This comprehensive text on working with groups is in its 9th edition and covers social skills training.

Humanistic Therapy Strategies: Active Listening

Active Listening (also known as Empathic Listening) is the counseling technique developed by Carl Rogers as a central part of Person-Centered Therapy. Rogers originally called his approach Client-Centered Therapy because of its strong focus on listening to the client's concerns and following the client's lead. *Active Listening* is an important couple and family counseling technique for building better communication between family members.

Definition: Active Listening is the skill of accurately summarizing the concerns and feelings of another person. Active Listening typically involves reflecting the content of what the other person said as well as reflecting the emotions or feelings associated with it. The term "reflecting" refers to the skill of mirroring back to someone what they just said. For example, if someone were to say to you: "I can't stand the way she is always criticizing me" a surface Active Listening response might look like this: "It really upsets you when she criticizes you." The Active Listening components here are: "It really upsets you" (Reflection of Feeling) and "when she criticizes you" (Reflection of Content). This is considered a surface *Active listening* response because the response is basically interchangeable with what the other person said. An underlying *Active Listening* response would look like this: "You feel hurt because you think she doesn't respect you." What makes this response underlying is that it shows a willingness of the listener to go deeper into what the other person may be experiencing. Throughout, the focus is on the listener demonstrating to the speaker that the listener wants to understand the speaker's point of view. Practicing *Active Listening* with others is an excellent way to strengthen one's Introversion. In making an *Active Listening* response it is important to avoid parroting (e.g., "You can't stand the way she is always criticizing you.") and to instead summarize in your own words what the other person has said.

Procedure:

Step 1   Teach the client how to make an Active Listening response.
Step 2   Have the client practice Active Listening in session with you playing the role of the Other Person with whom they want to have better communication.

Step 3 When the client is ready have them try out Active listening with the Other Person.

How This Approach Strengthens Introversion: In order to make an accurate Active listening response, the Extravert has to listen carefully to what the Other Person is saying. In addition, in order to make a really effective Active Listening response, the Extravert has to "put themselves into the other person's shoes" and attempt to see the world from the Other Person's perspective. This shift in focus from acting and speaking to listening and trying to see things from the Other Person's perspective, facilitates the development of Introversion.

Type Demand of This Approach:

For the Therapist: Introversion Intuition Feeling Perceiving. To use this approach the therapist must be skilled at listening (I), be able to intuit underlying emotions and concerns (N), model warmth and caring in responses that reflect feelings (F), and be flexible in following the client's lead during the roleplaying (P).

For the Client: Introversion Intuition Feeling Perceiving. To use this approach the client must be willing to listen (I), make an effort to understand underlying feeling and concerns of the Other Person (N), relate in a warm and caring way (F), and be flexible in following the Other Person's lead (P).

Case Study: Alice

In the following case study the therapist Jacques taught Alice how to use Active Listening with Gwen. Jacques did this by explaining what Active Listening is, inviting Alice to read about Active Listening, having Alice practice Active Listening during counseling sessions, and then having Alice practice with Gwen. The case study that follows illustrates how Jacques had Alice practice Active Listening during sessions and then had Alice try Active Listening with Gwen.

Jacques: *How did you feel about our session on Active Listening last week?*

Alice: *I really liked it. I think if I can learn to do this I will have a better relationship with Gwen. I also read one of the books you mentioned on Active listening and I have a better idea of how to do it.*

Jacques: *That's great! How would you feel about us practicing Active Listening together with me in the role of Gwen.*

Alice: *Sure. How do we do it?*

Strategies for Strengthening Introversion

Jacques: I will pretend to be Gwen and talk about something that you think she would typically talk about and you would keep the focus on me using Active Listening.

Alice: OK.

Jacques: What would be something Gwen might want to talk to you about?

Alice: Well it's kind of boring to me, but she loves to talk about her cat, Princess.

Jacques: OK, let's give it a try. I want you to make at least three Active listening responses. I'll now pretend I am Gwen and I have just phoned you. Hi Alice, nice to hear your voice.

Alice: Hi Gwen, how are things.

Jacques: (as Gwen) Well, you know Princess is getting up there in years and she has been throwing up a lot lately. I really don't know what is going on.

Alice: Sounds like she is not well. (Reflects Content)

Jacques: (as Gwen) Yeah, I don't know what I'd do if she were really sick.

Alice: Why don't you take her to a vet?

Jacques: Ok I'm going to stop the role play and give you some feedback. Instead of using Active Listening you just gave Gwen some advice. Try to reflect her concern.

Alice: Uh, ok. Gwen you think she might be really sick (Reflects Content).

Jacques: (as Gwen) Yeah, I live alone as you know and she is my best buddy. She even sleeps with me. I don't know what I would do without her.

Alice: Princess is really important to you (Reflects Content).

Jacques: Ok Alice, how do you think you did?

Alice: OK I guess. I didn't realize I had given her advice.

Jacques: You made a great correction, however, and you made three really good reflections of what Gwen's concerns were. You didn't reflect any of Gwen's feelings however. What do you think Gwen might feel about this topic with Princess.

Alice: I think she would be feeling scared.

Jacques: Let's continue, but this time try and reflect Gwen's feelings as well.

Alice: Alright. Gwen you must be feeling really scared about what might happen to Princess (Reflects Feeling and Content).

Jacques: (as Gwen) Yes, I don't know what I would do without her.

Alice: You really love Princess and you'd feel lost without her (Reflects Feeling and Content).

Jacques: That was a great response. You reflected Gwen's underlying feelings that time. If I were Gwen I would feel that you really understand what I am going through.

Alice: I can see that I have been treating Gwen's interest in talking about Princess as unimportant. I want to change that.

At the end of this session, Jacques discussed with Alice whether she felt ready to try using Active Listening with Gwen. Alice said she needed to think about it some more. The next conversation occurred at the next counseling session.

Jacques: How did your week go.
Alice: I spoke to Gwen!
Jacques: Please tell me about it.
Alice: It's been three weeks since we last spoke and I thought maybe she might not be so mad at me now, so I phoned her. She seemed glad to talk to me.
Jacques: How did it go?
Alice: Better than I expected. First, I made an effort not to talk about myself and instead focus on Gwen. I asked her how things were going and she told me that she was still having trouble with her physician. So I said to her: "That must be really upsetting to feel that your doctor doesn't listen to you." Then she talked for a while about how she had tried to find another doctor, but was reluctant to do so because she actually likes this doctor – she just thinks the doctor isn't listening to her on this particular issue. So I said to her: "You really want to stay with her, but you are frustrated that she doesn't see eye to eye with you on what is causing your leg pain." I also asked her questions a couple of times using the Two Question Rule I learned in group. The next thing I knew we had talked for an hour and none of it was about me. She thanked me for helping her and I don't feel like I really did anything special.
Jacques: Well, listening to a family member's concerns like you did is a very caring act and is something special. It sounds like you have really used your listening skills effectively with Gwen.
Alice: I feel really good about it.

Although this is a hypothetical example, it illustrates how a therapist can facilitate listening skills with a client. Often, multiple practice sessions will be needed before a client is ready to use Active Listening with a family member or friend.

Resources

Gordon, T. (2008). *Parent effectiveness training: The proven program for raising responsible children*. Harmony.
King, P. (2020). *How to listen with intention: The foundation of true connection, communication, and relationships*. Pkcs Media, Inc.
Nichols, M. P. (2009). *The lost art of listening: How learning to listen can improve relationships*. Guilford Press.
Nixaly Leonardo, L. (2020). *Active listening techniques: 30 practical tools to hone your communication skills*. Rockridge Press.
Sorensen, J. (2019). *Active listening: Improve your conversation skills, learn effective communication techniques, achieve successful relationships with 6 essential guidelines*. Joseph Sorensen.

Family Therapy Strategies: Unbalancing and the Talking Stick Exercise

Unbalancing and *The Talking Stick Exercise* are two family therapy techniques that can be used to promote Introversion.

Definition: *Unbalancing* is a technique developed by Salvador Minuchin, developer of Structural Family Therapy. It involves changing the extent to which particular family members talk in a family session. Family members who are very Extraverted and talk a great deal are encouraged to talk less. Family members who are very Introverted and talk very little are encouraged to talk more. When the therapist asks the opinion of an Introverted family member and an Extraverted family member interrupts, or attempts to speak for the Introvert, the therapist interrupts the Extravert using a *Blocking Directive* ("Father, it's your son's turn to speak," "Billie your mother hasn't finished sharing her concerns. We will get to you in a few minutes"). The Introverted family member is then encouraged to continue speaking. This type of therapist initiated intervention changes the balance of speech within the family, thereby "unbalancing" the usual pattern of who "dominates" the conversation.

Definition: The Talking Stick Exercise is based on a Native American tradition in which a council of elders would take turns speaking about important matters. Only the person holding the "talking stick" was allowed to speak while the others listened in silence. The Talking Stick would then be passed to the next person who wished to speak and this would be repeated until everyone had spoken. In a family session any object (such as a pen or pencil) could be used as the Talking Stick. A time limit for speaking could also be set (e.g., 1–2 minutes, etc.).

Procedure:

Step 1 Introduce the Talking Stick exercise to the family members. Emphasize the importance of taking turns and respecting the other person's point of view.

Step 2   Enforce the rules when someone speaks out of turn. Use Unbalancing and Blocking Directives to gently but firmly block interruptions.
Step 3   Make sure that everyone gets a chance to speak.
Step 4   When debriefing the exercise, encourage family members to give positive feedback to the Extraverted member who wants to learn to listen better.

How This Approach Strengthens Introversion: Because the Extravert can only speak when they are holding the Talking Stick, and there may be several others in the family of group who will speak also, the Extravert is exposed to a situation where they speak no more than the other group members. This facilitates listening and developing the ability to speak in shorter (e.g., 2 minute) time frames.

Type Demand of this Approach:

For the Therapist: Extraversion Sensing Thinking Judging. In order to use this technique the therapist must actively take charge of the session (E), pay close attention to who is speaking and for how long (S), be willing to block interruptions and enforce rules (T), and ensure everyone follows the structured approach (J).

For the Client: Introversion Feeling Judging. To use this approach the client must be willing to talk less and listen more (I), be willing to take turns to promote harmony in the group or family (F), and be accepting of the therapist's structured activity (J).

Case Study: **A family session with Alice and Gwen**

In the following case study involving Alice, the therapist will use Unbalancing and The Talking Stick Exercise to help Alice listen more (and Gwen to talk more).

At the beginning of the session with Alice and Gwen, Jacques has explained the Talking Stick Exercise and obtained Alice's and Gwen's consent to try it.

Jacques: We can use this pencil as our Talking Stick. You each will have 1 minute to speak and I will keep track of the time. Since we all agreed to meet today to talk about how both of you as sisters can get along better, why don't we talk about that? Gwen, why don't you go first (hands pencil to Gwen) (Talking Stick Exercise).

Gwen: Thanks. I am really glad to be here today because I really care about my sister and ...

Strategies for Strengthening Introversion 83

Alice: (*Interrupting*) *If you care about me so much why did you stop phoning me and ...*

Jacques: (*Interrupting*) *Alice I'd like you to hold with your comments because Gwen has the Talking Stick and only the person with the Talking Stick can speak (Blocking Directive).*

Alice: *Oh, yeah.*

Jacques: *Please continue Gwen.*

Gwen: *I really care about Alice but whenever we get on the phone she does all the talking and I never get a chance to talk much.*

Alice: (*Interrupting*) *That's not true! I always ...*

Jacques: (*Interrupting*) *You'll get your chance to speak soon Alice. Please let Gwen finish (Blocking Directive).*

Gwen: *This is what it's like on the phone. She always interrupts me.*

Jacques: *Gwen can you look at Alice while you are talking and also let her know why this upsets you (Unbalancing).*

Gwen: (*To Alice*) *When you interrupt me I lose my train of thought and then don't finish what I wanted to say to you. I feel unimportant when that happens.*

Jacques: *Thank you Gwen. It's been 2 minutes now so Alice it is your turn to take the Talking Stick and say whatever you want (Talking Stick Exercise).*

Alice: (*Taking the Talking Stick*) *But Gwen I am just trying to help you. When you tell me about all the terrible problems you are having I just want to help you find a solution. I know I talk a lot but then you hardly talk at all and someone needs to talk otherwise there would just be silence on the phone plus when I get an idea about how to help you solve your problems I don't want to lose it so I share it right away. Like for instance when you told me your were having difficulty with your doctor. I have lot's of experience with doctors so I know all kinds of things to help with that sort of thing. You may recall that when you were only 10 you got into ...*

Jacques: *A minute is now up! Alice please give Gwen the Talking Stick and let her respond to what you have said. You can continue when it is your turn next (Blocking Directive; Talking Stick Exercise).*

Gwen: (*receiving Talking Stick from Alice*) *I know that you are older than me and that you have a lot of good ideas that could help me and that you are only trying to help me. But sometimes you interrupt me before I have given you the*

84 *Strategies for Strengthening Introversion*

	full story and the advice you give me isn't helpful because you are missing important details. If you would let me talk more then you would know what is really going on and be in a better position to be helpful (*Hands Talking Stick to Alice*).
Alice:	I'm sorry Gwen, I didn't know you felt that way (*Hands Talking Stick back to Gwen*).
Gwen:	I do. When I am talking with you I pause when I am talking because I am collecting my thoughts, and it is in those moments when you interrupt me and start giving me all kinds of premature advice. I appreciate that you want to help me but I would like you to listen more before giving me advice (*Hands Talking Stick to Alice*).
Alice:	I am sorry. I really didn't know you were feeling that way. I really don't want to upset you. You are important to me (*Hands Talking Stick to Gwen*).
Jacques:	Gwen, I have noticed that Alice is talking less and has given you the Talking Stick after she has only spoken a little. Can you tell Alice how you experience that?
Gwen:	(*to Alice*) I really like it when you let me talk more just now and when you stopped talking and gave me the Talking Stick (*Talking Stick Exercise*).

Using *Unbalancing* and *The Talking Stick Exercise* requires that the therapist use his/her Extraversion, Sensing, Thinking, and Judging side in order to block interruptions, be firm with family members who interrupt, keep track of the time each person has spoken and stay with the alternating sequence of who gets to speak. The reason these techniques can be helpful in promoting Introversion (listening) in an Extravert is because they interrupt the normal "unbalanced" flow of conversation, provide feedback to the Extravert when they talk too long, and simultaneously encourage the more Introverted family member to Extravert more (talk more). In the above example both Alice and Gwen had an opportunity to relate differently to each other and to experience the benefits of balancing their interaction more equitably.

Additional Strategies: Box 5.1 lists five additional strategies for strengthening Introversion.

Box 5.1   Five Additional Ways to Strengthen Introversion

Approach	Example
Positive Reinforcement	Using the Premack Principle have the client reward themself with a favorite activity only when they do a good job of listening.
Decision Grid	Have the client develop a Decision Grid that weighs the consequences of not listening.
Ordeal Therapy	If the client monopolizes a conversation, or interrupts others, have the client agree to undergo a "positive" ordeal.
Family Sculpting	Have family members sculpt a current and ideal family sculpture showing how they experience the client who has underdeveloped Introversion (e.g., doesn't listen).
Caring Days	Encourage the client's partner to list constructive Introvert behaviors on the Caring Days list (e.g., invited me to share concerns, listened to me quietly, etc.).

Resources

Colapinto, J. (2015). Structural family therapy. *Handbook of Family Therapy*, 120–133. doi: 10.4324/9780203123584-7

This chapter gives a brief overview of Structural Family Therapy and the role of Unbalancing in restructuring families.

Minuchin, S. (2018). *Families and family therapy*. Routledge.

This text by the founder of Structural Family Therapy describes Unbalancing in Chapter 8: Restructuring the Family.

Talking Stick Exercise.

Hartina, S. (2020). Talking sticks as a technique to stimulate the students' speaking performance. *IDEAS: Journal on English Language Teaching and Learning, Linguistics and Literature*, *8*(1). doi: 10.24256/ideas.v8i1.1317

The authors used the Talking Stick approach with 22 EFL students and found that the students' speaking performance increased significantly on speaking tests and interviews.

Mehl-Madrona, L., & Mainguy, B. (2014). Introducing healing circles and talking circles into primary care. *The Permanente Journal*, *18*(2), 4–9. doi: 10.7812/TPP/13-104

A large sample of 1200 people used the Talking Stick exercise to share concerns. The results for improvement in reported symptoms and overall quality of life were statistically significant.

Wolf, P. R., & Rickard, J. A. (2003). Talking circles: A Native American approach to experiential learning. *Journal of Multicultural Counseling and Development*, 31(1), 39–43. doi: 10.1002/j.2161-1912.2003.tb00529.x

This article discusses the use of the Talking Stick exercise in counseling as a way to promote multicultural awareness.

6 Strategies for Strengthening Sensing

CHALLENGES OF UNDERDEVELOPED SENSING

A common challenge experienced by Intuitive types who have not developed their Sensing mental function is a failure to pay attention to detail. This can be experienced as absent-mindedness which can result in missing important meetings, forgetting where one has parked the car, and being unable to find important things like one's keys, wallet, passport, and other important documents. The family members of persons with underdeveloped Sensing may complain that the Intuitive type frequently forgets birthdays and important anniversaries, forgets to do common home chores in a timely fashion, and promises to do something and then forgets it. Friends and family will sometimes accuse the Intuitive type of being uncaring when they are forgetful, but the problem really is about not being good with remembering detail. Dealing with tax and financial details can be particularly challenging for Intuitive types who have underdeveloped Sensing.

WAYS TO STRENGTHEN SENSING

Cognitive-Behavioral Therapy Strategies: Charting and Positive Reinforcement

Charting and *Positive Reinforcement* are two behavioral strategies that can be used to strengthen Sensing.

Definition: *Charting* involves having the client track the frequency of a behavior using a simple chart that lists the date the behavior occurred, has a description of the behavior, and (often) keeps a tabulation of the frequency with which the behavior occurred. By maintaining a Chart of desired/undesired behaviors, the client's awareness of the occurrence of the behaviors is heightened. This close detailed tracking of behavior reduces the likelihood the client will not notice or forget these behaviors.

Definition: *Positive Reinforcement* is a behavior therapy technique that emphasizes rewarding desirable behavior and not rewarding undesirable behavior. A positive reinforcer is anything that follows a behavior and

DOI: 10.4324/9781003097167-6

causes it to increase in frequency. For example, if you are speaking with someone and they avoid eye contact with you and spend their time looking at their cell phone, you are likely to lose interest in talking with them. Your act of talking to them is not being reinforced or rewarded. Alternatively, if when you speak to someone they put away their cell phone, look at you without interrupting, and occasionally demonstrate that they are interested in what you are saying by nodding their head, smiling, or saying things like "Go on," "Tell me more," then you are likely to continue talking to them. Your talking is being rewarded or reinforced by the attention the other person is giving you. There is expensive research on the effectiveness of *Positive Reinforcement* and it has been used to help children and adults improve social skills.

The *Premack Principle* refers to having clients reward themselves by engaging in a frequent enjoyable behavior only if they first engage in a low frequency behavior they have been avoiding. This is sometimes called "Grandma's rule" and is expressed as: "If you eat the main meal then you can have dessert." In this instance getting dessert is contingent on first eating the main meal. Clients who are motivated to change enter into a contract with their therapist to only engage in the desirable behavior if they first engage in the more challenging behavior.

Procedure:

Step 1 Explain the Premack Principle to the client and obtain a commitment to try using it.
Step 2 Teach the client how to keep a chart of desirable (rewarding) and undesirable (in this case negative Intuition) behaviors.
Step 3 During each counseling session, have the client report on their chart and their progress in developing the new (Sensing) behavior.

How This Approach Strengthens Sensing: The client has to use their Sensing function in order to keep a chart. Charting requires that one: (a) make the chart, (b) record on it daily, and (c) write down a detailed description of behaviors that occurred. These are all concrete Sensing behaviors. The Premack principle strengthens Sensing by rewarding clients for engaging in Sensing behaviors (and not engaging in challenging Intuition behaviors, such as being forgetful).

Type Demand of This Approach:

For the Therapist: Sensing Judging. To use this approach the therapist must give detailed instructions (S) and must follow up by debriefing the use of the approach (J).

For the Client: Sensing Judging. To use this approach the client must be willing to keep a detailed chart during the week (S) and systematically apply the Premack Principle (J).

Case Study: **Benjamin**

Benjamin, age 35 comes for therapy with Amira because of problems he is experiencing with his extended family. Benjamin is a grade eight music teacher at a Middle school. Benjamin's wife Reji is frequently angry with him because he forgets to do his chores, such as cleaning up the cat's litter box and doing the dishes. He reports that Reji frequently complains that she resents having to do the chores he forgets to do. The event that precipitated Benjamin coming for therapy was that he forgot his wedding anniversary and Reji yelled at him and left the house for several hours. Benjamin also reported that he frequently gets into trouble at school because he forgets to turn his grades in on time. The principal Ms. Mitchell recently sent Benjamin a written warning about this. The following conversation takes place between Amira and Benjamin during their second session.

Amira: *What would you like to talk about today?*
Benjamin: *At our last session you helped me to understand that in terms of Psychological Type I am a strong Intuitive type and the fact that I haven't developed my Sensing side is why I am so absent-minded. I really want to change that and learn how to be better at remembering detail. Reji gets really mad at me when I am forgetful and she takes it personally.*
Amira: *It sounds like you are really motivated to change and strengthen your Sensing side.*
Benjamin: *Yes. How can I do that?*
Amira: *There are two things that I think might help you. How about I describe them to you and you can let me know if you would like to try them?*
Benjamin: *OK!*
Amira: *The first thing I would suggest is that you use something called Charting. This would involve you keeping a daily Chart that looks like this (see* Figure 6.1).

In the Desirable Behavior column you would write down the behaviors you want to improve. What would be examples of that?

Benjamin: *I want to remember to do the dishes every morning and evening and also to take out the garbage once a week. And if Reji asks me to do something, to not forget it.*
Amira: *What about at school?*
Benjamin: *Oh yeah. I want to turn my grades in each week on time.*
Amira: *That's great! So you just list all these desirable behaviors in the first column. Then each day you keep track in the What*

90 *Strategies for Strengthening Sensing*

Desirable Behavior	Week	What Happened?	Earned Reward?
	Week 1		
	Mon		
	Tues		
	Wed		
	Thurs		
	Fri		
	Sat		
	Sun		
	Week 2		
	Mon		
	Tues		
	Wed		
	Thurs		
	Fri		
	Sat		
	Sun		

Figure 6.1 Example of Form for Charting.

Strategies for Strengthening Sensing 91

	Happened column of each time you remembered to do one or more of the desirable behaviors or whether you forgot. If you remember to do at least one thing then you can engage in a rewarding behavior and would write Yes in the final column to note that you deserved a reward. However, if you forget to do anything you write No in the last column and you don't get a reward. What would be a good reward for you, ideally something that can happen each day?
Benjamin:	*I love watching TV. I have a favorite show I just started watching and it has run for six seasons with about ten episodes each season.*
Amira:	*That sounds excellent. It's a show you really like to watch and it can be watched every day if you remember to engage in your desirable behaviors and don't forget to do at least one of them. Would you like to try this?*
Benjamin:	*Very much.*

Benjamin and Amira meet two weeks later and review Benjamin's progress.

Amira:	*It has been two weeks since we last met. How did your Charting project go?*
Benjamin:	*I brought it in so we can look at it together (shows Amira the Chart in* Box 6.1*).*

Box 6.1 Example of Charting for Benjamin

Desirable Behavior	*Week*	*What Happened?*	*Earned Reward?*
Doing Chores, Completing Reji's requests, Doing grades, Not forgetting important tasks generally	Week 1 Mon	Forgot chores. Reji upset.	No
	Tues	Forgot to go to grocery store and get milk.	No
	Wed	Forgot to get up on time- didn't set alarm again! (I am really missing watching my show!)	No
	Thurs	Set alarm, got up on time and did the dishes after breakfast	Yes! Watched show 1 hour
	Fri	Forgot to hand in grades on time. Spoken to by principal.	No
	Sat	Remembered to go to grocery store. Reji happy.	Yes

92 Strategies for Strengthening Sensing

	Sun	Did dishes after breakfast and lunch.	Yes
Week 2			
	Mon	Turned in grades from Monday's test on time.	Yes
	Tues	Forgot to take garbage out	No
	Wed	Did dishes after Breakfast and dinner. Reji very happy.	Yes
	Thurs	Did dishes after breakfast and dinner. Reji thanked me.	Yes
	Fri	Remembered to update my personnel file as requested by the principal. Principal sent me email thanking me.	Yes
	Sat	Forgot Reji's request to buy a birthday card for Reji's mother. Reji upset.	No
	Sun	Set alarm, got up early and mowed lawn, did dishes all three meals.	Yes

Amira: So tell me what this means to you.

Benjamin: Well, at first in week 1 I didn't do so well. I was absent-minded three days in a row and Reji was mad at me. But what really bothered me was that I didn't get to watch my favorite show. I had only seen the first episode which ended quite dramatically so I was dying to know what happened next. Anyways I pulled it together on Thursday and got up on time so I rewarded myself that night by watching the second episode. I was forgetful at school on Friday so no show, but on the weekend I pleased Reji by remembering to go to the grocery store and on Sunday I remembered to do the dishes. So I rewarded myself both nights.

Amira: That's excellent. And I see you had quite a different week the second week.

Benjamin: Yes, I went from rewarding myself three times in week 1 to five times in week 2.

Amira: That is a significant improvement. Do you feel as though you are improving in strengthening your ability to remember detail and important tasks?

Benjamin: I do. What I especially like is that my relationships with Reji and with my principal seem to be improving.

Amira: What I see is that you are beginning to effectively strengthen your Sensing side so that you are better at remembering detail and not being as absent-minded.

Comment: For this technique to be successful the client must be motivated to change and be willing to self-administer the selected reward.

Resources

Books

Martin, G., & Pear, J. J. (2015). *Behavior modification: What it is and how to do it* (10th ed.). Psychology Press.

This behavior modification text is very through in describing a range of strategies for modifying behavior. Pages 69–72 give an overview of the different ways the Premack Principle can be used with clients.

Watson, D. L., & Tharp, R. G. (2013). *Self-directed behavior: Self-modification for personal adjustment.* Cengage Learning.

This behavior modification book gives practical suggestions for modifying one's own behavior, making it a useful book to recommend to clients. Chapter 7: Consequences describes how to use the Premack Principle, and other ways to reinforce (reward) desirable behaviors in oneself.

YouTube Video

ABA Strategy: The Premack Principle https://www.youtube.com/watch?v=EPodUlf6DGo

Behaviorist Rob Haupt explains the practical use of the Premack Principle in terms of how it can be used with children.

Humanistic Therapy Strategies: Multimodal Assessment

Multimodal Assessment is the assessment approach used in Arnold Lazarus' eclectic approach to therapy called Multimodal Therapy. Lazarus, who was originally trained as a behavior therapist, developed Multimodal Therapy as an antidote to what he felt was behavior therapy's overly narrow approach. Multimodal Assessment includes assessment of cognitive and behavioral factors that could justify its placement as a Cognitive-Behavioral Therapy assessment approach. However, it also contains assessment of feelings and sensations which would justify it as an Humanistic therapy assessment approach. We include it here as a Humanistic Therapy Strategy because of the eclectic nature of the approach overall.

Definition: Multimodal Assessment is an assessment of a client's functioning in seven basic aspects of personality: Behavior, Affect, Sensation, Imagery, Cognition, Interpersonal, and physiological (body) aspects represented by Drugs. The acronym represented by these seven core parts of personality is BASIC ID, which Lazarus intended as a convenient way to remember the seven parts. Table 6.1 illustrates typical questions a therapist can use to investigate how a client's personality is engaged when interacting with another person.

The purpose of Multimodal Assessment is: (1) to help the therapist develop a comprehensive treatment plan that draws upon different therapies and which target problems in any of the seven personality areas, and (2) to help the client understand how her/his personality is affected in

94 *Strategies for Strengthening Sensing*

Table 6.1 BASIC ID Assessment Questions

BASIC ID Category	Assessment Questions
Behavior	"What do you typically say or do with_____ (problematic situation or person)?"
Affect	"What sort of emotions or feelings do you typically have with_____?"
Sensation	"What sensations or tensions do you experience when_____?"
Imagery	"What images or fantasies do you have when dealing with_____?"
Cognition	"What does it mean to you when_____?" "What kinds of thoughts do you have about_____?"
Interpersonal	"What does (name person) typically do when_____?" "How does (name person) treat you when_____?"
Drug/Physiological	"When you are dealing with_____, how is your body affected?" (e.g. "Feel ill, sleep affected, need medication, etc").

relationships. Because Intuitive types who have not developed Sensing are sometimes unaware of how specific interpersonal behaviors impact themselves, teaching this client how to identify how specific parts of their personality interconnect helps strengthen their Sensation side.

Procedure:

Step 1 Teach the Client the BASIC ID.
Step 2 Use the BASIC ID to explore a relationship that the client finds puzzling and in which the client seems unaware of the detailed way their personality is affected in the relationship.
Step 3 Teach the client the firing order in which the parts of their personality are triggered when with others.
Step 4 Have the client for homework practice identifying their BASIC ID sequence.

How This Approach Strengthens Sensing: In order for a client to identify their BASIC ID sequence that have to develop skill in identifying specific triggering behaviors of the Other Person, and the specific behaviors the client makes in response. This detailed behavioral tracking relies heavily on the Sensing function. In addition, the client must also develop awareness of how their body is affected (Drugs modality), what their sensations are (Sensation modality), and what is happening at the cognitive level (Cognitions and Imagery). Finally, the client is asked to describe the sequence in which these different parts of their personality occur during encounters with others. This complex tracking of external and internal behaviors using precise language requires the extensive use of Sensing.

Type Demand of This Approach:

For the Therapist: Extraversion Sensing/Intuition Thinking/Feeling Judging. To effectively use this approach the therapist must adopt an active teaching role (E), be precise in identifying and labeling behaviors (S), images (N), thoughts (T) and feelings (F), and be able to organize the order in which the BASIC ID occurs (J).

For the Client: To benefit from this approach the client needs to be willing to keep track of the different parts of their personality (S).

Case Study: **Benjamin**

During her session with Benjamin, Amira teaches Benjamin the BASIC ID in relationship to an incident involving Reji.

Amira:	One way to strengthen your awareness of detail is to use an approach to understanding personality called the BASIC ID. This is an acronym for the seven different parts of one's personality: Behavior, Affect, Sensation, Imagery, Cognition, Interpersonal, and Drugs (D for the physical part of the body most affected by drugs and medication). If you like I can show you how to used the BASIC ID to heighten your awareness of what happens between you and Reji. Would you like to try it?
Benjamin:	Yes, I would.
Amira:	OK, the next step is that I will interview you using the BASIC ID about an incident that caused you stress with Reji. Can you describe a recent incident?
Benjamin:	Yes, on Saturday she was unhappy with me and it basically ruined my day I was so upset.
Amira:	I am going to start by asking you about the Interpersonal dimension which is what was the other person's behavior. What did Reji say and do that upset you? (Behavior)
Benjamin:	She said: "You forgot to take the garbage out again. Please take it out now!"
Amira:	What did her face look like and what was her voice tone like? (Behavior)
Benjamin:	She had an irritated look like she was clenching her teeth. Her voice tone was tense.
Amira:	Now I am going to ask you about Affect or Emotion. What feeling did you experience when she said this? (Affect)
Benjamin:	I felt she was being ridiculous!

96 *Strategies for Strengthening Sensing*

Amira: That is a thought you had. What emotion, like anxious, sad, angry did you have? *(Affect)*
Benjamin: I felt angry.
Amira: Did you have any other feelings, perhaps later?
Benjamin: I felt anxious, worried.
Amira: Ok, it's important to be aware of that. Now when you felt angry were you aware of any sensations in your body and was your breathing affected? *(Sensation)*
Benjamin: I felt a tightness in my chest and I think I was breathing more rapidly.
Amira: I am going to ask you now about Cognition which refers to thoughts or ideas. What thoughts were you having at the time? *(Cognition)*
Benjamin: I was thinking: "She doesn't love me any more."
Amira: Now I am going to ask you about Imagery. This refers to images or fantasies we have. Did you experience any images while talking with Reji? *(Imagery)*
Benjamin: Yes, I had an image of her getting so mad she would walk out the door and leave me.
Amira: Has this ever happened?
Benjamin: No.
Amira: So it is an image really based on your fear not on something likely to occur. *(Clarifying Image)*
Benjamin: Yes, that's true.
Amira: I am going to ask you now about your Behavior. What did you say or do in response? *(Behavior)*
Benjamin: I didn't say anything. I went and took the garbage out. Then I went for a long walk to get out of the house.
Amira: Finally I am going to ask you about the Drugs-Body dimension. How was your body affected? *(Drugs)*
Benjamin: Well, that night I was unable to sleep much.
Amira: Thank you that gives me a more detailed picture of how your personality was affected during this interaction with Reji. How did you experience my using the BASIC ID with you?
Benjamin: It was good. I can see that it tracks things in a really detailed way.
Amira: Now let's try and see if we can figure out the sequence in which the different parts of your personality were affected. What would you select as the beginning factor?
Benjamin: When she yelled at me.
Amira: That's the Interpersonal dimension. What part of you do you think was affected next?
Benjamin: I didn't act right away. I think I felt angry, then anxious.
Amira: Sometimes when we have a strong emotion it's because of

	a thought we are having. Is that possible what happened for you?
Benjamin:	Yes, maybe. I think I was thinking "she yelled at me and this means she doesn't love me."
Amira:	That's a thought that can trigger a strong emotion.
Benjamin:	Yes I think that's what happened.
Amira:	Can you see that your feeling anxious came from your thought "she doesn't love me"?
Benjamin:	Yes, it's not a happy thought.
Amira:	*(drawing on a piece of paper)* From what you told me it sounds like your BASIC ID sequence was like this and ending with your Behavior *(see* Figure 6.2*)*. Notice how after Reji criticized you there is something happening with your Cognition and Affect that seems connected with your Behavior.
Benjamin:	Yes, my Behavior seems to flow out of my upset thoughts and feelings.

INTERPERSONAL

(Yelled at by wife)

COGNITION

("She doesn't love me")

AFFECT

(Angry then anxious)

BEHAVIOR

(Said nothing, took out garbage)

Figure 6.2 Initial BASIC ID Sequence for Benjamin.

Amira: That's right. What we are trying to do here is put labels on what is going on with your personality so that you have a more accurate of understanding of yourself.

Amira then discussed with Benjamin a homework assignment in which he was asked to keep a diary and write down his BASIC ID sequence whenever he experienced stress with Reji. His homework assignment was to try and notice how all the parts of his personality were engaged when an "incident" with Reji occurred. The following discussion takes place at their next session.

Amira: How did your week go with tracking your BASIC ID?
Benjamin: It was interesting. I experienced stress with Reji twice and I got the same BASIC ID sequence each time. Here is the sequence I noted. I also tried to be more aware of how the other parts of my BASIC ID fitted in (see Figure 6.3).
Amira: So your BASIC ID sequence seems to be:

> Interpersonal > Imagery > Cognition > Sensation > Affect > Behavior > Drugs.

Benjamin: That's right.
Amira: Is there anything about this sequence that surprised you?
Benjamin: Yes. Previously I was aware that when Reji was upset with me I would feel upset in response and then keep silent and avoid her. Now I see that the images and thoughts I have are of a very strong, really overly strong, nature and that is why I react so strongly. Now that I am able to track my BASIC ID I have noticed that I am calmer and don't get as upset. I am able to step back from myself and examine what is going on better. I am also doing better at noticing Reji's behaviors and how they impact me.
Amira: Can you give an example?
Benjamin: Yes, the other day I almost forgot to take the garbage out. I noticed Reji looking at the kitchen garbage can and I had the thought: "She thinks I am going to forget to take the garbage out." So I immediately went and took out the garbage.
Amira: It sounds like using the Basic ID is helping you to be more focused and track better your relationship with Reji.
Benjamin: Yes, it's definitely helping.

This illustrates how Benjamin was able to develop his Sensation side further and become more aware of the connection between Reji's behavior, his own behavior, and his internal processes that produced his behavior with Reji.

Strategies for Strengthening Sensing 99

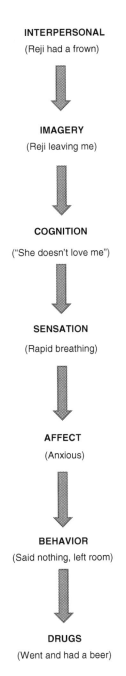

Figure 6.3 Complete BASIC ID Sequence for Benjamin.

Resource

Lazarus, A. (2006). *Brief but comprehensive psychotherapy: The multimodal way.* Springer Publishing Company.

Family Therapy Strategies: Caring Days

The *Caring Days* exercise is a useful technique that can be used to strengthen Sensing behaviors.

Definition: Caring Days involves having two family members (often a couple) identify frequent small caring behaviors that each would like to receive from the other person. These are monitored on a chart kept in a central place where each person writes the date on which the other person engaged in the caring behavior. This technique was developed by behavioral couples therapist Richard Stuart.

Procedure:

Step 1 Explain rationale for doing *Caring Days*.
Step 2 Have each family member make a list of small, easy to implement on a frequent basis, caring behaviors they would like to receive from each other.
Step 3 Assign the Caring Days exercise for homework.
Step 4 Debrief the Caring Days Exercise.

How This Approach Strengthens Sensing: When Caring Days is used to strengthen Sensing in a client, it is essential that the Other Person list as the behaviors they want to receive be Sensing behaviors. These typically would be behaviors that are the antithesis of being absent-minded and could include behaviors that the Intuitive type frequently forgets. Because the Intuitive type also gets to list behaviors they want from the Other Person, engaging in this exercise is rewarding. As the Other Person on a daily basis engages in behaviors that the Intuitive type likes, the Intuitive type will be more motivated to engage in the Sensing behaviors that the Other Person would like to receive. As Richard Stuart puts it, the "coin of the realm" in a marriage (and we would add – a family) consists of small caring behaviors that are repeated daily. In addition, because the Caring Days List is posted somewhere central it helps the absent-minded Intuitive type to remember to initiate behaviors on the list.

Type Demand of This Approach:

For the Therapist: Sensing Judging. To use this technique the therapist must teach the Caring Days approach using concrete examples (S) and be willing to follow up on assigning it as homework (J).

For the Client: The clients must be willing to identify concrete behaviors they would like to see from each other (S), be willing to show caring through these behaviors (F), and be willing to systematically engage in the exercise on a daily basis (J).

Case Study: **Benjamin**

At a joint counseling session with Benjamin and Reji, Amira introduces *Caring Days*.

Amira: As you have both told me that you would like to strengthen your relationship, I would like to tell you about an exercise you can do that will help with that. It is called Caring Days. It involves our making a list of about ten different things that each of you would like the other person to do during the week. These behaviors should be small, caring behaviors that would let you know the other person cares about you. They should be something you could do ideally on a daily basis and should not be something you are fighting about. For example, Reji you could list behaviors Benjamin could do that show he remembers things you consider important. And Benjamin, you could have in your list behaviors that Reji could do that show she cares about you. After we make this list we will post it somewhere central in your home, like on the refrigerator or the mirror in the bathroom. Then each time your partner does one of the behaviors, you keep track of it on the chart by writing in the date the caring behavior was done. *(Step 1: Explain the Rationale for Doing Caring Days)*.

Amira than worked with the couple and together they made the list shown as Table 6.2. As can be seen from the lists, Reji's list is very different from Benjamin's list. Reji's requested caring behaviors mostly involve actions that involve helping Reji with things around the house – things he normally forgets to do. Benjamin's list involves affectionate behaviors and collaborative couple activities. Since Benjamin had indicated that he wanted to become less forgetful and remember to do chores and behaviors valued by Reji, Amira gently encouraged Reji to include these items on her request list. Table 6.2 also shows how the couple completed the *Caring Days* chart which they taped to the refrigerator. It can be seen that although they did not complete all the requested activities, they did attempt many of them. The following discussion with Amira takes place at the next session.

102 *Strategies for Strengthening Sensing*

Table 6.2 Caring Days List for Reji and Benjamin

Behaviors Reji Will do for Benjamin	Date Done (Recorded by Benjamin)	Behaviors Benjamin Will do for Reji	Date Done (recorded by Reji)
Give a compliment	May 3, 4, 6, 8	Wash dishes at breakfast	May 2, 4, 6
Hold hands in public	May 9, 10	Wash dishes at dinner	May 2
Massage his back	May 3	Ask Reji if he can help with anything	May 3, 8
Say I love you		Watch TV together	
Cuddle in bed	May 8	Make breakfast	
Play scrabble game		Help with gardening	May 10
Go for an evening walk	May 4, 6, 8	Get Chinese take-out for dinner	May 8
Ride bicycles together	May 10	Clean cat's litter box	May 2, 3, 4, 5
Ask me what I'd like for dinner		Vacuum the house	
Watch an "action" movie with me		Get up at 8 am on the weekend so we can have breakfast together	
Give me a hug	May 3, 4, 6, 8	Wash her car	
Give me a smile and a kiss	May 4, 8, 10	Pick up his socks from the floor	May 3, 4, 5, 6
Send me a text message	May 2, 6	Tidy books in the den	May 6
Give me a foot rub		Flea comb the cat	
Put a note-message for me in my briefcase to surprise me at work		Shop for groceries	May 8

Amira: So how did the Caring Days exercise go last week? (*Step 4*: *Debrief the Caring Days Exercise*)

Reji: It went really well.

Benjamin: Yes it was good.

Amira: I see from the Caring Days chart you brought in that you each attempted quite a few items with each other. Which ones did you enjoy most?

Reji: I really liked it when Benjamin did the dishes so many times. This is a big help to me.

Benjamin: She gave me a lot of surprise hugs and massaged my back. I really liked that.

This sample dialog is typical of how couples and family members experience doing Caring Days. The central posting of the Caring Days list makes it an easy reminder for family members to participate. In addition, receiving a desired behavior from a family member motivates the client to also provide them with a desired behavior.

Additional Strategies: Box 6.2 shows five additional ways to strengthen Sensing.

Box 6.2 Five Additional Ways to Strengthen Sensing

Approach	*Example*
Ordeal Therapy	If the client is absent-minded more than "x" times a day, they have to agree to undergo a positive ordeal.
Active Listening	Have the client active listen to a partner/family member who is upset by the client's absent-minded behavior.
Empty Chair Technique	Ask the client to have a dialog between Absent-minded Self and Detailed Self.
The Miracle Question	Ask the client what would be the smallest behavior that would indicate that a miracle had occurred and their absent-mindedness problem no longer existed.
Method III Problem Solving	Explore with the client and family members using brainstorming different ways the client could help develop their detailed (Sensing) side.

Resources

LeCroy, C. W., Carrol, P., Nelson-Becker, H., & Sturlaugson, P. (1989). An experimental evaluation of the caring days technique for marital enrichment. *Family Relations, 38*(1), 15. 10.2307/583603
This study provides evidence-based support for the effectiveness of the Caring Day technique.

Lorenzo, J. M., & Barry, R. A. (2019). Caring days in couple and family therapy. *Encyclopedia of Couple and Family Therapy,* 381–383. 10.1007/978-3-319-49425-8_77
This encyclopedia entry gives a concise overview of Caring Days.

7 Strategies for Strengthening Intuition

CHALLENGES OF UNDERDEVELOPED INTUITION

Common challenges experienced by clients who have not developed their Intuition are: Expressing their Sensing function in a critical, nitpicking way and becoming upset with persons not adhering to close attention to detail. Clients with underdeveloped Intuition regard the use of imagination, feelings, gut instinct, or hunches as not valid ways to gather information about others. Sometimes they become easily upset if a friend or family member is late for a meeting or forgets some detail that the Sensing type regards as critical (but the other person does not). The Sensing type with underdeveloped Intuition often regards the Intuitive type's absent-mindedness as a sign of not caring, leading to tension and arguments. A common problem experienced when someone has not developed their Intuition is to fail to consider solutions that are not immediately obvious. This can lead to ineffective problem-solving.

WAYS TO STRENGTHEN INTUITION

Cognitive Behavioral Therapy Strategies: Cognitive Restructuring

A Cognitive Behavioral Therapy technique that can be used to strengthen Intuition is *Cognitive Restructuring.*

Definition: Cognitive Restructuring is the technique of disrupting negative or dysfunctional beliefs of the client and replacing them with more positive or functional beliefs.

Procedure: There are a number of different ways of doing cognitive restructuring with clients. The approach used here is based on Albert Ellis' Rational Emotive Behavior Therapy technique of Disputation. Disputation is a way of disputing or challenging a client's dysfunctional belief. Disputation is typically done by conveying to the client that perhaps they are wrong in their belief. There are several ways to do this, but asking the client questions is a common approach.

DOI: 10.4324/9781003097167-7

Table 7.1 Common Dysfunctional Beliefs

Dysfunctional Belief	Common Emotional Reaction
1. If I am not loved or approved of it's awful	Anxiety, depression
2. If I am rejected or lose a partner I will never find love	Depression, sadness
3. Making mistakes is terrible	Anxiety
4. I can't stand the way some people act	Anger
5. People who behave in ways I disapprove of should be punished	Anger
6. I am a worthless person	Depression
7. I am incapable of being happy	Depression
8. Terrible things are going to happen to me	Anxiety
9. I can't stand it	Anxiety
10. Because of what happened in the past I cannot change	Apathy

Step 1 Identify the client's dysfunctional belief and have the client rate the extent to which the client believes it (See Table 7.1).

Step 2 Teach the client the ABCDE's of behavior: Activating Event, Belief, Consequence, Disputation, Effect (see Table 7.2).

Step 3 Dispute the Client's dysfunctional belief using one or more disputation strategies. (see Table 7.3).

Step 4 Following disputation have the client rate the extent to which they now believe the dysfunctional belief to be true.

Step 5 Request the client use the ABCDE chart for homework (see Figures 7.1 and 7.2).

Step 6 Debrief with the client the ABCDE homework assignment.

How This Approach Strengthens Intuition: This cognitive therapy technique can be used to address any dysfunctional belief. In the case of the Sensing client whose Activating Events are absent-minded behaviors of an Intuitive type, Disputation can help the Sensing type to adopt less catastrophic thinking about the Intuitive's absent-minded behavior. This may increase the Sensing type's tolerance for the Other Person's lack of attention to detail and open the door to appreciating the role intuition could play in their own personality.

Type Demand of This Approach: For the Therapist: Extraversion Intuition Thinking Judging. To use this approach the therapist must take

Table 7.2 The ABCDE's of Behavior

Category	Description	Examples
Activating Incident	An incident that triggers the client Becoming upset or stressed	Someone criticizes the client The client makes a mistake Someone behaves in a way that the client disapproves of
Belief	A dysfunctional or irrational belief	"I am worthless" "I am no longer loved" "I will never be happy again" "He/she is a bad person"
Consequence	The client's behavior and emotions in response to the Belief	Excessively depressed, angry, anxious Isolating self Acting aggressive Experiencing very high stress on a 1–10 Scale (e.g. 9, 10)
Disputation	Most typically a question that Challenges the dysfunctional belief	"What is the evidence this belief is true?" "How does this make me worthless?"
Effect	The positive effect of the client disputing the dysfunctional belief	Feeling only slightly upset Being able to concentrate on other activities Experiencing lower stress on a 1–10 scale (e.g. 2, 3)

Table 7.3 Disputational Strategies

Strategy	Questions for Disputation
1. Evaluate Dysfunctional Thought	"Does that thought help you or hurt you?"
2. Prompt for coping thought	"What would be a more positive thought?"
3. Challenge Activating Event	"Why is that Activating Event so terrible?" "I realize that the Activating Event was stressful. But why is it catastrophic?"
4. Catastrophe Scale	"Imagine a Catastrophe Scale that goes from 1 to 100. On this scale what would be a 100, a 75, a 50, a 25? Now where would you place the Activating Event?" If the client places it below 50 say: "So it's not that catastrophic."

Strategies for Strengthening Intuition 107

5. Previous Coping Incident	"Can you think of a time when a similar Activating Event occurred and you didn't get so upset?" If the client can, say: "What thoughts did you have at the time that calmed you?" "Is that a coping thought you could use for this recent Activating Event?"
6. Personal Growth Opportunity	"Can you think of any positive things that could come from you having to deal with this Activating Event?"
7. Counteracting Imagery	"Can you think of any positive image that would counteract your dysfunctional belief that (state dysfunctional belief) (e.g. if the client's belief is "If I am not loved it's terrible" a counteracting image would be for the client to imagine a situation in which they do feel loved).

Date	Activating Event	Belief (Dysfunctional)	Behavior	Disputation	Effect (Positive)

Figure 7.1 The ABCDE Chart.

an active role teaching the ABCDE model to the client (E), be able to uncover the client's underlying dysfunctional belief (N), challenge the client's dysfunctional beliefs in a gentle but firm manner (T), and help the client to follow a structured Disputation procedure (J).

108   *Strategies for Strengthening Intuition*

Date	Activating Event	Belief (Dysfunctional)	Behavior	Disputation	Effect (Positive)
June 5	Partner forgets our anniversary	If I'm not loved or approved of it's awful	Acted angry, Didn't talk to them for several hours Felt depressed Tension 10/10	Being absent-minded doen't mean they don't care about me	Felt better, we agreed to go out and celebrate on the next day Tension 2/10

Figure 7.2 The ABCDE Chart: Example.

For the Client: Introversion Intuition Thinking Judging. To use this approach the client must be willing to be contemplative about themselves (I), to be introspective about underlying thoughts as opposed to surface and obvious behaviors (N), to consider their thoughts and behaviors objectively (T), and to carry out structured homework assignments using the ABCDE chart (J).

Case Study: Marcus

Marcus, age 30, comes for therapy with Lee because of problems Marcus is having with his partner Alain, who is 27. Marcus is an accountant and Lee is a designer and artist in an advertising firm. Marcus' specific reason for therapy is explained in the following interaction in Lee's office.

Lee: What would you like to talk about today?
Marcus: My partner Alain is constantly forgetful. I ask him to go grocery shopping and I give him a list and he comes back and he has missed one or more items on the list. He forgets dates like our closest friend Emily's birthday. Once he forgot our anniversary.
Lee: So is the problem that you want him to change?
Marcus: No! I want to change and not always be so upset with him. I am a detail person. As an accountant I have to be. If I make a mistake around the placement of a single figure it could ruin someone's tax report that I am preparing. Alain is an artist and I love him for his creativity. But along with

	that creativity is this flakiness, this lack of attention to detail. Originally, when we first met, I really liked this side of him. He is very imaginative and I am not.
Lee:	Can you give me an example of something specific where you liked his imaginative side?
Marcus:	Sure. When we moved in together my idea of furniture was very functional and basic. But he had all these wild ideas about using color and different furniture styles and he would describe his visions of what our house could look like. I really couldn't imagine what he was talking about but I told him to "go for it" and now we have the most beautiful furniture and decorations. Our friends love to visit because our place is like an art gallery!
Lee:	So at the beginning of your relationship you really valued his creative side. Were you aware that with that imaginative creativity it came with a lack of attention to practical detail?
Marcus:	Well yes, but it didn't bother me so much. Now it irritates me constantly and I am frequently critical of him and it is hurting our relationship.
Lee:	This is my understanding of your goal: you really value the creative, imaginative side of Alain but the absent-minded side of him is upsetting you to the point that it is having a negative effect on your relationship. To solve this you want to learn to be more tolerant of his absent-mindedness.
Marcus:	That's right.

Lee than explained to Marcus the ABCDE model of cognitive restructuring and obtained Marcus' permission to dispute his dysfunctional beliefs about Alain.

Lee:	Let's take a specific recent example of when you felt upset with Alain. What would that be?
Marcus:	Last Monday when he forgot to buy milk at the grocery store.
Lee:	OK, that was the Activating Event on the ABCDE form. What was your behavior in response?
Marcus:	I got very angry! I shouted at him: "What is the matter with you. How can you be so forgetful?" Then I didn't talk to him for the rest of the day.
Lee:	On a one to ten scale with ten being very stressed and one not at all stressed what was your tension level?

Marcus: It was a nine immediately, then maybe a seven the rest of the day.

Lee: Now let's examine what you were telling yourself at the B – the dysfunctional Belief – level. Here is a list of common dysfunctional beliefs (shows Marcus Table 7.1). Which of these do you think was affecting you?

Marcus: Number 4: I can't stand the way some people act, in this case Alain.

Lee: Would it be alright if I ask you some questions to help you challenge this belief?

Marcus: Yes.

Lee: Did your belief "I can't stand the way Alain acts" help you or hurt you? *(Disputation)*

Marcus: It hurt me.

Lee: How did it hurt you?

Marcus: It brings alienation into our relationship. When I get that upset I then make mistakes in my accounting. It fails to take into account all the good things in our relationship that are more important.

Lee: What more rational or calming thought could you have instead? *(Disputation)*

Marcus: We have a good relationship and I need to focus on that.

Lee: That sounds like a great coping thought. Now I understand that Alain's forgetting the milk was upsetting, but why was it terrible? *(Disputation)*

Marcus: Because he does it all the time.

Lee: I can see why that would be upsetting, but why is it catastrophic? *(Disputation)*

Marcus: OK, I get it. Alright, it's not really catastrophic.

Lee: Let's imagine a catastrophe scale from 1 to 100 where 100 is the very worst thing you can imagine. What would be a 100 on your scale?

Marcus: Death of a loved one, like Alain or my parents.

Lee: What would be a 75?

Marcus: Getting a serious illness where you have to be hospitalized.

Lee: What would be a 50?

Marcus: Being reprimanded by my boss for doing bad work.

Lee: What would be a 25?

Marcus: Finding a small dent on my car.

Lee: Ok, so where on this scale would you put Alain forgetting the milk?

Marcus: A ten!

Strategies for Strengthening Intuition 111

Lee: Definitely not catastrophic! Now can you think of a time when Alain forgot to do something and you didn't get so upset? *(Disputation)*

Marcus: Yes, and it involved groceries. He once forgot to buy a cake for a party we were holding for our friend Emily.

Lee: What sort of thoughts were you having that time?

Marcus: I realized that he was under an important deadline at his office and that being as creative as he is not easy for him when under pressure.

Lee: Is that sort of thought something you could use in the future to be calmer?

Marcus: Yes.

Lee: Can you think of any good things that could come from you having to deal with Alain being forgetful? *(Disputation)*

Marcus: Yes. It could help me to learn patience and to be more tolerant of someone behaving very opposite to me. Like a test really. It's sort of a reminder that Alain is a creative type and that kind of person is often forgetful.

Lee: When Alain is forgetful and you begin to feel stressed, is there an image you can focus on that would contradict your thought "I can't stand the way Alain acts"?

Marcus: Let me think for a minute. Well, I could focus on this time he remembered my birthday and presented me with a surprise party.

Lee: That's a good one because it shows Alain isn't always forgetful. Now I have used a number of different approaches to help you dispute or challenge your dysfunctional belief. Which of these do you think would be the most helpful for you to try between now and our next session.

Marcus: There were two that stood out for me: asking me what good things could come from my dealing with Alain's forgetfulness and the Catastrophe scale.

At the next session Marcus shared with Lee the following ABCDE Chart and reported that even though Alain had been forgetful three times during the week, Marcus had used Disputation to challenge his dysfunctional belief and remain calmer (Figure 7.3).

Comment: Although Disputation may not actively build Intuition in a client, it can be used to develop greater acceptance of Intuition in others and therefore potentially in oneself.

112 *Strategies for Strengthening Intuition*

Date	Activating Event	Belief (Dysfunctional)	Behavior	Disputation	Effect (Positive)
July 1	Alain forgets to buy bananas	I can't stand how someone (Alain) acts	Acted angry, Didn't talk to him for 2 days Felt depressed Tension 10/10	Did not dispute	
July 5	Alain forgot to mail a letter containing a bill payment	I can't stand how someone (Alain) acts	Initially upset, but then I challenged my belief	This behavior is typical of creative types who are creatively absorbed I can stand it	Felt calmer, more forgiving We had a nice dinner together Tension 3/10

Figure 7.3 Marcus' ABCDE Chart.

Resources

DiGiuseppe, R. A., DiGiuseppe, R., Doyle, K. A., Dryden, W., & Backx, W. (2013). *A practitioner's guide to rational-emotive behavior therapy.* Oxford University Press.

This book is a practical handbook containing detailed examples of how to effectively dispute clients dysfunctional beliefs.

Burns, D. (2020). *Feeling great: The revolutionary new treatment for depression and anxiety.* Pesi Publishing & Media.

This book describes a Cognitive Therapy approach to Cognitive Restructuring and Disputation. Like REBT this is an evidence-based approach. Although the book is written for clients, it contains many useful forms and activities that therapists can use with their clients.

Humanistic Therapy Strategies: Imagery Meditation and Guided Visualization

Imagery Meditation and *Guided Visualization* are humanistic therapy approaches that can be used to develop one's Intuitive (imaginative) side.

Definition: Imagery Meditation is a version of meditation that involves visualizing peaceful scenes. *Guided Visualization* is an Imagery meditation in which the therapist guides the client in visualizing.

Procedure: The following are instructions that the therapist can give during an in-session *Guided Visualization.* They can also be provided to the client to use as a between session exercise. It may be helpful for the therapist to first use a *Guided Visualization* with the client and then follow

Strategies for Strengthening Intuition 113

up with the suggestion that the client try the *Imagery Meditation* on their own between sessions.

Step 1 *Sit or lie in a quiet, comfortable place where you will not be disturbed.*

Step 2 *Close your eyes and begin to breathe slowly and deeply. One way to do this is to breathe in for 3 seconds (counting to yourself "1 and 2 and 3"), hold your breath for a 3 second count, then breathe out to a 3 second count. Do this for a few minutes then increase to 4 seconds, then later 5. Increase the number of seconds only if it feels comfortable to do so. This helps you to breath at a slower rate which produces a sense of relaxation.*

Step 3 *At any point imagine the most peaceful scene you can think of. Let yourself fully enter into being present in that scene by noticing details (for example, notice if your scene involves your lying on the sand at a beach, visualize the color of the sky and the water, notice any birds flying above the waves, try to experience the warmth and texture of the sand, etc.). Do this for about 5 minutes.*

Step 4 *Now imagine yourself moving within your peaceful scene. For example, if you are visualizing being at the beach, imagine yourself walking along the shoreline and gazing at the waves as they crash and foam on the sandy shore. Notice how your bare feet feel when the water touches them. Imagine yourself looking at and picking up interesting shells on the sand. Do this for about 5 minutes.*

The length of this exercise can be varied in time but you should not fall asleep, but instead use it to both relax and to develop your imagination.

In order to effectively conduct a Guided Visualization it is helpful if the therapist has experienced the type of scene the client is being asked to visualize.

How This Approach Strengthens Intuition: This exercise strengthens Intuition by exercising the client's imagination. Interestingly, it calls for the use of Sensing function within the visualization ("Notice the color of the sky").

Type Demand of This Approach: For the Therapist: Extraversion Sensing Judging. To use this technique where the therapist directs the client in a guided visualization, the therapist must guide the visualization (E), instruct the client in detailed observation within the visualization (S), and provide instructions in a sequence (J).

For the Client: Introversion Intuition Judging. To engage in a Guided visualization with the therapist, the client needs to listen to the therapist's instructions (I), use imagination to visualize details (N), and follow a sequence of instructions (J).

Case Study: **Marcus**

At the end of one session Marcus asked Lee if there was an exercise he could do to develop his Intuition. Lee recommended that Marcus try Imagery Meditation and explained the steps involved (outlined in the Procedure above). During that session Lee used a Guided Visualization to help Marcus learn the approach.

Lee: *To get you started there is an exercise we could do called Guided Visualization. This is a form of Imagery Meditation where I describe to you something peaceful for you to visualize as you concentrate on developing your imaging of the scene. Would you like to try it?*

Marcus: *Yes. I would.*

Lee: *If you were to think of a very peaceful scene what would that be?*

Marcus: *It would be in the mountains when I am skiing.*

Lee: *Is there a particular scene you would like to imagine?*

Marcus: *I am not really good at imagining. I would rather watch a film.*

Lee: *Ok, I am going to guide you in imagining this. Try closing your eyes and take a slow deep breath hold it for 3 seconds...1...2...3 now breathe out for three seconds 1...2...3.*

Lee then has Marcus extend his breathing to a 5 second period over the next few minutes and then begins the visualization (Steps 1 and 2).

Lee: *I want you to imagine that you are on a chairlift riding up the mountain at your favorite ski resort. It is a beautiful spring day and you can feel the warmth of the sun and the chairlift ascends. The sun is glistening off the snow and there are beautiful spruce trees on either side of the lift and you can smell the fresh scent from the boughs of the forest. You can hear the whirring of the lift cable passing through the towers as the lift gently swings as it passes each tower (Step 3).*

Lee continues for several minutes with Step 3 which involves the client passively visualizing the peaceful scene. Then he implements Step 4 which involves the client taking some action within the scene.

Lee: *Now as you approach the top of the lift you raise your ski tips and gently ski off the lift and stop at the edge of the run. You put your hands through the straps on your ski*

> *poles and wait until other skiers have gone and then you push off down an easy run. Now go ahead and visualize yourself skiing down a long groomed slope making graceful turns and feeling the sensation of flying across the snow. I am going to be quiet now as you continue to ski down the slope (Step 4).*
>
> Lee: *(after 3 minutes): OK, I'd like you to bring your awareness back to the room and open your eyes. Were you able to visualize skiing?*
>
> Marcus: *Yes, but your guiding me helped. I was actually able to experience the sense of riding the chairlift as well as coming down the slope.*

At a follow-up session Lee and Marcus have the following discussion.

> Lee: *It has been 3 weeks now that you have been practicing Imagery Meditation. What has been your experience of doing this?*
>
> Marcus: *It was hard at first because I am not someone who uses their imagination much. However, doing the Guided Visualization with you in our sessions and then listening to some of the Guided Visualizations on the internet helped a lot. On my own I have used the skiing one we first did together and I have tried it about four times each week. I find that I can now easily visualize skiing down different runs.*
>
> Lee: *Has this new ability of your to use your imagination showed up in any other contexts?*
>
> Marcus: *It's interesting you ask that. Yesterday Alain showed me a painting he has bought and asked me where I thought would be a good place for it. Normally I would have needed to take it and place it against the wall in different parts of the house to know where it should go. However, I found that I was able to imagine it in different spots and I quickly said I think it should go on the wall facing the dining room. And it was perfect there! Actually, Alain said to me: "You are developing an artistic eye."*

Resources

Gajdamaschko, N. (2005). Vygotsky on imagination: Why an understanding of the imagination is an important issue for schoolteachers. *Teaching Education*, 16(1), 13–22. 10.1080/1047621052000341581
This article explains Vygotsky's position on why the widely held view of many educators that imagination is innate and cannot be taught is incorrect. Vygotsky

held that an important role of teachers is to promote the development of children's imagination and that imagination is a very important part of the personality.

Guided Imagery Meditation – HelpGuide.org. https://www.helpguide.org/meditations/guided-imagery-meditation.htm

This 5 minute guided imagery meditation combines deep breathing with verbal instructions on visualizing in detail a peaceful lake scene.

Nguyen, J., & Brymer, E. (2018). Nature-based guided imagery as an intervention for state anxiety. *Frontiers in Psychology, 9.* 10.3389/fpsyg.2018.01858

This study describes a comparison group study on the effectiveness of guided imagery on reducing anxiety. The study contains a summary of the evidence-based support for using guided imagery for anxiety reduction.

Zittoun, T., & Gillespie, A. (2015). *Imagination in human and cultural development.* Routledge.

The authors describe how collective community action can result when many different persons participate in the same imaginary scenario about a possible future. "Communities of imagination can become galvanized by a vision of the future and seek to institute it, leading to sociogenesis, that is, the development of society itself."

Family Therapy Strategies: Method III Problem Solving

Method III Problem Solving is a brainstorming approach to problem solving that encourages participants to come up with a creative solution that satisfies both parties.

Definition: *Method III Problem Solving* was developed by psychologist Thomas Gordon as an alternative to what he called Method I (we solve this my way) or Method II (we solve this your way). In Method III Problem Solving both parties win in the sense that they may not get exactly what they want, but that because there is compromise each party obtains something and no one is clearly the "loser."

Procedure:

Step 1 Define everyone's needs

This is a very important step because it differentiates between needs and solutions. People often come to the negotiating table prematurely committed to a particular solution which the other person may reject out of hand. By identifying each person's needs everyone is in a more flexible position to generate alternative solutions that might meet a particular need. The underlying principle is that for any particular need a person has there are likely several ways that need could be met.

Step 2 Brainstorm solutions

This is the step where Intuition comes into play. During this phase each person should try to generate at least five to eight solutions, including "off the wall" ones that could be used to meet both person's needs. This is the type of creative brainstorming that is called for when one is asked to generate as many different uses for a paper clip as one can think of (e.g. repair a broken zipper, remove hair from a hairbrush, hold flowers in place, open an envelope, repair eyeglasses, clear a spray bottle, etc.).

Step 3 Evaluate the solutions

During this phase place a + beside the solutions you both agree on, an x beside any you both find unacceptable, and a ? beside the solution you disagree on. Next discuss with each other your likes and dislikes about each solution.

Step 4 Decide on final solutions

This step will likely require some compromise. However, if enough different solutions have been brainstormed then the likelihood that there is one solution that both persons can agree on is more likely. Reaching this sort of compromise requires a measure of caring between the persons involved.

Step 5 Implement solutions

This step involves making clear who does what to implement the solution.

Step 6 Evaluate solutions

Set a date at which you will meet again to discuss the effectiveness of the solution. If the solution did not work to everyone's satisfaction, then a repeat of Method III steps is warranted with a need to re-examine other previously generated solutions to see if they are worth trying and to perhaps generate some additional solutions.

How This Approach Strengthens Intuition: The step where Intuition is called for is Step 2 Brainstorming. Brainstorming calls for the generation of different possibilities. However, when doing this step, it is important to legitimize creative and unusual solutions as one makes one's list.

Type Demand of This Approach: For the Therapist: Extraversion Intuition Judging. To use this technique the therapist must teach it to the clients (E), emphasize creativity (N), and ask the clients to strictly follow the six problem solving steps (J).

For the Clients: Intuition Feeling Perceiving. To benefit from this technique the clients must be willing to suspend judgment in order to brainstorm creative alternatives (N), care enough about the other person to compromise (F)), and be flexible when considering alternatives (P).

Case Study: **Marcus**

At a joint session Lee is having with Marcus and Alain, the following problem comes up.

Lee: *What would you both like to discuss today.*
Marcus: *I would like to discuss Alain's plan to have his parents come for a two week visit!*
Alain: *It's not just my plan. You agreed to it!*
Lee: *Marcus, you sound unhappy with this visit. Can you say more about it?*
Marcus: *Yes. I work out of my home office and I need quiet during the day so I can concentrate. Alain has invited his parents to come visit during the two weeks before taxes are due which is the busiest time of the year for me. Alain's parents love to talk and watch football and while I generally enjoy their company, their coming at this time will make it hard for me to work in a quiet house. I think Alain should ask his parents to cancel their visit.*
Alain: *But you agreed to these dates and they have already bought their airline tickets which are not refundable!*
Marcus: *Yes that's true. But my boss has unexpectedly asked me to take on extra tax work that is new for me and I will be in big trouble if I screw this up!*
Lee: *I would like to suggest we try to solve this in a way that works for you both. May I tell you about it?*

Lee then explains the six steps of Method III Problem Solving and Marcus and Alain agree to try it. The following dialog will illustrate Steps 1, 2, and 3.

Lee: *Let's do Step 1. First let's clarify what needs each of you has rather than what solution you want. Marcus let's start with you.*
Marcus: *I need peace and quiet so that I can complete my work and not have my boss mad at me.*
Alain: *I want to spend time with my parents and not insult them by canceling their visit.*
Lee: *Ok, now let's do Step 2 which is brainstorming. This involves each of you making five to eight different suggestions which may be very creative, even "off the*

Strategies for Strengthening Intuition 119

wall." By generating a lot of different solutions it increases the chance we can find one satisfactory to both of you. Let's take 10 minutes while each of you writes down your ideas then we will share them.

After 10 minutes Marcus and Alain share their lists of brainstormed solutions (see Table 7.4).

Their resulting Step 3 evaluation is summarized in Table 7.5.

During Step 4 Deciding on a Final Solution, Marcus and Alain agreed on trying one solution they both had recommended: having Alain take his parents on a week-long trip somewhere (either Nashville or Key West). This would give Marcus a week by himself to focus on his work. During the second week when Alain's parents would be at Marcus' and Alain's house, Marcus agreed to try the soundproof headphones, and Alain agreed to try and take his parents out for a few hours each day. Following the parent's visit, Lee met with Marcus and Alain again and learned that Step 5 Implementation of the Solution had gone fine. Their overall evaluation (Step 6) was that this was a solution that they could effectively use again in the future.

Table 7.4 Step 2 Marcus' and Alain's Brainstormed Solutions

Person	Alternate Solutions
Marcus	Reschedule visit and pay for their tickets
	Alain takes them on a trip to Key West
	Alain goes to visit them instead
	We put them up in a nice hotel for two weeks
	We move the TV room to the other end of the house
	We outfit the TV room with wireless headphones to eliminate TV noise
	Each day Alain takes his parents out somewhere for 3–4 hours exploring the city
Alain	Marcus asks his boss to let him work at the main accounting office
	Marcus wears soundproof headphones while working
	We rent a nice hotel room for Marcus to work out of during the day
	I take my parents on a holiday to Nashville for at least one week
	My parents go to bed early and Marcus works until midnight because he is a night owl and is generally up to midnight anyway
	We soundproof Marcus' office
	We buy a white noise machine to place outside Marcus' office to muffle noise

120 *Strategies for Strengthening Intuition*

Table 7.5 Step 3 Marcus' and Alain's Evaluation of Brainstormed Solutions

Person	Evaluation by Marcus & Alain	Alternate Solutions
Marcus	x	Reschedule visit and pay for their tickets
	+	Alain takes them on a trip to Key West
	x	Alain goes to visit them instead
	x	We put them up in a nice hotel for two weeks
	x	We move the TV room to the other end of the house
	?	We outfit the TV room with wireless headphones to eliminate TV noise
	+	Each day Alain takes his parents out somewhere for 3–4 hours exploring the city
Alain	x	Marcus asks his boss to let him work at the main accounting office
	?	Marcus wears soundproof headphones while working
	x	We rent a nice hotel room for Marcus to work out of during the day
	+	I take my parents on a holiday to Nashville for at least one week
	x	My parents go to bed early and Marcus works until midnight because he is a night owl and is generally up to midnight anyway
	x	We soundproof Marcus' office
	?	We buy a white noise machine to place outside Marcus' office to muffle noise

Additional Strategies: Box 7.1 shows five additional ways to strengthen Intuition.

Box 7.1 Five Additional Ways to Strengthen Intuition

Approach	Example
Charting	Ask the client to keep a daily chart of instances where they act in a more imaginative way.
Paradoxical Intention	Ask the client to deliberately do something safe but in a somewhat negligent way that fails to pay attention to detail (e.g. sloppy paint job, poor typing, etc.) then to try and make themselves feel anxious for 30 minutes about this "error."
Multimodal Assessment	Have the client carry out a homework assignment in which they track the sequence of their BASIC ID, but paying particular attention to imagery.
Active Listening	When having the client practice Active Listening with a family member, encourage the client to intuit the

The Miracle Question	family member's underlying feelings by using therapist prompts (e.g. "What do you think she is feeling?"). Ask the client what very small behavior would indicate that a miracle had occurred that indicates they were able to be more Intuitive and imaginative.

Resources

Gordon, T. (2010). *Parent effectiveness training: The proven program for raising responsible children.* Harmony.

Chapter 11. *"The "no lose" method for resolving conflicts" and Chapter 13 "Putting the 'No lose" method to work" describe in detail how Method III can be used to resolve conflict between parents and children. However, the same approach can be used with adults.*

Brainstorming: Generating many radical, creative ideas. (1996, November 11). Management Training and Leadership Training - Online. https://www.mindtools.com/brainstm.html

This website describes the business use of brainstorming, but contains many creative strategies for giving imagination free play: the Stepladder Technique, Brainwriting, Online Brainstorming, Rolestorming, and more.

Relationship communication blocked? Play the brainstorming game. (2013, October 9). GoodTherapy.org TherapyBlog. https://www.goodtherapy.org/blog/relationship-communication-blocked-play-brainstorming-game-1009134

This website provides an interesting example of how brainstorming can be used with a family.

8 Strategies for Developing Thinking

CHALLENGES OF UNDERDEVELOPED THINKING

Feeling types who have not developed their Thinking function typically experience a number of challenges. First, they ofter experience difficulty in analyzing a situation rationally and objectively which can lead to errors in judgment about persons and important tasks. Second, they have an emphasis on mercy and forgiveness that can lead to a failure to promote justice. Third, an abhorrence for conflict can lead them to lack courage in speaking up for themselves in close personal as well as work situations. Thinking types are often described as tough-minded and assertive and as persons who are not easily pushed around. A common reason Feeling types, who have not developed their assertive, tough-minded Thinking side, seek therapy is because of their inability to handle aggressive behavior from others to which they may respond in a non-assertive and submissive manner.

WAYS TO STRENGTHEN THINKING

Cognitive-Behavioral Therapy Strategies: Assertion Training and Behavior Rehearsal

Assertion Training and *Behavior Rehearsal* are two useful Cognitive-Behavioral Therapy techniques for strengthening Thinking.

Definition: Assertion Training teaches clients ways to develop and use social skills so that they have courage to stand up for themselves and express their opinions without being paralyzed by the fear of rejection. *Behavior Rehearsal* is the technique of having the client role play an assertive behavior with the therapist as a way to build competency in the social skill.

Procedure

Step 1 Teach the client the difference between submissive, aggressive, and assertive behavior.

DOI: 10.4324/9781003097167-8

Submissive behavior occurs when someone wants to say or do something but remains silent and does nothing. As a result they don't get what they want and the Other Person gets what they want. For example, you have been patiently waiting in line for a long time to purchase something and the Other Person, without going to the end of the line, cuts in front of you and you say nothing. Aggressive behavior occurs when someone dominates the Other Person in such a way that they achieve what they want in the social situation and the Other Person loses (doesn't get what they want). For the cutting in line situation, an example of aggressive behavior would be for you to yell at the person cutting in and call them names. Assertion behavior is appropriate socially skilled behavior in which someone stands up for their rights without violating the rights of the Other Person. In this situation, assertive behavior would involve you calmly pointing out to the Other Person that there is a line and that you would like them to respect that by behaving like everyone else and take their place at the back of the line. The important thing about being assertive is that you stand up for your rights without violating the rights of others.

Some examples of the types of assertive behaviors that Feeling types may find challenging are:

- Expressing opinions
- Making requests
- Confronting others
- Saying no

You should determine through discussion which of these assertion behaviors is most appropriate for your client's situation.

Step 2 Help the Client Develop an Appropriate Assertive Response.

Discuss with the client what they would like to say and do to be more assertive.

Since one of the most difficult assertion skills for Feeling types to develop is confronting others, we will focus on that skill for illustrative purposes. A useful approach for addressing confrontation situations is the *DESC Confrontation* (Bower & Bower, 2008) (see Boxes 8.1 and 8.2).

Step 3 Role Play the Assertive Response with the Client.

This step is called *Behavior Rehearsal.* That is, the client, like an actor, rehearses their lines in practice with the therapist.

Step 3A Easy Role Play

The therapist plays the role of the Other Person while the client practices their assertive response. However, the therapist role plays a cooperative Other Person to make it easy for the client to experience success.

Box 8.1   How to Make a DESC Confrontation

The acronym DESC stands for Describe, Express, Specify, and Consequences. Each word describes a step for handling a situation in which the Other Person has violated your rights in some way.

Describe: This is the step of describing the Other Person's behavior in neutral, objective language without adding in any aggressive messages.

> Right way: "When we were just talking now you interrupted me before I was finished speaking."
>
> Wrong way: " How dare you interrupt me – what is the matter with you?"

Express: This is the step of explaining the effect the other person's behavior is having on you. This may involve a description of any inconvenience caused to you as well as a statemnet of the feeling impact it has on you.

> Right way: " I lose track of the point I want to make when you do that and I feel upset by it."
>
> Wrong way: " Your inconsiderate behavior is unacceptable."

Specify: This is the step of making a specific request for the Other Person to change their behavior.

> Right way: "I would like you to wait until I have finished speaking before you take your turn."
>
> Wrong way: " You need to keep your mouth shut."

Consequences: For this step you point out the positive consequences for both of you if they are willing to honor your request.

> Right way: "If you do that I will really appreciate it and we will be able to both enjoy our conversation."
>
> Wrong way: "If you continue being rude I won't talk to you any more."

A form that clients can use to write out a DESC confrontation is shown in Box 8.2.

Box 8.2 DESC Confrontation Form

Activating Event: Briefly describe the Other Person's behavior that you would like to confront.
_____
_____
_____
_____

Write out a sample DESC Confrontation you could make to handle this situation.
DESCRIBE: e.g. When you_____
_____
_____

EXPRESS: e.g. It had this effect on me_____
_____
And I felt_____

SPECIFY: e.g. I would like you to_____
_____

CONSEQUENCES: e.g. If you do that it will have a positvive effect of our relationship because
_____
_____

Step 3B Feedback

The therapist gives the client feedback on how to improve their assertive response (e.g. by maintaining eye contact, by not hesitating while speaking, etc.).

Step 3C Challenging Role Play

The therapist role plays the Other Person in a slightly more challenging way. This is to prepare the client for dealing with defensiveness and resistance which may occur.

Step 3D Feedback

The therapist provides additional feedback on how the client's role play went. It is important to give positive feedback to encourage the client, but to also point out any areas for improvement.

Steps 3A–D may be repeated as necessary to build up the client's confidence in using this approach.

How This Approach Strengthens Thinking
It is quite common for Feeling types to become "tongue-tied" during confrontation and other assertion situations. Having a script of what to say and do helps the client to stay focused on the task at hand. Behavior Rehearsal helps to build client self-efficacy: the belief that one can be efficacious in doing something. By allowing the client to experience success in the easy role play, the client acquires more confidence to try the more challenging role play. The therapist should be careful not to prematurely present an Other Person role play that is too intimidating for the client to respond to. From a behavior therapy point of view, the therapist provides positive reinforcement for the client's practice steps towards more assertive behavior. From a cognitive therapy point of view, the client comes to understand that in the role plays they are actually able to be successful. This changes their belief from "this is too hard for me to do" to "I did a good job of this!"

Type Demand of This Approach:
For the Therapist: Extraversion Sensing Thinking/ Feeling Judging. To use this approach the therapist must take on an active teaching role (E), give specific feedback to the client (S), be firm in playing the challenging version of the Other Person (T), encourage the client in trying new behavior (F), and follow the necessary structure of this approach (J).

For the Client: Extraversion Sensing Thinking Judging. To use this approach the client must speak up (E), be specific about what they would like (S), be firm and persistent (T), and follow-through with their assertive agenda (J).

Case Study: Camila

Isabella's client Camila, age 45, comes to a therapy session because she is feeling depressed. During the first session Isabella discovers that Camila is very non-assertive and has difficulty dealing with persons who are aggressive or critical. Camila describes a co-worker Beatrice who frequently criticizes Camila's work in front of other co-workers.

Strategies for Developing Thinking 127

Isabella: When Beatrice criticizes you, what do you typically do?
Camila: I put my head down and don't say anything.
Isabella: How do you feel when that happens?
Camila: I feel angry at her and angry at myself. Then I feel depressed for several days. It's affecting my work. I make a lot of mistakes.
Isabella: It sounds like you find it very hard to stand up for yourself.
Camila: Yes, I have always been like that.
Isabella: Is this something you would like to change?
Camila: Yes, very much.

Isabella then discusses with Camila the difference between submissive, aggressive, and assertive behavior and then teaches her how to make a DESC confrontation. Isabella writes out the DESC script shown as Box 8.3.

Isabella: Now how would you feel about us role playing your DESC response. I will role play Beatrice and you will be yourself and confront me using the DESC confrontation. This type of practice will help you to gain confidence. I will role play Beatrice as cooperative initially, then as we continue, I will push back a bit as that is what sometimes happens when one is confronted. In-between our role plays I will give you feedback on how you did. Would you like to continue?
Camila: I'm nervous, but yes.
Isabella: OK, let's imagine that you are approaching Beatrice when she is alone in her office. (*Initiating Behavior Rehearsal*)
Camila: Excuse me Beatrice, but may I speak with you for a moment?
Beatrice: Certainly, please have a seat.
Camila: I want to talk to you about the aggressive thing you did to me on Monday.
Beatrice: Whatever do you mean?
Camila: You said to me that I was stupid and I don't like that. In the future I would like you to not criticize me in front of others. It completely messes me up for the rest of the day.
Isabella: OK, how do you feel you did?
Camila: I thought I was ok. I felt very nervous standing up for myself like that.
Isabella: I thought you did an excellent job of speaking firmly. I would like to suggest you do two things to improve your confrontation. When you called her behavior "aggressive" she is likely to disagree with you. She may think she was trying to be helpful. It's better to stick to a simple

	description of her behavior as you did in the Describe part of your confrontation. You may also want to share that you felt angry and that it affected your work. Saying it "messes you up" is a little vague. (Provides Feedback)
Camila:	OK, I see what you mean.
Isabella:	Let's role play again and I will role play a slightly more challenging Beatrice. During the challenge, try to stay on course and don't let "her" sidetrack you. (Initiates second Behavior Rehearsal)
Camila:	OK. Excuse me Beatrice, may I speak to you for a moment.
Isabella:	You know I am really busy right now.
Camila:	This will only take a few minutes.
Isabella:	Oh, all right. What is it?
Camila:	Last Monday in front of Carmen and Judy you said to me that I made stupid mistakes on a letter I typed.
Isabella:	Yes, I could not believe your work was so poor.
Camila:	I felt angry at you because I felt embarrassed at being criticized publicly. You are not my supervisor. And you used the word stupid which I did not appreciate.
Isabella:	I was only trying to help you.
Camila:	It did not help me. It upset me and had a negative effect on my work the rest of the day. In the future I would like you to not criticize my work in front of our co-workers.
Isabella:	I'm sorry, I didn't mean to upset you.
Camila:	If you will do that I will really appreciate it and we will have a better work relationship.
Isabella:	OK, how did it feel that time?
Camila:	It felt good. I hesitated a bit when you said you were busy, but once I got into it, it felt ok.
Isabella:	I thought you did really well. You sounded confident. This time you maintained eye contact throughout, which is very assertive, and you were very specific about what I said that upset you. This made it hard for me to disagree with you. I also liked the way you pointed out to me the benefits of me complying with your request. (Provides Feedback)

As can be seen in the second role play, Isabella acted challenging at two points: at the beginning when she acted too busy to see Camila and when she made the excuse "I was only trying to help you." Following this, Isabella let Camila experience success by making no further challenging responses and instead made a conciliating response ("I'm sorry, I didn't mean to upset you."). By moving gradually from an easy role play to a more difficult one, the therapist's use of Behavior Rehearsal can significantly strengthen Thinking (tough-mindedness).

Box 8.3 DESC Confrontation Form for Camila

Activating Event: Briefly describe the Other Person's behavior that you would like to confront.
   In the presence of two other co-worker's Beatrice said to me: "Look at the stupid mistakes you made on this letter – don't you know how to use spellcheck?
   Write out a sample DESC Confrontation you could make to handle this situation.
   DESCRIBE: e.g. When you *said to me on Monday that I had made stupid mistakes in a letter that I typed you did so in the presence of our co-workers.*
   EXPRESS: e.g. It had this effect on me: *I felt embarassed to be criticized publically by someone who is not my supervisor.*
   And I felt *angry towards you. In addition it made it hard for me to focus on my work the rest of the day.*
   SPECIFY: e.g. I would like you *to not criticize my work in front of our colleagues or use words like "stupid" with me.*

   CONCEQUENCES: e.g. If you do that it will have a positive effect of our relationship because *I will be able to concentrate on my work and I will really appreciate it.*

Resources

Bower, S. A., & Bower, G. H. (2008). *Asserting yourself-updated edition: A practical guide for positive change.* Addison-Wesley.
   This book give a detailed description of how to make a DESC confrontation.
McFall, R. M., & Marston, A. R. (1970). An experimental investigation of behavior rehearsal in assertive training. *Journal of Abnormal Psychology, 76*(2), 295–303. 10.1037/h0030112
   This was an important randomized control group study demonstrating the effectiveness of behavior rehearsal with non-assertive undergraduate students.
Behavioral rehearsal. (2017, November 30). Counseling Practices. https://counselingpractices.wordpress.com/2017/10/17/behavioral-rehearsal/
   This website provides a thorough overview of the history and use of Behavioral Rehearsal.

Humanistic Therapy Strategies: Empty Chair Technique

The *Empty Chair Technique* (also called the Two Chair Technique) is a useful Gestalt therapy technique for strengthening Thinking by promoting assertive behavior.

Definition: The *Empty Chair Technique* is used by Gestalt therapists to help clients become aware of different parts of themselves. The therapist places an empty chair opposite the client and then asks the client to engage in a dialog with the underdeveloped or different parts of the self. For example, a client who feels conflicted about whether to end a relationship, might be asked to have a dialog between their head (Thinking) and their heart (Feeling). The Empty Chair Technique can also be used to have a client practice assertion with another person by having the client play themselves in one chair and the other person in the second chair.

Procedure

Step 1 Place an empty chair opposite the client's chair so that both chairs are facing each other (with the therapist sitting off to one side).

Instruct the client that when they are in chair A they are to play the role of (for example) their Heart or Feeling side. When they are in chair B they are to play the role of (for example) their Head or Thinking side. Ask the client to engage in a back and forth dialog between these two aspects of their self. Explain the rationale for this exercise by indicating that it will help to clarify what the client is thinking and feeling about their situation. Instruct the client to engage in this dialog for at least 5 minutes.

Step 2 Ask the client to begin speaking from one chair and to imagine that they are addressing in the second chair the self that will represent a different perspective.

If the client falters after a short period of time, encourage the client to continue.

Step 3 Debrief the exercise with the client.

How did they experience being in each role? What thoughts and feelings did they have? Did they have any insights into their behavior or the behavior of others? If the client is open to it offer coaching on ways to develop the personality aspect they wish to strengthen.

Step 4 If there was something the client wanted to say, but did not, have them continue the exercise and try to say what they wanted to.

Step 5 Conduct a final debriefing with the client.

About how they experienced doing the final role play. Discuss with the client any implications for a homework assignment.

How this Approach Strengthens Thinking
The Empty Chair Technique can strengthen Thinking in two ways. First a dialog between one's Heart and one's Head is essentially a dialog between one's Feeling side and one's Thinking side. Role playing one's Thinking side can help strengthen that aspect of a client simply by the therapist encouraging its expression. Second, the therapist can encourage the client to "stay with" the Thinking side of themselves by asking the client to stay longer in the chair where they are speaking from the Head perspective.

Type Demand of this Approach
For the Therapist: Extraversion Intuition Thinking Judging. To use this technique the therapist must direct the session (E), be able to intuit underlying feelings and thoughts that the client might have as they role play (N), be able to encourage the client to "stay with" a difficult part of the role play (T), and follow through with the structure of the exercise (J).

For the Client: Extraversion Sensing Thinking Perceiving. To use this technique the client must be willing to "take the stage" and engage in the role play (E), must focus on specifics as they express the different role play perspectives (S), be willing to challenge each perspective as they switch chairs (T), and be willing to follow the structure of the exercise (J).

Case Study: **Camila**

Camila told her therapist Isabella that she was having conflicted feelings about confronting Beatrice at work. Isabella explained how the Empty Chair technique might help clarify what Camila's feeling of conflict are about and Camila agreed to try the exercise.

Isabella: OK Camila, when you are in the chair you are currently sitting in I would like you to role play what your Heart has to say about the situation with Beatrice. When you are sitting in the other chair I would like you to role play what your Head has to say about things. Try to keep the conversation between your Heart and your Head going for at least 3 minutes and just say whatever you think your

Heart and your *Head* would have to say. Ok, go ahead *(Step 2 Ask Client to begin role play)*.

Camila: (as *Heart*) It feels wrong to confront Beatrice because I might hurt her feelings.

Isabella: That's great! Now sit in the other chair and speak as your *Head* (Coaching).

Camila: (changing chairs, as *Head* What! Are you going to let Beatrice walk all over you. Are you a mouse?

Camila: (changing chairs, as *Heart*) No I'm not a mouse. But I am a kind person and I would never want to hurt Beatrice's' feelings.

Camila: (as *Head*) Oh you are definitely a mouse. And what you are doing that is so wrong is that by remaining silent you are preventing yourself and Beatrice from clearing the air and having a better relationship.

Camila: (as *Heart*) I am afraid Beatrice will get angry at me if I criticize her.

Camila: (as *Head*) Oh so you are not afraid you will hurt her, you are afraid she will hurt you.

Camila: (as *Heart*) Why shouldn't I protect myself?

Camila: (as *Head*) Well you won't be protecting yourself if your remain silent. Beatrice will just criticize you again and again. You need to have the courage to stand up for your self.

Camila: as *Heart*: (Remains silent)

Isabella: Ok let's stop here. What are you experiencing right now? *(Step 3 Debriefing)*

Camila: I really don't have a *Heart* response to what my *Head* said about needing courage and that if I do nothing I really won't be protecting myself.

Isabella: Do you think that your *Head* side is becoming stronger with respect to confronting Beatrice?

Camila: I do.

Isabella: How did you experience doing this exercise?

Camila: It was difficult at first, but then I got caught up in it. I really do have these two different sides about dealing with someone being aggressive. I generally don't listen much to my "*Head*" side. But now I am beginning to see that side of me has something important to say. I feel challenged though by my *Heart* feeling that my *Head* side is cruel.

Isabella: Would you like a suggestion on how to handle that?

Camila: Yes I would.

Isabella: Could you from a *Head* perspective describe to your *Heart* side more about how standing up to Beatrice could lead to you having a better, more caring relationship with

	Beatrice. That is, have your Head side develop a rational argument that might appeal to your Heart side. *(Step 3 Debriefing-coaching)*.
Camila:	I think I understand.
Isabella:	OK, please continue as your Head talking to your Heart. *(Step 4)*
Camila:	*(as Head)* I know you think my being firm is cruel but that is not the case. When you let someone abuse you, you open the door to contempt and fear in the relationship.
Camilla:	*(as Heart)* What do you mean?
Camilla:	*(as Head)* When you let Beatrice be rude to you it's unlikely she will respect you. In addition, when you avoid confronting her it's because you are letting fear become the core of your relationship with her. When contempt and fear are what a relationship is all about that's a terrible loss of what could be a better relationship. If you stand up to Beatrice she is more likely to respect you and you will be more likely to respect yourself. Those are the ingredients that make for a better relationship.
Isabella:	How did you experience it this time? *(Step 5 Debriefing)*
Camila:	My Heart side was silent because my Head side was making sense. It's sort of strange but my Head side gave my Heart side a Heart reason for being confrontive with Beatrice.

As a result of doing the Empty Chair Technique Camila was able to see that being assertive could help meet a Heart goal: having a better relationship with Beatrice.

Resources

Gestalt therapy: The empty chair technique - Mental health recovery. (n.d.). Mental Health, Depression, Anxiety, Wellness, Family & Relationship Issues, Sexual Disorders & ADHD Medications. https://www.mentalhelp.net/blogs/gestalt-therapy-the-empty-chair-technique/

This article gives a brief overview of the Empty Chair Technique and its Gestalt Therapy origins.

Gestalt therapy roleplay – two chair technique with the internal critic. (March 9, 2016) YouTube. https://www.youtube.com/watch?v=X4OEhMWbSss

In this 12 minute video Dr. Todd Grande demonstrates how to help a "client" use the two chair technique to find a way to deal more effectively with her internal critic. The "client" carries out a conversation between her career self and he internal critic self. Dr. Grande also illustrates how the therapist can ask the client to accent hand movements and other non-verbal behaviors to strengthen a particular side of the client's personality.

Family Therapy Strategies: Unbalancing

Unbalancing is a Structural Family Therapy technique developed by Salvador Minuchin that can be used to help a family member become more assertive and restructure the power dynamics within a family.

Definition: Unbalancing is the technique of temporarily taking sides with one family member in order to rebalance the distribution of power in a family. Typically, the family therapist using this technique will coach the submissive family member to take a more assertive stance with a more dominant family member. The therapist asks the submissive family member to turn and speak directly to the dominant family member. If the dominant family member tries to cut the submissive family member off, the therapist may use a Blocking Directive to ask the dominant family member to wait their turn to speak. A fundamental requirement for using this technique is that the therapist have first establish rapport with the family members, especially the dominant family member. The therapist is therefore seen as taking sides with one family member, but only temporarily. Another requirement for this technique is that the therapist must be correct in the assumption that the submissive family member would like to have a more equal relationship with the dominant family member.

Procedure

Step 1 Ask the client to turn and speak directly to the dominant family member about the issue the client is concerned about.

Step 2 If the dominant family member interrupts, politely request them to listen without talking and let them know that they will have a chance to reply (Blocking Directive). If the client falters in asserting themselves, coach them in how to respond using phrases like:

"Tell her how you feel."
"Tell him why it upsets you."
"Say a bit more about why this is important to you."
"Tell her what you would like her to do."
"Can you tell him how this would help the two of you have a better relationship." (Encouragement/Coaching)

How This Approach Strengthens Thinking: By asking the client to assert themselves directly with the Other Person in the safety of a therapy session where the therapist can block the Other Person's interruptions, clients feel safe in expressing their thoughts and concerns. This expression of assertiveness is a hallmark of Thinking types who are tough-minded in "telling it like it is" and "speaking truth to power." When this happens – even on a small scale – in a family therapy session, the client experiences success in using their Thinking side.

Type Demand of This Approach:
For the Therapist: Extraversion Intuition Thinking/Feeling Perceiving. To use this technique the therapist must take charge of the session and direct family members when to speak or remain silent (E). Intuition is required to determine the right moment to use the technique: the therapist must be accurate in their judgment that the client is ready to speak up and that the dominant family member will listen (N). The therapist must be willing to encourage the submissive family member to be confrontive, but must also use their Intuition and Feeling functions to ensure that the dominant family member is not attacked (F). Therapists who are skilled at using this technique will know when to let the conversation continue or stop (P).

For the Client: Extraversion Sensing Thinking. To use this technique the client must speak up (E), be specific about their concerns (S) and be willing to state hard truths (T).

Case Study: Camila

After Camila reveals that she has a problem with her mother Grace, who is constantly interrupting her, Isabella invites Camila to bring Grace to a session. During the session, Isabella uses Unbalancing.

Grace:	*Camila's problem is that she lets other people walk all over her.*
Camila:	*Well actually, I…*
Grace (interrupting):	*Oh you know it's true. Even as a little girl you always let the other girls take your toys. Remember that dreadful girl, what was her name, Brenda I think. She used to make you cry.*
Camila:	*That's not true, I…*
Grace:	*(interrupting) And now you let that dreadful woman at work bully you. What you really need to do is…*
Isabella:	*(interrupting) Grace, your opinion is important, but could we hear from Camila for a moment? (Blocking Directive)*
Grace:	*Oh, sorry. (remains silent).*
Isabella:	*Grace, could you please turn your chair towards your mother.*
Camila:	*(Turns chair to face mother).*
Isabella:	*What would you like to say to your mother?*
Camila:	*(to Isabella) I don't like it when she interrupts me.*
Isabella:	*Please tell that to your mother.*

Camila:	I don't like it when you interrupt me.
Grace:	I am just trying to help you.
Isabella:	Grace, please let Camila talk now. You can respond later. Camila, tell your mother how you feel when she interrupts you. *(Coaching)*
Camila:	*(to mother)* I feel hurt and angry. It really upsets me.
Isabella:	Can you tell your mother why you feel that way?
Camila:	*(to mother)* When you interrupt me, it breaks up my train of thought and I am unable to say what I want to you. Then I give up and become silent and you never hear what it was I wanted to say. The effect this has on me is that I avoid telling you about things that are important to me because I have the impression you really don't want to listen, you just want to give me advice.
Isabella:	Can you tell your mother what you would like her to do? *(Coaching)*
Camila:	I would like you to stop interrupting me when I am speaking and wait your turn to speak.
Isabella:	Could you also tell your mother why this would be positive for both of you? *(Coaching)*
Camila:	If you will do that I will really appreciate it and I will be more likely to share things with you. It will bring us closer together.
Grace:	I didn't know you felt that way. I am sorry I upset you. I didn't know I was doing that.

In this exchange the therapist was coaching Camila to use elements of a DESC Confrontation with her mother. Isabella's encouragement of Camila to be specific about what she wants from her mother and to describe how this could help their relationship, softens Camila's confrontation with her mother so that it becomes an assertive rather than an aggressive exchange. The therapist must be an active participant in Unbalancing and be able to steer the confrontation in productive directions. In this example Isabella assisted Camila in providing Grace with objective reasons (Thinking) for why Camila was upset at being interrupted. Since Grace was a Thinking type (compared to Camilla), Camilla's providing objective reasons as to why she was upset was an example of "Talking in Type."

Additional Strategies
See Box 8.4 for five additional ways to strengthen Thinking.

Box 8.4 Five Additional Ways to Strengthen Thinking

Approach	Example
Cognitive Restructuring	Teach the client to dispute dysfunctional thoughts that block assertive behavior (e.g. "If I express my opinion and someone disagrees with me it will be terrible.").
Systematic Desensitization	Desensitize the client to images of other persons disagreeing with the client.
Guided Visualization	Ask the client to visualize having a successful confrontation with someone who has treated then unfairly. (This is also known as Covert Rehearsal).
Narrative Therapy	Ask the client for an example of when they were once successful in being tough-minded or objective, then explore this incident in depth.
Positive Reinforcement	Arrange for the client to reinforce incidents in which the client acted more assertive. For example, the client can watch a favorite TV show only if they have engaged in a certain number of assertive behaviors.

Resources

Restructuring in structural family therapy. (n.d.). Brighton Counselling. https://www.brighton-counselling.co.uk/2020/02/19/restructuring-in-structural-family-therapy/

This article gives a brief overview of the important role of Unbalancing in restructuring a family where there is a power hierarchy that some family members are unhappy with.

Minuchin, S. (2018). *Families and family therapy*. Routledge.

Chapter 8: Restructuring the Family provides clear examples of how to use Unbalancing with different families.

9 Strategies for Strengthening Feeling

CHALLENGES OF UNDERDEVELOPED FEELING

The hallmark of the person who has developed their Feeling function is one who is warm, sympathetic, kind, sensitive to others' feelings and someone who promotes cohesion and harmony in any group. When Feeling is underdeveloped, we see the opposite: the person who appears cold, unsympathetic, callous, blunt, overly confrontive, and often says things that make group members feel tense and uncomfortable. This can lead the person with underdeveloped Feeling (typically a Thinking type) to be shunned by co-workers, experience marital discord, and have conflict with other family members.

WAYS TO STRENGTHEN FEELING

Cognitive Behavioral Therapy Strategies: Ordeal Therapy

Ordeal Therapy is a technique that can be used to strengthen Feeling.

Definition: Ordeal Therapy is a Strategic Therapy technique developed by Milton Erickson and made popular by Jay Haley. The technique involves getting the client to agree to engage in a positive ordeal (defined as a task that they know is good for them, but which they would rather avoid) if they fail to engage in a new desired behavior. Because the technique is very behavioral in nature, we are including it as falling within the Cognitive Behavioral Therapy category.

Procedure

Step 1   Identify the behavior the client wishes to engage in and derermine their motivation to change. On a one to ten scale their motivation should be high, in the eight to ten range.

Step 2   Ask the client to identify a behavior that would be beneficial for them to engage in, but which they are really not motivated to carry

DOI: 10.4324/9781003097167-9

out. For some clients this might be cleaning the house, doing exercise, doing yard work, etc. The important thing is that this constructive activity must be an "ordeal." That is, the ordeal activity must be something the client really doesn't want to do even though doing it might be beneficial for them. The therapist's role is to make sure the activity the client wishes to avoid lasts long enough for the client to experience it as an ordeal (e.g. 3 hours of exercise as opposed to 15 minutes of exercise). Milton Erickson gives a classic example of the technique in a case involving a man who wanted to be cured of insomnia which had affected him all his life. The ordeal Erickson and the client decided on was that if the client was not asleep by midnight, he had to get up and wax his floors until morning. This client felt that having nicely waxed floors would be a good thing to have, but because he hated the smell of wax it would be a real ordeal. After waxing the floors all night several times, the client reported that he was able to fall asleep, which he preferred to do rather than face the ordeal.

Step 3 Draw up a contract specifying the exact degree to which the desirable new behaviors must occur each day/week and the exact positive ordeal the client must undergo if they fail to reach the agreed upon frequency of desirable new behaviors. The therapist and client should each sign and date the contract and each have a copy.

Step 4 At the next therapy session debrief how the exercise went.

In order for this technique to work the client must be motivated to change and be willing to make a commitment to undergo the ordeal if the client fails to sufficiently engage in the new desired behaviors (e.g. sharing feelings or expressing affection).

How This Approach Strengthens Feeling: In order to avoid the ordeal, the client must engage in a new desired behavior (e.g. expressing affection). If the client engages in the new desired behavior, then they avoid the ordeal, which is a relief, and they experience the positive benefits of having engaged in the new behavior. If, for example, the new behavior is expressing affection to others, that behavior tends to draw a positive response from other people and this is rewarding to the client. A behavioral explanation as to why this technique works is that avoiding the ordeal (which the client would experience as punishment) reinforces engaging in the new behavior (which in turn may receive positive responses from others, i.e. positive reinforcement).

Type Demand of This Approach: For the Therapist: Thinking Judging. To use this approach the therapist must insist that the client follow through on their commitment to engage in the ordeal if they fail to engage in the new behavior. This requires toughmindedness from the therapist (T). In addition, the therapist should closely follow up on whether the client is following the change contract (J).

For the Client: Thinking Judging. To use this approach the client must be willing to make a commitment that they will follow up on (T J).

Case Study: Vladimir

Vladimir is a 30 year old computer systems engineer, married to Mei, age 26. Mei is a university student enrolled in a Bachelor's degree in English. They have been married for 4 years and have been experiencing marital problems. In an initial joint session with Vladimir and Mei, the therapist Thomba learns that Mei is unhappy with Vladimir because he "has a problem showing affection."

In a follow up session with Vladimir, Thomba discusses this.

Thomba: In our last session you and Mei discussed problems in your relationship and she expressed some concerns with you. What are your thoughts about that?

Vladimir: Well, Mei believes I don't express affection enough to her.

Thomba: Do you agree with her?

Vladimir: Yes, it's true. Even as a child I was never one to go around hugging family members or asking them about their feelings or saying "I love" you. We just were not that kind of family. I know I am deficient in this area, but I don't know how to change.

Thomba: On a scale from one to ten with ten being you strongly want to change and one being it's not that important, how would you rate your motivation to change? (Step 1 Identify Motivation to Change)

Vladimir: A 10+. I really want to be more warm and affectionate to Mei but these behaviors don't come easy to me. I have tried to act more affectionate towards Mei in the past but I seem to just fall back on bringing her flowers which is not what she wants.

Thomba: What does your wife want? (Step 1 Identify Desired Change)

Vladimir: She wants me to say things like: I care about you", "I love You," and hug her and hold her hand, stuff like that. It's hard for me to be so touchy-feely.

Thomba: I can tell that you are very motivated to change. There is an exercise we can do that I believe would help you become more affectionate to Mei. Would you like to hear about it?

Vladimir: Yes, absolutely.
Thomba: Ok, now can you think of something that you are not at all motivated to do, maybe a one to five on the one to ten scale, but which if you were to do it would be very good for you? *(Step 2 Identify Positive Ordeal)*
Vladimir: Exercise at the gym. I hate to do it but I really need to do it for my health. I sit too much. And I really dislike going to the gym. I have a membership, but I never go. I dislike all the jock types in there and doing the machines is so boring. I haven't been in months.
Thomba: So if you were to have to go to the gym for 2 hours that would be a real ordeal?
Vladimir: Absolutely.
Thomba: So this is how this works. You and I would make an agreement that for every day that you fail to express affection a certain number of times to Mei, you have to go to the gym and do 2 hours of exercise.
Vladimir: Good grief!
Thomba: You said that you really wanted to make this change.
Vladimir: I really do. I'll try anything!
Thomba: Ok the next step is for us to draw up a contract specifying the caring behaviors you want to do with Mei and the positive ordeal you will undergo if you fail to engage in a certain number of the caring behaviors. *(Step 3 Positive Ordeal Contract)*

Thomba and Vladimir then drew up and signed the Change Contract shown as Box 9.1.

At their next session Thomba and Vladimir discuss the exercise.

Thomba: So how did your week go? *(Step 4 Debriefing)*
Vladimir: Very interesting! Tuesday, the first day of my contract I only did one affection behavior: I cuddled Mei in bed in the morning as we were waking up. She said: "You are very affectionate today!" and seemed pleased. When I got back from work at 6 pm I forgot to do any more of the affection behaviors. At 9 pm I went to the gym and did 2 hours of exercise. I didn't get home until 11:30pm. Mei told me: "I am so glad you are going to the gym again. It's something you really need to be doing." My muscles were really sore and it was hard to get to sleep. Wednesday I did three behaviors: I said "I love you" before we each went to work, I left a love note in her lunch bag, and I asked her how her day went during dinner.

Box 9.1 Positive Ordeal Behavior Change Contract Between Valdimir and Thomba

Behavior Change Contract Between Valdimir and Thomba

Desired Behavior Change:
Each day Vladimir will carry out at least three of the following behaviors showing affection towards Mei before 9 pm each day:

- Give Mei a hug
- Hold Mei's hand
- Kiss Mei
- Ask Mei about her day
- Say: "I love you"
- Cuddle in bed
- Leave a "love note" for Mei to find

Positive Ordeal:

Each day Vladimer does not carry out three or more of the above affection behaviors, Vladimir agrees to go to a 24 hour gym and engage in 2 hours of exercise: 1 hour on the treadmill and 1 hour using weight training machines. The exercise must be done that evening or sometime the next day.
Signed:
Vladimir
Valdimir
Thomba
Thomba
Date April 27

Thomba: How did you feel about engaging in these new behaviors?
Vladimir: Well, at first I was just relieved I didn't have to exercise again. But then when I saw how happy Mei seemed, I was pleased with myself. That night she made me my favorite dinner.
Thomba: How did the rest of the week go?
Vladimir: Thursday I slipped up and only did two behaviors: so I went to the gym for 2 hours on an extended lunch break. My muscles were still sore from before so I had to take it easy on the weight training. But I did a full workout. I know it's good for me but it was horrible being there! Thursday evening I did three behaviors: I hugged her, asked her how

> Thomba: her day was, and I added a new behavior: I cooked dinner for her – something I normally don't do. The rest of the week I did at least three behaviors each day.
> Thomba: That's impressive. How is Mei responding to this?
> Vladimir: Well, she seems happier. Normally I am the one who usually initiates sex, but last Saturday she did.
> Thomba: Do you think the Positive Ordeal Contract is helping?
> Vladimir: Yes. And the interesting thing is that the exercise has been giving me more energy. I have been thinking about how I could exercise more at home rather than at the gym.

Resources

Haley, J. (2011). *Ordeal therapy: Unusual ways to change behavior.* Crown House Pub.

In this book Haley describes how he learned about ordeal therapy from psychiatrist Milton Erickson. The book gives numerous examples of how to use the technique and discusses contraindications for use.

Milton Erickson – Utilizing Ordeal Therapy for Insomnia (May 8, 2020). YouTube. Retrieved April, 23, 2021 from https://www.youtube.com/watch?v=qy67PSaGRc8

Dr. Erickson describes one of his most famous cases in which he used ordeal therapy to cure a client's intractable case of insomnia.

Humanistic Therapy Strategies: Doubling

Doubling is a technique that can be used in couples or group therapy to uncover a client's unexpressed feelings and concerns.

Definition: Doubling is the technique where a therapist or therapy group member acts as a client's "double" and assumes the role of expressing underlying feelings or concerns that the client may have. This technique was widely used in Joseph Moreno's Psychodrama approach to therapy.

Procedure:

A. *Group Therapy Procedure*

Step 1 Identify a relationship concern that the client has and one which they want to improve. Have the client describe the relationship challenge and describe how they and the Other Person typically behave.

Step 2 Invite the client to participate in conversation with another group member who will play the Other Person with whom the client is having difficulty. Have the client and the "Other Person" sit in chairs facing each other. Invite a different group member to be the client's Double, a sort of alter ego who will have the role of sharing any feelings and concerns that the double believes the client has but may not be expressing. The double is instructed to sit slightly to one side and behind the client and when sharing what they believe to be the client's feelings and concerns, to address the "Other Person" as though they were the client. Clarify with the client that they do not have to accept any interpretation that the Double makes.

Step 3   Ask the client and the "Other Person" to talk for about 10 minutes about an area of concern. Instruct the Double to comment whenever they wish, but to avoid dominating the conversation.

Step 4   Debriefing. Ask the client how they experienced the exercise and whether they agreed with any of the Double's comments. Ask the "Other Person" how they experienced the exercise and whether the Double's comments changed how they viewed the client. Finally, ask the Double to share their experience of the exercise and their understanding of the client' situation.

B.   *Couples Therapy Procedure: In couples therapy the therapist would play the role of Double and the Other Person would play themself.*

How This Approach Strengthens Feeling: When the client is a Thinking type with underdeveloped Feeling, the effectiveness of this technique depends on the ability of the Double to accurately reflect underlying feelings and concerns that the Thinking type actually has. For this reason it is important that the therapist select as a Double someone who is an Intuitive type and a Feeling type, or is a Thinking type who has developed their Feeling side. When the client hears the Double accurately share the client's underlying feelings and concerns this may help the client to recognize and identify emotions that they were only dimly aware of. Even if the Thinking type client does not acknowledge to the group the presence of these feelings, the client may benefit from hearing about them. The goal is to promote the client's acceptance of their Feeling side. In addition, the person playing the Other Person may share underlying feelings and concerns that are accurate for the actual Other Person. This may promote further client insight into themselves and the relationship.

Type Demand of This Technique: For the Therapist: Extraversion Intuition Feeling Judging. To use this technique the therapist must identify the right person to act as the Double (N) and see that everyone sticks to their roles, much as a director of a play would do (E J).

For the Client: Extraversion Feeling Judging. For the client to benefit from this technique the client must be willing to be "on-stage" (E), be open to hearing the Double describe their possible underlying emotions and concerns and show acceptance towards the "Other Person's" role play (F), and consent to the structure of the exercise (J).

For the Double: Intuition Feeling. To be successful as a Double in assisting someone who has underdeveloped Feeling, the Double must be able to intuit the client's underlying feelings and concerns (N) and be able to express them in a sensitive fashion (F).

Case Study: **Vladimir**

At a group therapy session facilitated by Thomba, Vladimir volunteers for the doubling exercise.

The group members are already familiar with Doubling. They are also familiar with Vladimir's desire to learn to be more Feeling focused in his relationship with Mei.

Thomba: Thank you Vladimir for being willing to do this. Could you pick someone to play the role of Mei.
Vladimir: Charlotte
Thomba: Is that ok with you Charlotte?
Charlotte: Yes.
Thomba: Carlos, would you be willing to be Vladimir's Double?
Carlos: I would be honored.
Thomba: Vladimir, is that ok with you?
Vladimir: Yes.

Thomba then arranges the seating with Charlotte and Vladimir facing each other and Carlos sitting next to, but slightly behind Vladimir. Thomba reviews the roles and the instructions for the role play and asks Vladimir and Charlotte to begin.

Vladimir: Well I guess we should talk about our relationship and why you are so unhappy with me.
Charlotte: (as Mei) Well, it's just that sometimes I feel that you aren't aware of me.
Vladimir: Well, sometimes you know I am preoccupied with work and I bring it home with me.
Charlotte: (as Mei) Yes but I am in the same home and I frequently feel ignored by you when you go in your office for hours.
Vladimir: I am not trying to ignore you it's just that I am overwhelmed with work problems.

Carlos:	*(Doubling)* I am sorry I caused you to feel ignored. You are very important to me.
Vladimir:	It upsets me that you think I don't care. I care a lot. I don't know what I would do without you.
Charlotte:	*(as Mei)* Your saying that means a lot to me because that's not something you say very often.
Vladimir:	Well it's because I am preoccupied with work.
Charlotte:	*(as Mei)* Sometimes I think your work is more important that me.
Vladimir:	That's not true!
Carlos:	*(Doubling)* I feel sad when I hear you say that.
Charlotte:	*(as Mei)* I didn't know you felt sad about my feeling this.
Vladimir:	I do but sometimes I am not aware of it as much as I would like.
Charlotte:	*(as Mei)* When you don't share your feelings with me I just feel like I am a maid working in the house. That's why sometimes I go shopping by myself frequently on the weekends.
Vladimir:	You are not a maid!
Carlos:	*(Doubling)* The thought that you feel you have to leave the house sometimes to get away from me saddens and frightens me.
Vladimir:	I want to change. I don't want to make you feel bad.
Carlos:	*(Doubling)* I really love you and want us to be closer.
Charlotte:	*(as Mei)* I sense that you do and I appreciate that.
Vladimir:	I really care about you and want to show it better.
Thomba:	Let's stop here and debrief. Vladimir, how did you experience this exercise?
Vladimir:	It was difficult, but insightful. Carlos did a great job describing my feelings. And Charlotte said a lot of things that Mei would have said.
Thomba:	Charlotte, can you give Vladimir some feedback?
Charlotte:	*(to Vladimir)* I thought you did great. You were slow at first to express your feelings, but when Carlos doubled for you, you did a great job of following up with your own way of sharing your feelings. In my role as Mei I felt your sadness and caring.
Thomba:	Carlos, can you please give Vladimir some feedback.
Carlos:	Well, I was sort of guessing your feelings and wasn't sure if I was accurate. I just tried to put myself into your shoes and see things from your point of view.
Vladimir:	It surprised me when you said I was sad. I hadn't really thought about that but I think you are right. It helped me to get in touch with that.

> Although this is a hypothetical example of Doubling, it is typical of what occurs in a Doubling session where the group therapy members care about each other and are willing to take risks to help each other. As can be seen in the case study, the Doubling facilitates Vladimir's getting in touch with his Feeling side.

Resources

Gershoni, J. (Ed.) (2003). *Psychodrama in the 21st century: Clinical and educational applications.* Springer Publishing Company.

This book provides a modern update on applications of psychodrama to a wide variety of situations: disasters, art therapy, women, children and adolescents, the LGBTQ community, etc. There are several sections dealing with doubling.

Carnabucci, K. (2014). *Show and tell psychodrama: Skills for therapists, coaches, teachers, leaders.* Nusanto Publishing.

This book has a valuable "how to" focus that will benefit readers interested in learning specific psychodrama techniques.

Family Therapy Strategies: Intentional Dialog

Intentional Dialog is a structured communications technique that assists couples in sharing concerns and feelings with each other.

Definition: Intentional Dialog (also known as Imago Couples Dialog) is an Imago Therapy technique developed by Harville Hendrix and Helen LaKelly Hunt. It is a highly structured couple sharing exercise guided step by step by the therapist.

Procedure:

Step 1 Orientation and Invitation.

Invite the couple to try the Intentional Dialog. Briefly describe the different steps in the exercise. Emphasize that each will have a turn as Sender to share a concern while the other takes the role of Active Listener. The Sender should calmly explain their concern and the feelings underlying the concern. The Receiver should practice Mirroring, Validating, and Showing Empathy (Reflecting Feelings). The therapist will act as a coach and give occasional prompts to assist the Sender and the Receiver. The entire exercise should take about 20 minutes.

Step 2 Ask the Sender to Request an Appointment.

Ask the Sender to request a time to discuss a concern. This is helps the couple become used to requesting appointments to discuss concerns at home. Asking for an appointment gives the Receiver an opportunity to negotiate a convenient time for the Intentional Dialog.

Step 3 Ask the Sender to Describe Their Concern.

Instruct the Receiver to listen without talking and to not interrupt the Sender.
Use prompts to encourage the Sender to share feelings:

> "and that makes me feel."
> "and I also feel."
> "Can you say more about that?"
> "The reason I feel that way is because…"

Generally the Sender should be asked to talk for no more than 5 minutes as the Receiver must summarize the Sender's concern and if the Sender talks for too long it may be difficult for the Receiver to make an accurate response.

Step 4 Receiver's three Step Response.

Step A *Summary*

Ask the Receiver to summarize what the Sender said.

> "Could you mirror back what your partner just said to you."

If the Receiver begins to offer advice or defend themselves, gently steer them back to the listening role.

> "When you said_____, you are giving advice about something you think your partner should do. Can you instead stay in your listener role and just focus on showing your partner that you understand what was said to you?"

Check with the Sender for the accuracy of the Receiver's summary.

> "How did your partner do with their response?"

> "Was your partner's response accurate?"

If the Sender feels something important was left out, have them clarify it and then ask the Receiver to attempt their Summary again.
Do not require the Receiver to make a perfect response.

> "It sounds like your partner got most of it."

Step B *Validation*

Strategies for Strengthening Feeling 149

Ask the Receiver to validate what the Sender said by making a statement like:

"What you say makes sense."

"I can understand why this is important to you."

"It makes sense that you would feel that way."

Emphasize to the Receiver that they do not need to agree with everything the Sender has said. What they are acknowledging is that the Sender has a valid concern.

Step C *Empathy*

Ask the Receiver to reflect what they think the Sender is feeling.
If necessary use prompts:

"What I believe you must feel is..."

"If I were in your shoes I would feel..."

Optional Step

Step 4.1 Ask Sender to Relate Concern to a Childhood Wound

A childhood wound is a vulnerability developed when one was a child and which still affects one in the present. The therapist can use prompts to initiate this step, but should be sure to have discussed it in Step 1.

"and this reminds me of when I was young and..."

"and this reminds me of my childhood wound which is..."

Then Step 4 is repeated with the Receiver summarizing, validating and empathizing with the Sender.

Step 5 Behavior Change Request

Ask the Sender to request three changes in behavior from the Receiver. The requests should be for small, specific positive behaviors that could be done on a daily basis. Requests to stop a negative behavior should be handled by asking the Sender what positive behavior would address their concern. Requests that are of a general nature ("to treat me nice") should also be avoided and replaced with specific examples of what would indicate "nice" behavior.

Step 6 Invite the Receiver to Consider Granting One Request as a Gift

The Receiver may grant more than one request. If the Receiver is reluctant to agree to a behavior change request, ask the Receiver if they would be willing to "think about it" until the next session.

Step 7 Debriefing the Exercise

Discuss with the couple how they experienced the exercise. Then repeat the exercise with the couple reversing roles as Sender and Receiver.

How this Approach Strengthens Feeling: This approach strengthens Feeling by encouraging the client to make guesses about their partner's emotions and to validate the situation that produces those emotions. A critical feature of this technique is the ability of the therapist to coach the Sender in sharing underlying feelings and concerns and coach the Receiver in reflecting and validating the partner's feelings and concerns. The structure of the exercise provides a safe space for the couple to discuss their issues without the Sender talking for too long or the Receiver interrupting.

Type Demand of This Technique: For the Therapist: Extraversion Sensing/Intuition Thinking/Feeling Judging. To effectively use this technique the therapist must take charge of the session (E) and ensure that the couple follow the steps (J). The therapist must make frequent use of prompts (), especially prompts for expression of feelings (N F), be able to block interruptions (T) and identify accuracy in the Receiver's responses ().

For the Client: Introversion Sensing/Intuition Feeling Judging. To benefit from this technique the client must be willing to listen to their partner share concerns (F) without interrupting (I), be willing to make guesses as to the partner's feelings (N F), and be willing to follow the structure of the exercise (J).

Case Study: Vladimir

At a couples session with Vladimir and Mei, Thomba introduces the Imago Therapy Intentional Dialog exercise and invites them to try it. The couple agrees. (Step 1: Orientation and Invitation)

Thomba: Mei, would you be willing to be the Sender?
Mei: OK.
Thomba: Go ahead and make your invitation to Vladimir. (Coaching)
Mei: May I have an appointment now to discuss something with you? (Step 2 Request an Appointment)
Vladimir: Yes, of course.
Mei: Thank you.

Thomba: Ok, Mei, go ahead and express your concern. Vladimir, your role as Receiver is to listen quietly. *(Coaching)*

Mei: I know you love me but you often don't show it. You show it when I have a birthday by buying me a gift and giving me flowers. But what is missing are everyday expressions of love. Like last Saturday we were home all day and you were in your office for hours. I asked you after dinner if you would watch a movie with me but you wanted to keep working on something from the office. *(Step 3 Describe Concern)*

Thomba: and that makes me feel... *(Prompt)*

Mei: That makes me feel angry like I am not important.

Vladimir: Mei you know I care about you. Sometimes I just...

Thomba: *(interrupting)* Remember Vladimir, as the Receiver your role is to not express your point of view but to focus on listening to and understanding Mei's point of view.

Vladimir: Sorry.

Thomba: *(to Vladimir)* Can you ask Mei if there is more?

Vladimir: Is there more?

Mei: Yes. I am always the one who initiates hugging and touching, and watching movies together.

Thomba: and that makes me feel...

Mei: Alone, lonely.

Thomba: Ok Vladimir, Mei has said some important things to you. Can you be like a mirror and summarize back to Mei what you heard her say? *(Coaching)*

Vladimir: I heard her say...

Thomba: Please say this directly to Mei.

Vladimir: I heard you say that you are upset with me because I didn't watch a movie with you and I don't initiate things enough with you. *(Step 4A Summary)*

Thomba: *(to Mei)* How was Vladimir's response?

Mei: It was pretty good.

Thomba: Did he miss anything important?

Mei: Yes, that it makes me feel alone.

Thomba: Vladimir, could you do your summary again and add that?

Vladimir: *(to Mei)* You were upset with me when I didn't watch the movie with you and you feel alone because I don't initiate things with you very much.

Thomba: How was that Mei?

Mei: Good.

Thomba: OK Vladimir, the next step is for you to validate what Mei said.

Vladimir: Mei, it makes sense that you would feel alone and be upset with me when I don't do things with you. *(Step 4B Validation)*

Mei: *(nods her head)*

Thomba: Now Vladimir, can you make a guess about what you think Mei might be feeling about this?

Vladimir: I think you must sometimes feel very lonely and wonder if you are important to me. *(Step 4C Empathy)*

Mei: Yes, that's right.

Thomba: What Mei is saying is that was a really good response you made Vladimir. Mei, can you now share with Vladimir what this reminds you of when you were young? *(Step 4.1 Childhood Wound)*

Mei: When you don't seem to want to do things with me it reminds me of when I was 12 and my parents sent me to bording school. I often didn't see them for months. I had no friends at the school – it was a very strict school, and I felt very alone.

Thomba then asked Vladimir to Summarize, Validate and Empathize with Mei's latest statement. What follows is Vladimir's empathy response.

Vladimir: When you think I don't want to do things with you it reminds you of when you were in boarding school and that makes you feel very isolated, lonely and lost.

Thomba: Was Vladimir accurate Mei?

Mei: Yes, I feel he really understood me.

Thomba: Mei would you like to make a Behavior Change request of three specific gifts Vladimir could consider giving you that would address your concerns?

Mei: I would really like it if each day when you come home from work you would ask me how my day was, give me a hug when you greet me, and after dinner watch a movie with me.

Thomba: *(To Vladimir)* OK, Mei has asked for three gifts. Is there at least one you would be willing to grant?

Vladimir: I would be willing to ask you how your day was and give you a hug when I come home from work. About the movie, maybe on the weekends.

Thomba: OK so he is willing to grant you two of the gifts and part of the third. How do you feel about that?

Mei: I like it!

In the debriefing Mei expressed her appreciation to Vladimir for "really listening to me and understanding my feelings." Vladimir, in turn, indicated that he had not realized the feeling impact his behavior had had on Mei and that the Intentional Dialog exercise had helped him to understand Mei better.

Additional Strategies

See Box 9.2 for five additional strategies for strengthening Feeling.

Box 9.2 Five Additional Ways to Strengthen Feeling

Approach	Example
Solution Focused Therapy	Ask the client "If a miracle occurred overnight and when you woke you were now a more sensitive person in dealing with others, what would be the smallest behavior that would indicate this?"
Cognitive Restructuring	Teach the client to dispute dysfunctional beliefs that block treating others with empathy (e.g. "I can't stand the way certain people act.", "People who make mistakes deserve to be punished.").
Caring Days	Encourage the client to include on their caring Days list numerous small behaviors that indicate sensitivity to the partner's feelings and expressions of affection (e.g. saying "I love you.").
Family Sculpting	Emphasize when debriefing family members' Ideal Family sculptures the family members wish that the client be "closer" and "more warm" in the relationship.
Decision Grid	Help the client to generate (brainstorm) alternative ways to show empathy and warmth in a relationship and assist the client in identifying multiple advantages to being more warm and empathic.

Resources

Hendrix, H., & Hunt, H. L. (2021). *Doing imago relationship therapy in the space-between: A clinician's guide.* W. W. Norton & Company.

This book by the founders of Imago Therapy provides many examples of the Intentional Dialogue.

Imago Dialogue between a husband and a wife. (March 3, 2017). YouTube. https://www.youtube.com/watch?v=bu7L_BySRgY

This brief video illustrates mirroring and validation between a couple.

Love, Pat (2009). *Imago Couples Dialogue* [DVD]. Couples Therapy with the Experts Series with Jon Carlson and Diane Kjos.

This 1 ½ hour video of therapist Pat Love using the Imago Couples Dialogue with the couple is available from psychotherapy.net but can be watched for free on Kanopy with a library card or university login.

10 Strategies for Strengthening Judging

CHALLENGES OF UNDERDEVELOPED JUDGING

Persons who have developed their Judging side are organized and decisive. Persons who have underdeveloped Judging are typically unorganized and indecisive. They have difficulty following a structured sequence, such as might be required at work. Their filing systems tend to be chaotic and they have difficulty finding things on their computer or elsewhere. Decision-making can cause them to become very anxious and hesitant. This, in turn, can be annoying to family members and work colleagues who are eager to get on with a particular activity or task. Inability to make a decision in a romantic situation can be particularly painful for persons who have not developed their Judging function and are torn between what their Heart (Feeling) and Head (Thinking) sides dictate.

WAYS OF STRENGTHENING JUDGING

Cognitive Behavioral Therapy Strategies: Decision Grid

The *Decision Grid* is a problem-solving technique that can be used to strengthen Judging.

Definition: The *Decision Grid* was developed by Robert Carkhuff as a systematic way to promote client decision making. It involves systematically generating alternatives and then evaluating the advantages and disadvantages of each alternative.

The following procedure for constructing a Decision Grid is adapted from Carkhuff's approach. It has the addition of a rating scale to indicate degree of advantage and disadvantage.

Procedure*

Step 1 *Describe the Decision Grid Technique*

Describe the technique to the client and invite the client to try it.

DOI: 10.4324/9781003097167-10

Strategies for Strengthening Judging 155

"You've been struggling with what to do in this situation. I have an exercise called the Decision Grid that you might find helpful. Would you like to hear about it?"

Step 2 *Draw a Decision Grid*

Draw a decision grid like that shown in Table 10.1

Table 10.1 The Decision Grid

ALTERNATIVES	ADVANTAGES	DISADVANTAGES
1.		
2.		
3.		
4.		

Step 3 *Have the Client Generate Alternatives*

Try to generate from two to four alternatives.

"What do you see as your alternatives for handling this situation?"
"What is one thing you could do to deal with this situation with_____?"
"What would be another thing you could do?"

Step 4 *If the Client is Having Difficulty, Suggest Alternatives*

"I have an idea about an alternative. Would you like to hear it?"
"Another alternative would be to_____. What do you think about that?"
"Sometimes people in this type of situation will _____ (mention alternative). What do you think of that?"
"Would you like to add it to your list?"

Step 5 *Generate Advantages and Disadvantages*

During this step you should encourage the client to take their time. If the client has difficulty thinking of an advantage or disadvantage, or there is an advantage/disadvantage that you think may be relevant, you should suggest it to the client. You should make clear that placing any suggested advantage/disadvantage on the grid is strictly up to the client.

"OK let's take your first alternative which is_____. What do you see as the advantages of doing this?"

156 *Strategies for Strengthening Judging*

"Can you think of any more advantages?"
"OK, now what do you think are the disadvantages of this alternative?"
"Would you consider_____ to be an advantage?"
"Would you like to add that to your advantage list?"
"Are there any changes you would like to make to your list of advantages and disadvantages for your first alternative?"
"Now let's look at the advantages and disadvantages for your second alternative."

Step 6 *Have the Client Rate the Strength of Each Advantage or Disadvantage Using a +10 to −10 Scale*

The purpose of this step is to give you and the client a clearer picture of the degree to which the client regards something as an advantage or disadvantage.
Advantages are rated on a scale from +1 to +10.

+10 Very strong advantage
+8 Strong advantage
+6 Moderate advantage
+4 Mild advantage
+2 Slight advantage

Disadvantages are rated on a scale from −1 to −10.

−10 Very strong disadvantage
−8 Strong disadvantage
−6 Moderate disadvantage
−4 Mild disadvantage
−2 Slight disadvantage

As your client rates each advantage/disadvantage you should write the rating beside the item being rated.

"Let's rate each advantage and disadvantage for how strong it is using a scale from −10 to +10."
"Starting with your first alternative, the first advantage you listed was_____. How strong an advantage is that on your +1 to +10 scale, with +10 being a very strong advantage and +2 being a slight advantage?"
"How would you rate the second advantage which is_____?"

Continue until all the advantages for Alternative #1 have been rated.

Strategies for Strengthening Judging 157

"Now let's rate the disadvantages for Alternative #1. We will use a scale from −1 to −10, with −10 being a very strong disadvantage and −2 being a slight disadvantage."
"How would you rate the first disadvantage?"

Continue until all the disadvantages for Alternative 1 have been rated. Repeat Step 6 for each Alternative.

Step 7 *Compute the overall advantage and disadvantage scores*

Total the ratings for the advantages and then the disadvantages for each alternative. Subtract the disadvantage total from the advantage total and place this summary total beside the alternative.

Example: A Decision Grid for a client in Grade 9 who is deciding whether to skip school to hang out with friends to skateboard is shown in Table 10.2.

Step 8 *Review the totals with the client*

Summarize the total scores for each alternative and then ask the client to comment on this. Review whether the result matches the client's view of what the best alternative is. Check to see if there are any changes the client wants to make in the ratings or in the alternatives, advantages, or disadvantages. Be flexible in accommodating any changes the client might like.

"When you look at your total scores for your alternatives, what do you conclude?"
"Based on your total scores, your alternative with the most advantages and least disadvantages appears to be_____. Does this fit how you feel?"

Table 10.2 Example of a Completed Decision Grid

ALTERNATIVES	ADVANTAGES	DISADVANTAGES
1. Skip school Total: −19	• Fun with friends +10 **Total: +10**	• May get caught −10 • Grounded by parents −9 • Get detention −10 **Total: −29**
2. Don't skip school Total: +5	• Stay out of trouble +8 • Get better grades +7 **Total: +15**	• Miss fun with friends −10 **Total: −10**
3. Don't skip school and ask parents for more weekend time with friends Total: +15	• Stay out of trouble +8 • Get better grades +7 • Fun with friends on Weekend +10 **Total: +25**	• No fun with friends during week-days −10 **Total: −10**

"Now that we are looking at your overall evaluations for your alternatives, are there any changes you think you should make in your ratings or any of your advantages or disadvantages?"

"Based on this exercise, what alternative do you think would be best for you?"

*Reprinted with permission from:

Gerrard, B. A., Carter, M. J., & Ribera, D. (2019). *School-based family counseling: An interdisciplinary practitioner's guide*. Routledge.

How This Approach Strengthens Thinking:

The problem-solving of clients who have not developed Judging is typically haphazard and may consist of consideration of only two alternatives with a lack of thorough analysis of advantages and disadvantages. The Decision Grid is a very structured activity, which – when done by the client as a homework exercise – follows the same sequence (but without therapist prompts). This assists the client in developing an organized way of problem-solving.

Type Demand of This Approach:

For the Therapist: Extraversion Intuition Thinking Judging/Perceiving. To use this technique the therapist must guide the client through the detailed problem solving sequence (E J), be able to generate alternatives, advantages, and disadvantages that the client might not have thought of (N P), and help the client to objectively rate their advantages and disadvantages (T).

For the Client: Intuition Thinking Judging/Perceiving. To use this technique the client must be able to follow the steps of the exercise (J), brainstorm alternatives, as well as advantages and disadvantages (N P), and evaluate the importance of each advantage and disadvantage (T).

Case Study: Kaycee

Kaycee, age 20, is a university student in a general arts program at a local university. Kaycee comes for therapy with Ling at the Student Counseling Center.

Ling: *What would you most like to talk about today Kaycee?*
Kaycee: *I am a first year general arts student and I live on campus with a room-mate Jane. I'm here because I am really confused about whether to stay in university or not. I am doing ok in my classes and all, but I just don't know whether to continue and graduate or get a job and have more of a social life. I go round and round and I just can't figure it out. My room-mate Jane, who is a good friend, thinks I am nuts.*

Strategies for Strengthening Judging 159

Ling: Why do you think she says that?

Kaycee: She says I am a flake because I am indecisive about everything, not just about being in university or not. I hate making decisions generally. Jane will say to me: "Do you want to go to restaurant x or restaurant y for dinner" and I have the hardest time making a decision about something simple like that. And she is right. I am a flake and I am very indecisive generally. I think this is why I am always unhappy.

After gathering more information on Kaycee and her concerns, Ling introduces the Decision Grid to Kaycee.

Ling: As I understand it the decision you most want to make in your life right now is whether to continue your university work or leave and find a job. But that when you try to make a decision you get very confused, pulled this way and that way, and you end up indecisive and upset with yourself. Is that correct?

Kaycee: Yeah, I'm a flake at making decisions.

Ling: Well, you don't have to be weak at making decisions. There is an exercise called the Decision Grid that many of my clients have found very helpful in making difficult decisions. And they report to me that it is very effective in helping them to make decisions about all kinds of problems. Would you like to hear more about it?

Kaycee: Very much.

After hearing Ling's description of the Decision Grid, Kaycee decided to try it. Ling then drew a beginning Decision Grid (similar to Table 10.1) on a piece of paper.

Ling: Now what do you see as your alternatives around the university/work question?

Kaycee: Either I complete my 3 years of university or I quit and get a job.

Ling: OK, that's two alternatives. Can you think of a third alternative?

Kaycee: No.

Ling: I can think of one. Would you like to hear it? *(Step 4: Suggest Alternatives)*

Kaycee: Yes.

Ling: Well, a third alternative would be for you to drop out for a year or two while you get work experience and then return and complete your degree. Many people do that.

Kaycee: I hadn't really considered that.
Ling: A fourth alternative would be to work part-time to earn money and get job experience, but stay enrolled in university.
Kaycee: Would the university allow that?
Ling: Sure, many students at this university work part-time. You just have to get the right part-time job that allows you to attend classes.
Kaycee: That's interesting.

Following this discussion, Kaycee decided to add Ling's suggestion of a university/part-time work alternative to the list. Ling then asked Kaycee to list what she saw as the Advantages and disadvantages of each alternative and rate them using the one to ten scale (see Table 10.3).

The following discussion took place.

Ling: When you look at your total scores for your alternatives, what do you conclude?
Kaycee: It's no contest: completing university while working part-time has many advantages and fewer disadvantages.
Ling: I also see that the overall advantages for being at university full-time and working full-time are almost the same. This explains why you were feeling stuck about what to do.
Kaycee: Yeah, that's really interesting!

The conversation then moved to a discussion about what sort of part-time work might be feasible for Kaycee while completing her studies. This example illustrates how the Decision Grid facilitates a client in systematically identifying and evaluating alternatives so that a decision can be made.

Resources

Carkhuff, R. R. (2009). *The art of helping*. Human Resource Development.
This book describes Carkhuff's Decision Grid technique.
Make better decisions: Use the systematic problem-solving model. (n.d.). California State University, Long Beach. https://web.csulb.edu/~tstevens/wsps.htm
Tom G. Stevens PhD, a Psychologist/Professor Emeritus, at California State University, Long Beach presents his adaptation of the Carkhuff Decision Grid model.

Table 10.3 The Decision Grid for Kaycee

ALTERNATIVES	ADVANTAGES	DISADVANTAGES
1. Complete university degree *+9*	+10 Helps get a good paying job +7 Get to hang out more with Jane +8 Really like my sociology courses +10 Parents will be happy **+ 35**	−10 Financially dependent on parents −8 Not really sure about what career to pursue −8 Can't afford a car **−26**
2. Work full-time (quit university) *+10*	+10 Financial independence from parents +10 Have more of a social life +10 Gain valuable work experience +9 Able to buy a car **+39**	−8 University graduates earn more −8 Lack of a degree may be obstacle to job promotion −5 Might be hard to get an interesting job −8 Parents will disapprove **−29**
3. Complete university degree and work part-time *+32*	+ 10 Helps get a good paying job + 7 Get to hang out more with Jane +8 Really like my sociology courses +10 Parents will be happy + 8 Some financial independencefrom parents +10 Gain valuable work experience +8 Working might help me decide on career path **+ 61**	−10 It would be challenging doing both −8 Have less of a social life −5 Won't be able to buy car right Away −6 Still partly financially dependent on parents **−29**

Humanistic Therapy Strategies: Paradoxical Intention

Paradoxical Intention is an existential therapy technique that can be used to strengthen Judging.

Definition: Paradoxical Intention is the technique of asking the client to deliberately intend to experience the behavior they fear and are trying to overcome. This technique was developed by the psychiatrist Victor Frankl as part of his existential approach to psychotherapy called Logotherapy. Frankl states: "For instance, when a phobic patient is afraid that something

162   *Strategies for Strengthening Judging*

will happen to him, the logotherapist encourages him to intend or wish, even if only for a second, precisely what he fears." The technique was especially intended for use with anxious clients. (Frankl, 1960, p. 522). Paradoxical interventions became very popular in Strategic approaches to therapy in the 1970s and 1980s and were used by therapists like Jay Haley, Cloe Madanes, Richard Fisch, John Weakland, and Lynn Segal.

Procedure: For clients who are anxious about something, ask them to try and make themselves feel more anxious than they usually would. A rationale that can be given to the client to explain this unusual request is that if they are able to make themselves more anxious they will be demonstrating that they can control their anxiety. The client can be instructed to use paradoxical intention whenever they begin to feel anxious. Alternatively, the therapist can instruct the client to set aside a time each day (e.g. from 7:00 to 7:30 pm) during which they practice making themselves feel as anxious as possible. Typically, the client will report that they failed at the task. In the event that the client reports that they are able to make themselves feel more anxious, discontinue use of this technique and try something else (e.g. Cognitive Restructuring).

Caution: this technique should not be used to ask the client to engage in any behavior that would be unsafe or dangerous (e.g. to engage in more drinking, drug use, etc.). The focus should be on the feelings of anxiety experienced by the client.

How This Approach Strengthens Judging: For clients who are anxious about making a decision, *paradoxical intention* may lead to a reduction in their anxiety over making a wrong decision and thus free them to make a decision (decisiveness being the hallmark of the Judging type).

Type Demand of this Approach: For the Therapist: Thinking Judging. To use this technique the therapist must present it as a prescription (e.g. "I recommend you do this.") that is delivered in a decisive (J) and rational (T) manner.

For the Client: Judging. The client must be willing to implement the technique as instructed by the therapist (Judging).

Case Study: Kaycee

Kaycee reported to Ling that whenever her roommate Jane asks her what activity she wants to do on the weekend (e.g. go to a party, movie, out for dinner, etc.) Kaycee becomes extremely anxious because she is afraid she will pick the "wrong" activity.

Ling: How often do you feel anxious about Jane asking your opinion about weekend activities?

Kaycee:	Almost every day. I know she is going to ask me on Thursday or Friday because we always do something together on the weekend. But I am afraid I'll pick something boring and she'll get upset with me.
Ling:	On a scale from one to ten with ten extremely anxious and one not at all anxious, how anxious do you get during the week when you think about this?
Kaycee:	About a seven.
Ling:	And how long does it last?
Kaycee:	An hour or two.
Ling:	So feeling anxious about making a weekend decision really takes up a lot of your time.
Kaycee:	It causes me a lot of stress.
Ling:	I have an exercise that I think might help you to feel less anxious. Would you like to hear about it?
Kaycee:	Definitely!
Ling:	This is going to sound a little unusual, but I think if you try it, it will help. Once a day for 30 minutes, when you are alone in your room, I want you to try and make yourself feel extremely anxious – 9 or 10 out of 10 – on the anxiety scale.
Kaycee:	What…you want me to make myself feel anxious!
Ling:	Extremely anxious. I want you to think about making a weekend decision and then for 30 minutes try to go to the top of the anxiety scale.
Kaycee:	I don't know.
Ling:	Right now you have no control of your anxiety, right?
Kaycee:	That's true.
Ling:	Practicing making yourself feel anxious is a way to get control of your anxiety. If you can control it by making it happen, then maybe you can control reducing it. Other clients of mine have found it helpful. Will you try it for 1 week?
Kaycee:	Alright.
Ling:	During the day when would be a good time for you to practice being anxious?
Kaycee:	Each night after 9pm.
Ling:	Excellent. Could you also write down each day how anxious you were able to make yourself?

At their next counseling session, Ling checked on Kaycee's assignment.

Ling:	So how did your homework assignment go?

> Kaycee: It was very strange. I started Monday night and spent 30 minutes trying to make myself extremely anxious. But I was only able to get an anxiety rating of four. The next night the same thing happened, maybe a three or four. Wednesday and Thursday I wasn't able to make myself feel anxious. I actually found myself laughing that I couldn't do it. So Friday when Jane said: "Shall we go to a movie or a party?" I thought "What the hell have I got to lose" and I quickly said "Let's go to a movie!"
> Ling: Interesting! How anxious were you when you made the movie decision?
> Kaycee: About a three! I was also trying to make myself feel anxious by telling Jane quickly what I thought we should do, but nothing happened. We went to the movie and had a good time.
>
> Ling then asked Kaycee to continue the exercise for another week. At their next session Kaycee reported that she was not able to make herself feel anxious and that she seemed to now be more relaxed at making weekend decisions.

Resources

Frankl, V. E. (1960). Paradoxical intention. *American Journal of Psychotherapy, 14*(3), 520–535. 10.1176/appi.psychotherapy.1960.14.3.520

This is Frankl's original article explaining the use of paradoxical intention as a logotherapy technique.

Lewis, M. H. (2016). Amelioration of obsessive-compulsive disorder using paradoxical intention. *Logotherapy and Existential Analysis: Proceedings of the Viktor Frankl Institute Vienna*, 175–178. 10.1007/978-3-319-29424-7_16

This article describes a modern case study in which paradoxical intention was used to cure a client's obsessive-compulsive behavior.

Family Therapy Strategies: Contracting, Ignoring, and Positive Reinforcement

Contracting, Ignoring, and *Positive Reinforcement* are behavior modification techniques frequently used in Behavioral Parent Therapy and which can also be used in relationship therapy.

Definition: *Ignoring* is the technique of not paying attention to an unwanted behavior. *Positive Reinforcement* is the technique of rewarding a desired behavior so that it is likely to increase. *Contracting* is defined as drawing up an agreement between the client, family/friend(s), and the therapist as to specific behaviors that will be selected for ignoring and positive reinforcement. In Behavioral Parent Therapy, the therapist will

Strategies for Strengthening Judging 165

typically teach the parents to ignore a child's tantrum behaviors by going into another room, or not looking at or speaking to the child. However, when the child is calm the parent will reinforce the calm behavior by doing something that the child experiences as rewarding (for example, playing with the child, giving the child a hug, playing a favorite movie for the child, etc.). *Ignoring* and *Positive Reinforcement* can also be used to strengthen a client's behavior by enlisting the support of friends.

Procedure:

Step 1 Describe to the client and the family or friend(s) the behavior modification techniques of Ignoring and Positive Reinforcement and how they could be used to help the client strengthen their behavior.

Step 2 Invite the client and family/friend(s) to participate in the behavior change activity.

Step 3 Identify how the family/friend(s) will ignore the client's undesirable behavior.

Step 4 Identify how the family/friend(s) will reinforce the client's desirable behavior.

In determining Steps 3 and 4 it is essential the client fully cooperate with the decision. That is, the client should be the initiator for the behavior change program.

Step 5 Each week debrief with the client and family/friend(s) how the behavior modification program is going. Make any necessary adjustments as to how ignoring and positive reinforcement are being used.

How This Approach Strengthens Judging: This approach strengthens a client's Judging function by enlisting the aid of significant others in the client's life (family and friends) to provide the client with rewarding behavior for demonstrating stronger Judging behaviors (such as being more decisive and organized).

Type Demand of This Approach: For the Therapist: Extraversion Sensing Thinking, Judging. To use this technique the therapist must play an active, directive role (E T), be able to identify specific ignoring and reinforcing behaviors (S) and help the client and family/friend(s) stay with the behavior modification program (J).

For the Client: Judging. The client must be motivated to want to strengthen Judging behaviors and be willing to engage – even in a small way – in new Judging behaviors such as making decisions and being more organized.

> ### *Case Study:* **Kaycee**
>
> At Kaycee's request her roommate Jane came to a therapy session to discuss ways of helping Kaycee become more organized in her life.
>
> *Ling:*   *Thank you Jane for coming to this meeting with Kaycee and me. Kaycee could you describe what you would like to accomplish at today's session.*
>
> *Kaycee:*   *Jane has agreed to help me be more organized. I have been getting into trouble with some of my professors because I arrive at class late and turn in assignments late. I have a part-time job working in the university library, but last week I was put on notice because I was filing books incorrectly.*
>
> *Ling:*   *Jane how do you see Kaycee's situation?*
>
> *Jane:*   *Kaycee is my best friend but she is like a bit of a flake. She isn't organized in the way she conducts her life and because of that she is having problems. I am worried that she will get poor grades or lose her job at the library. Even her room is a mess – she can never find anything and she asks me to come and search for things.*
>
> *Ling:*   *Kaycee, what do you think about what Jane said?*
>
> *Kaycee:*   *Guilty on all counts!*
>
> *Ling:*   *My understanding Kaycee is that you really want to become more organized so that you can get better grades and keep your library job and that you would like Jane to assist you in this.*
>
> *Kaycee:*   *That's right.*
>
> *Jane:*   *I am here for Kaycee.*

At this point Ling explains to Kaycee and Jane how ignoring and positive reinforcement could be used to help Kaycee. Normally when Kaycee was "flakey" and was criticized by a professor for being late to class or late with an assignment, Kaycee would complain to Jane who would listen patiently and try to comfort her. Ling got Kaycee and Jane to agree that in the future Jane would ignore Kaycee's "late" complaints by going to her own room and closing the door. Ling then discussed how Jane could positively reinforce (reward) Kaycee when she engages in more organized behaviors. Box 10.1 shows the contract Ling prepared specifying

Box 10.1   Behavior Modification Contract for Kaycee

Change Contract for Kaycee

Goal: To help Kaycee become more organized in her life.

Example of Desired Behaviors Showing Organization:

Getting up each day by 8am
Getting to class on time
Handing in assignments on time
Keeping my room tidy
Getting to work on time
Filing books correctly

Ignoring:
If Kaycee complains to Jane about failing to do any of the desired behaviors, Jane will ignore Kaycee by changing the topic or withdrawing to Jane's room and closing the door.

Positive Reinforcement:
Each weekday that Kaycee shows good organization by reporting that she has accomplished three or more of the desired behaviors, Jane will spend at least 1 hour that evening doing fun things (e.g. watching TV, playing cards, learning new dance routine, etc.) with Kaycee. If Kaycee reports less than three desired behaviors, Jane will not spend any time doing fun things with Kaycee.

Bonus reinforcer:
Each week that Kaycee has three or more weekdays with at least three desired behaviors each day, Jane will do a fun activity of Kaycee's choice on the weekend.

Signed:
Kaycee: *Kaycee*
Jane: *Jane*
Ling: *Ling*
Date: September 8

168 *Strategies for Strengthening Judging*

Kaycee's desirable (organized) behaviors and how Jane would reinforce them if they occurred during the week.

During the next six weeks, Ling met weekly with Kaycee and Jane. Several adjustments were made to the behavior modification contract. It became clear to Ling that both Kaycee and Jane were disturbed if Jane used withdrawing to her room as an ignoring strategy. Since changing the topic seemed to be working as Jane's ignoring strategy, the contract was modified to include that as the sole ignoring approach. During the first week of the program Kaycee only had 2 days in which she demonstrated "good organization." She reported that when she tried to complain about being late to Jane, that Jane was quite effective in changing the topic to something else. In week 2 Kaycee had 3 "good organization" days during each of which Jane spent an hour practicing a dance routine with Kaycee. During that week Kaycee received the bonus reinforcer of attending a modern dance performance on the weekend with Jane. During week 3 Kaycee completely tidied her room and had 5 "good organization" days. As a result, Ling and Kaycee decided to require 5 "good organization" days in order to get the bonus reinforcer in future weeks. During the 6th week, Ling met with Kaycee and Jane and had this discussion.

Ling: How do you feel your behavior modification program has been going?

Kaycee: It's really good. I got an "A" on my mid-term assignment - which I handed in on time and so had no points deducted for lateness. My attention to filing in the library has improved and the Head Librarian complimented my work last week.

Jane: You should see her room now. You can actually find things!

Ling: It sounds like your behavior modification project has been helpful.

Kaycee: Having Jane engage in fun behaviors each day that I demonstrated "good organization" made a big difference. It really got my attention when I had a bad day and Jane, instead of spending an hour with me just went to her room and studied.

Additional Strategies
See Box 10.2 for five additional strategies for strengthening Judging.

Box 10.2 Five Additional Ways to Develop Judging

Approach	Example
Ordeal Therapy	Arrange with the client a positive ordeal the client must undergo each day the client fails to remember important daily tasks.
Empty Chair Technique	Heighten the client's awareness of their "indecisive side" by having them role play a discussion between their Organized Self and their Less Organized Self.
Active Listening	In a session with a concerned family member, have the client active listen to the family member's feelings about the client being indecisive (perhaps forcing other family members to make difficult decisions).
Solution Focused Therapy	Ask the client "If a miracle occurred overnight and when you woke you were now a more organized person in dealing with others, what would be the smallest behavior that would indicate this?"
Cognitive Restructuring	Teach the client to dispute dysfunctional beliefs that block the client from making decisions (e.g. "If I make a mistaken decision it would be awful.")

Resources

Martin, G. & Pear, J. (2019). *Behavior modification: What it is and how to do it.* Routledge.

This comprehensive text now in its 11th edition gives a thorough overview of the history of behavior modification, detailed examples of how to do it, and provides evidence-based support for the techniques.

Watson, D. L., & Tharp, R. G. (2013). *Self-directed behavior: Self-modification for personal adjustment.* Cengage Learning.

This book describes how individuals can learn to apply behavior modification techniques to themselves as a way to improve their relationships and personal growth.

11 Strategies for Strengthening Perceiving

CHALLENGES OF UNDERDEVELOPED PERCEIVING

Clients who have developed their Perceiving side are flexible in their decision-making. They are able to consider alternative plans of action and recognize that "there are many roads to Rome." However, clients who have not developed their Perceiving side may have premature closure in their decision making. They can fail to gather enough information on alternatives and they frequently, too quickly, decide on a course of action – for themselves and for others. As a result the client with underdeveloped Perceiving can become rigid and arbitrary in decision making and will often impose their rigid decisions on others in a "one size fits all" manner.

Cognitive-Behavioral Therapy Strategies: Decision Grid

The *Decision Grid* discussed in Chapter 10 can be used to strengthen Perceiving.

Definition: The reader is referred to the previous definition in Chapter 10 where the Decision Grid was used to promote Judging (being more decisive).

Procedure: The Decision Grid procedure for the client with underdeveloped Perceiving is basically the same as for the person with underdeveloped Judging. However, for the client with underdeveloped Perceiving, the therapist should spend more time helping the client generate different alternatives. This is because the client with underdeveloped Perceiving is more prone to make decisions too quickly without considering alternate solutions. The therapist should also help the client take time to consider the advantages and the disadvantages of each alternative. This is because the client with underdeveloped Perceiving has a tendency to not gather enough information on advantages and disadvantages. Statements like the following may be useful in helping clients to expand their thinking about possibilities.

"Can you think of any other alternative?"
"Have you considered _____ as a possible alternative?"

DOI: 10.4324/9781003097167-11

"I know you think that _____ is the only likely alternative, but what if _____ were to occur?"
"Would _____ be a disadvantage?"
"Would _____ be an advantage?"

How this Approach Promotes Perceiving: The therapist who has a good client relationship is likely to be more effective with the technique because it involves an element of gentle confrontation. Because the client with underdeveloped Perceiving tends to overlook important information, the therapist must be somewhat tough-minded in pointing out the overlooked alternatives and details. If there is sufficient rapport between the client and therapist, the client will be more likely to consider the therapist's suggestions.

Type Demand of This Approach: For the Therapist: Extraversion, Intuition Thinking Perceiving. To effectively use the Decision Grid in promoting Perceiving, the therapist must be active (E) in generating creative options (N P) and must be willing to make suggestions when the client acts as if no alternatives exist (T).

For the Client: Introversion Intuition Perceiving. To benefit from this approach the client must be willing to listen to suggestions from the therapist (I) and be open to considering alternatives that the client has overlooked (P).

Case Study: Carlos

Carlos, age 60, is seeing therapist Judy because of complaints from his wife Sarah that he is too "unbending" in their family life. Other family members are Casey (age 14) and Lisa (age 13). At the first therapy session Judy explores the "unbending" issue with Carlos.

Judy: What would you like to talk about today?
Carlos: My wife is very upset with me and thinks I need therapy.
Judy: Can you tell me more about that?
Carlos: She has threatened to leave me because she says I am patriarchal and bossy with her and the children.
Judy: Would she be willing to come to a session so we can talk about this?
Carlos: She says no. It's my problem and I have to go and fix this.
Judy: Do you agree with her that you are patriarchal and bossy?
Carlos: Well, I was raised to believe that a man should protect his family and make decisions on their behalf.
Judy: And is that working out for you?
Carlos: I guess not.

During the rest of their session, Judy explored with Carlos examples of his bossy behavior and how it related to his upbringing, in particular his parent's marriage in which his father was autocratic. At the end of the session Carlos acknowledged that he wanted to change but that he didn't know how. The following conversation takes place at their second session.

Judy: At the end of our last session you told me that you would like to learn to be more flexible in your relationship with your wife and your family. Do you still feel that way?

Carlos: I am tired of the fighting that happens whenever I try to get everyone to do what I think is the right thing. I know that I am too much like my father: I always think there is just one way to do anything. I would like to make my family happier with me.

Judy: Would you agree that when you make decisions in your family you tend to make them for everyone and then they get upset with you and argue with you?

Carlos: Yes, that is what happens when I try to discuss with the family that we need a new car. I have thoroughly researched this and picked the best one for us: a truck that pulls a big load. They all say no! Sarah wants a SUV.

Judy: There is an exercise we can do called the Decision Grid that I think might help you look more systematically at the car buying decision that is a source of conflict in the family. Would you like to hear about it?

Carlos: Sure.

Judy then explained the steps in doing the Decision Grid and Carlos agreed to try it.

Judy: With respect to buying this car, what do you see as your alternatives?

Carlos: Buy a truck or don't buy a truck. Keep the old car that is falling apart.

Judy: Can you think of any other alternatives?

Carlos: No.

Judy: What about buying an SUV that could hold as much as a truck? They come in different sizes.

Carlos: Maybe.

Judy: What about not buying a new car, but buying 2 used cars: a truck and a SUV. Something you want and something your wife wants?

Carlos: That's interesting. I hadn't thought of that.

Strategies for Strengthening Perceiving 173

Table 11.1 Decision Grid for Carlos (Car Situation)

ALTERNATIVES	ADVANTAGES	DISADVANTAGES
1. Buy a truck **+10**	+10 Carry heavy loads +10 Good for work projects +10 My friends will like it **+30**	−5 Expensive −10 Wife won't be happy −5 My kids won't like it **−20**
2. Keep our old car **0**	+10 Save money	−10 Expensive repairs
3. Buy large Sports Utility Vehicle (SUV) **5**	+10 Wife will like it +10 My children will like it **+20**	−10 I don't want a SUV −5 Expensive **−15**
4. Buy used truck and SUV **+18**	+10 I will be happy +10 My wife will be happy +10 Probably affordable **+30**	−5 Additional cost of insurance for 2 cars −7 Possible repairs in the future **−12**

Judy and Carlos then developed the Decision Grid shown as Table 11.1.

Carlos decided to implement alternative #4 and buy a used truck for himself and a used SUV for his wife. He reported that everyone in the family was happy with the decision. In a later session, Carlos described a problem with his son Casey, age 14. Casey was playing baseball in the back yard and accidently hit a ball through a neighbor's window. Carlos had initially decided to ground his son for a month (that meant after coming home from school Casey was not allowed to go outside and play with his friends and would have to remain in the house). Sarah disagreed with Carlos' decision and the two had an unpleasant argument. When Carlos reported this, Judy suggested they make a decision grid. Judy assisted Carlos in coming up with five alternatives for handling his son's behavior (see Table 11.2). Carlos ultimately decided on alternative #5 to consult his wife about what to do.

At the next session, Judy checked in with Carlos on how things went.

Judy: So Carlos, how did things go with Sarah?
Carlos: They went very well! I think she was shocked when I asked her for her opinion instead of doing what I usually do which is to just decide for others.
Judy: What did you and Sarah decide to do with Casey?

Table 11.2 Decision Grid for Carlos (Broken Window Situation)

ALTERNATIVES	ADVANTAGES	DISADVANTAGES
1. Ground son for a month **+9**	+10 What I usually do +8 Punish son's bad behavior **+18**	−7 May cause son's resentment −10 Wife not supportive of this −10 Son may not learn responsibility **−27**
2. Make son repay damage bill **+25**	+10 Son learns to be responsible +10 Son pays for window +10 Wife would support this **+30**	−5 Son would need to find a part-time job, might be difficult given his age **−5**
3. Have son do neighbor's yard work for 2 months **+10**	+10 Son learns to be responsible +8 Wife might support this **+18**	−8 I would need to pay for Window **−8**
4. Give son choice of #2 or #3 **+22**	+10 Son learns to be responsible +10 Son has a say in how he makes reparations +10 Wife would support this **+30**	−8 I might need to pay for window if son chooses # 3 **−8**
5. Involve Sarah in which alternative to select **+40**	+10 Will help improve my marriage +10 Sarah will be very happy +8 Likely Sarah will support #2,#3, or #4 +10 Son will learn to be Responsible +10 Children will see parents cooperating not fighting **+48**	−8 Possibility Sarah might not support a disciplinary action for Casey

Carlos: We decided on alternative four to let him have a choice. We thought this would be a way to help Casey be more responsible because we were treating him more like an adult who should have some say in what happens.

Judy: How did it turn out for Casey?

Carlos: He decided to get a part-time job delivering newspapers Saturday mornings. I will drive him to get the newspapers

	and then he will use his bike to go around the neighborhood and deliver them. Sarah and I are very proud of how responsible he is acting.
Judy:	Carlos, when we first met you were concerned about the fact that your family did not like that you always made quick decisions for everyone and that this was causing friction in your family. You have done a really great job using the Decision Grid in coming up with alternatives for handling different situations, for example, buying a car and disciplining your son. How do you feel about your ability to be more flexible in considering different possibilities for finding solutions?
Carlos:	It has helped me a lot. My quick decisions are not always good and I see the value of considering other options. Plus Sarah seems a lot happier with me. She loves her SUV!

The reader will note that the Decision Grid was used with the client with underdeveloped Judging as well as the client with underdeveloped Perceiving. The reason this technique can be effective with both types of clients is that the Decision Grid requires a systematic step by step procedure that facilitates being organized (Judging) and it also requires brainstorming of alternatives which facilitates being flexible (Perceiving).

Resources

Carkhuff, R. R. (2009). *The art of helping*. Human Resource Development.
  This book describes Carkhuff's Decision Grid technique.
Make better decisions: Use the systematic problem-solving model. (n.d.). California State University, Long Beach. https://web.csulb.edu/~tstevens/wsps.htm
  Tom G. Stevens PhD, a Psychologist/Professor Emeritus, at California State University, Long Beach presents his adaptation of the Carkhuff Decision Grid model.

Humanistic Therapy Strategies: The Miracle Question

The Miracle Question is a Solution-Focused Therapy approach that can be used to strengthen Perceiving.

Definition: The Miracle Question is a technique developed in the 1970s by Solution-Focused therapists Insoo Kim Berg and Steven de Shazer. The technique involves asking the client to consider what would be different in their life if, overnight, a miracle occurred and their problem no longer existed. The therapist helps the client identify a small, but significant behavior that the client can then implement. The change principle involved is that small changes can lead to bigger changes.

Procedure: This procedure is based on Professor Emilio Santa Rita, Jr.'s adaptation of the Miracle Question (Santa Rita Jr., 1998).

Step 1 Ask the client to describe their problem.

Step 2 Ask the Miracle Question.

> "Suppose tonight, while you were sleeping, a miracle occurred and your problems disappeared. When you wake up how could you tell the miracle had occurred? What about your life would you notice that was different? What would someone who knows you well notice that was different about you?"

Make brief notes on the behaviors the client mentions.

Step 3 Compliment the client on their answer.

Step 4 Ask the client to identify the smallest behavior that would indicate the miracle has occurred. Have the client do this during a 10 minute period while you leave the room.

Step 5 Return to the room and find out what the client regards as the smallest behavior indicating a miracle has occurred. Compliment them on identifying a smallest behavior.

Step 6 Leave the room again for a short break and write the client a short note (a) complimenting them for coming to therapy, (b) complimenting them for their response to the Miracle Question, and (c) asking them to focus on writing down instances during the next week in which the smallest behavior indicating the miracle occurs.

Step 7 At the follow up session a week later, explore with the client the instances in which the smallest behavior had occurred. Maintain a focus on the smallest behavior rather than on the presenting problem. Congratulate the client on their carrying out the smallest behavior. Ask them during the next week to note any additional small behavior miracles that occur.

How this Approach Strengthens Perceiving: This approach can strengthen any positive client characteristic by focusing on small, concrete behaviors that the client identifies with success (i.e. a miracle). Each small success builds the client's sense of self-efficacy – in this case the client's belief that they can strengthen their Perceiving side and become more flexible, and better able to consider and act on alternatives.

Strategies for Strengthening Perceiving 177

Type Demand of This Technique:
For the Therapist: Sensing, Feeling. To effectively use this technique the therapist must be able to help the client identify small, specific behaviors (S) that indicate "miracles." In addition, the therapist must be able to compliment the client on taking small steps (F).

For the Client: Sensing Perceiving. To benefit from this technique the client must be able to identify different (P) small, concrete (S) behaviors that indicate a positive future.

Case Study: Carlos

Judy:	*How would you describe your problem? (Step 1: Ask Client to Describe Problem)*
Carlos:	*My wife says I am too rigid and always want things done one way, my way.*
Judy:	*Do you agree with her?*
Carlos:	*Yes, that's why I am here. I can't help it. That's just the way I am.*
Judy:	*Suppose tonight while you were sleeping a miracle occurred and your problems disappeared. When you wake up how could you tell the miracle had occurred? What about your life would you notice that was different? What would someone who knows you well notice that was different about you? (Step 2: Ask the Miracle Question)*
Carlos:	*Well, we would be smiling in the morning when we wake up and greet each other, I would ask her: "What would you like to do today?" If it were the weekend, we would go out for dinner together without the children, we would all watch a movie together as a family, my son and I would play baseball together, we would all plan a vacation together.*
Judy:	*That is a wonderful answer to the "miracle." (Step 3: Compliment Client on their Answer). Now of all these things that would indicate a miracle has occurred, which one do you think would be the smallest sign that the miracle had occurred and your problem had ended? I am going to leave the room for 10 minutes so you can really focus on this as this is really important. (Step 4: Ask Client to Identify the Smallest Behavior Indicating Change)*

178 *Strategies for Strengthening Perceiving*

Judy (on returning to the room):	Were you able to identify the smallest behavior that would indicate a miracle has occurred?
Carlos:	Yes, we would all watch a movie together as a family. That hasn't happened for a long time.
Judy:	You have done an excellent job of identifying a small behavior that would indicate the miracle has occurred. I am going to leave the room again in order to write you a short note recommending something I would like you to think about doing during the next week. (Step 5: Complement Client on Identifying a Smallest Behavior)
Judy:	(returning to the room) Here is the note I wrote you (see box 11.1). You have done a wonderful job of selecting a small behavior that would reveal the presence of your miracle in your family. My recommendation for you is that you look for opportunities during the next week where that small behavior can begin to appear. (Step 6: Write a Note Encouraging the Client to Engage in the Smallest Behavior)

Box 11.1   Judy's Miracle Question Note for Carlos

To: Carlos
From: Judy
Date: July 15
Re: Your Miracle

I was very impressed Carlos on your ability to identify several behaviors that would indicate that a miracle had occurred in your life: (1) Your greeting your wife with the invitation: "What would you like to do today?", (2) your playing baseball with your son, (3) you and your wife going out for dinner together, (4) You and your family watching a movie together, (5) The entire family planning a vacation together. I also thought you did an impressive job of narrowing things down to the smallest behavior that would indicate to you that a miracle had occurred: your family watching a movie together.

Here is what I recommend you do during the next week: each day look for signs that any of these miracle behaviors have occurred, but especially the behavior of watching a movie together. I would like you to write down on notepaper your observations of any signs of these miracle behaviors occurring or almost occurring.

Judy

At their following session a week later, Judy checks in with Carlos.

Judy: So how did your week go?
Carlos: On Wednesday evening during dinner I suggested to my family that we all watch a movie together. And I suggested that my children make a recommendation. Everyone, including Sarah seemed surprised at my suggestion because we haven't watched a movie as a family for over a year. We watched a Walt Disney movie that they selected and it was quite good. On Friday I suggested that we watch a movie as a family again and I asked Sarah if she would choose one. She selected a murder mystery and she made popcorn for us to eat during the movie. She even held hands with me during the movie!

The solution-focused therapy literature contains many case studies suggesting that by restricting clients to a very small change in behavior that represents a "miracle" they are often able to engage in the small behavior. However, because the small behavior is highly symbolic of successful change to the client, it significantly increases their sense of self-efficacy and their expectation of further success.

Resources

Santa Rita, E., Jr. (1998). What do you do after asking the miracle question in solution-focused therapy? *Family Therapy, 25*(3). 189.
This article describes a refinement to the Miracle Question technique in which additional steps taken by the therapist help to promote client change.
De Shazer, S., Dolan, Y., Korman, H., Trepper, T., McCollum, E. & Berg, I. K. (2021). *More than miracles: The state of the art of solution-focused therapy.* Routledge.
This is one of the classic texts in solution-focused therapy with founding authors Steve deShazer and Insoo Kim Berg. Chapter 3 The Miracle Question gives a deeper perspective on this useful technique.

Family Therapy Strategies: Family Sculpting

Family Sculpting is a Psychodrama and Communications Family Therapy technique that can be used to strengthen Perceiving.

Definition: Family Sculpting is the technique of placing family members into positions that reveal the sculptor's view of the psychological reality of the family. The sculptor, who may be the therapist or a family member, asks the family members to pretend that they are clay that the Sculptor will shape and arrange in different positions to reveal how the Sculptor views the family members and their relationship to each other. For example, if a family is very close together and has harmonious relationships, the Sculptor might ask the members to stand in a close circle holding hands. If the family members are not at all close together, the Sculptor might ask the members to stand in opposite corners of the room with their backs to each other. This technique, which originated in psychodrama, was made famous by therapist Virginia Satir who used her intuition to create family sculptures that revealed the inner dynamics of the family.

Procedure: This procedure demonstrates how the therapist can assign the family members to do the Sculpting rather than the therapist. It has the advantage of allowing the therapist to build up a comprehensive picture of how the family members see each other and what changes they would like to see in the family.

Step 1 Invite the Family to Participate in Family Sculpting.

> "I would like to invite you to try an exercise called Family Sculpting. This exercise asks you to pretend you are made of clay and then each family member in turn will Sculpt how they view the family by placing each family member in a position that shows how the Sculptor views them in the family. For example, if you believe that there are two family members who have a close relationship, you might place them standing next to each other and have them holding hands and looking at each other. If you think two family members are not at all close to each other then you might place them standing at opposite sides of the room and ask them to turn their backs to each other. Families tell me that they enjoy doing this exercise because it helps them, and me, to develop a clearer picture of how they see each other. I will be asking each of you to have a turn as Sculptor. While the Sculptor is placing you in different positions you are not permitted to talk (as clay doesn't talk!). Each member will do two sculptures: first, how you see the family as it is now, second, how you ideally would like to see the family."

Step 2 Ask for a Volunteer to do the First Sculpture.

Step 3 Guide the Sculptor in Developing the Family Sculpture.

> "Ok, _____, go ahead and make a Family Sculpture showing how you currently see your family."
> "Who do you want to sculpt first?"
> "Where would you like them to stand or sit?"
> "Which way do you want them to face and look?"
> "Go ahead and place them where you want them in the sculpture."

Strategies for Strengthening Perceiving 181

"What facial expression (smiling, frowning, etc.) do you want them to have?"
"Who do you want to sculpt next?"

Continue until all the family members except the Sculptor have been positioned.

Step 4 Have the Sculptor place themself in the Family Sculpture and give it a Name.

"Now place yourself in the Family Sculpture."

"Sculptors often give a name to their sculptures. What name would you give your sculpture?"

Step 5 Ask the Family to Focus Their Awareness on the Sculpture.

"Please take a moment and notice how you are feeling about the family sculpture and your place in it."

Step 6 Debrief the Family's Feeling about the Sculpture.

"I am now going to ask each of you how you feel about the sculpture and your place in it."

"Please talk only about your thoughts and feelings, what you like or dislike, about the sculpture."

During this step discourage any discussion about what is actually happening in the family. Only allow comments about the sculpture. The purpose of this is to maintain a focus on the symbolism of the sculpture as it reveals underlying relationships and to prevent family members from becoming defensive should they feel they have to defend themselves from criticism. To begin the debriefing select a family member other than the Sculptor (who you should debrief last). Use Active Listening to draw out the member's feelings and thoughts. Begin by asking how the member experienced the entire sculpture, then ask them how they are experiencing the position of each other family member. This process typically takes 3–5 minutes for each member.

"Susie, how are you experiencing being in the sculpture?"
"You like being next to your mother but you are feeling too far apart from your Father."
"How are you experiencing your brother in the sculpture?"
"You don't like that his back is to you."

"Mother, how are you experiencing being in the sculpture?"

Step 7 Ask the Sculptor to Create a Second Sculpture Showing How They Ideally Would Like the Family to be.

Repeat Steps 3–6 to help the family members create their vision of how they would like the family to be (Ideal Family Sculpture). This is a very important step. While creating the Current Family Sculpture showing how family members perceive the family as it is currently functioning, unhappy family relationships are typically revealed. These strong feelings are somewhat diffused by the therapist repeatedly emphasizing that the members focus on their feelings about the sculpture, not the presenting problem that brought them to therapy. When the sculptures showing how family members ideally would like the family to be are done, they typically involve healing images of family members being closer together and relating more positively to each other. This desire for closeness and positive relationships should be drawn out by the therapist during the debriefing.

"So Susie, what you are saying is that you really like how you and your brother are standing next to each other and facing each other."

Step 8 Debrief the Entire Exercise.

" How did you experience the Family Sculpting?"

Step 9 Conclude the Family Sculpting by Complimenting the Family.

"Thank you for doing the Family Sculpting exercise with me. It really helped me see how each of you views the family and more importantly how all of you would like the family to be in the future."

How This Approach Strengthens Perceiving: Whether Family Sculpting strengthens Perceiving or any other psychological type characteristic depends on the sculptures done by family members and whether the sculptures highlight a family member's Perceiving or other function. The Family Sculpture displays symbolically how each family member perceives other family members. If a family member is conspicuously weak in a type behavior (e.g. Perceiving) they are likely to be perceived as overly strong in the type opposite behavior (e.g. Judging). In the current Family Sculptures for, e.g. the client who has underdeveloped Perceiving, it is therefore likely that the client will be pictured in some way that indicates their overly rigid behavior within the family. Conversely, in the ideal Family Sculpture, the client is likely to be pictured as behaving more flexibly toward other family members. For the client in question, being sculpted in this manner is likely to raise their awareness of how the family currently sees them and how the family would like to see them behave.

Type Development Demand of This Approach: For the Therapist: Extraversion Sensing Feeling Judging. To use this technique effectively the therapist must stage-manage the exercise directing family members (E) through the steps in a uniform sequence (J), help members create their sculpture detail (S), and reflect members' experiences of being in the sculpture (F).

For the Client: Intuition Sensing Judging. During this technique the family member doing the sculpting must intuit a posture that reveals something important about the other family member's relationship to the family (N), give explicit instructions to the family members as they adopt their sculpture postures (S), and follow the therapist's instructions for the exercise (J).

***Case Study*: Carlos**

At a session with Carlos' family, Judy decided to try Family Sculpting. The family agreed to try the exercise. Carlos' son Casey developed the current and ideal Family Sculptures shown as Figure 11.1.

What follows is Judy's debriefing of Casey's sculptures which he named "Misery" and "Joy."

Debriefing of Current Family Sculpture:

Judy: *Lisa, how are you experiencing being in the sculpture?*
Lisa: *I don't like it. My father's back is to me and I can't see Casey.*
Judy: *That must feel lonely.*
Lisa: *(Nods head).*

Figure 11.1 Current and Ideal Family Sculptures for Casey.

Judy: Are you aware of your mother behind you?
Lisa: Yes, I know she is there, but I don't like that I can't see her.
Judy: Sarah, how are you experiencing being in the sculpture?
Sarah: I don't like it. I am facing away from everyone.
Judy: So you must feel a little isolated.
Sarah: Yes, very isolated.
Judy: Are you aware of Lisa next to you?
Sarah: Yes, but I don't like that I can't see her.
Judy: Are you aware of Carlos and Casey?
Sarah: I know they are there but I don't know what is happening with them.
Judy: How does that feel?
Sarah: It makes me sad.
Judy: Carlos, how are you experiencing being in the sculpture?
Carlos: I do not like being cut off from half my family.
Judy: I notice your son is next to you. How are you experiencing him in the sculpture?
Carlos: It's good, we are close.
Judy: Are you aware of Sarah and Lisa behind you>
Carlos: No, not really. I know they are back there but I feel alienated from them.
Judy: I hear you saying that you really don't like being separated from them.
Carlos: That's right.
Judy: Casey, how are you experiencing being in the sculpture?
Casey: I don't like it. I can't get everyone together.
Judy: I notice that you are facing your father, but cannot see your mother and sister. How are you experiencing that?
Casey: I don't like that Dad isn't facing Lisa and mother.
Judy: So you really don't like the way your family members are separated.
Casey: Yeah.

Debriefing of Ideal Family Sculpture:
 The next dialog sequence illustrates part of Judy's debriefing of Casey's ideal Family Sculpture.

Judy: Lisa, how are you experiencing the ideal sculpture?
Lisa: It's great! I can see my Dad easier and my mom too. And they are both together. And we are all dancing!
Judy: You really like the way your parents are together and everyone is dancing.

Strategies for Strengthening Perceiving 185

Lisa:	*Yeah, we are doing Hip Hop!*
Judy:	*Sarah, how are you experiencing the sculpture?*
Sarah:	*I like that Carlos no longer has his back to me and we are dancing side by side in harmony. Plus I can see everyone.*
Judy:	*Carlos, how are you experiencing the sculpture?*
Carlos:	*It's happy. It's the way we should be – happy and dancing.*
Judy:	*Casey, how are you experiencing being in the sculpture?*
Casey:	*This is how I want us to be – everyone together and no one alone.*
Judy:	*What I hear you all saying is that you really like this sculpture because you are all doing something happy and together.*

In an actual Family Sculpting session the therapist would then move to the next family members and have them create a current and an ideal Family Sculpture and continue with a debriefing as illustrated above.

At a family session a week later, Judy has this discussion:

Judy:	*How did you experience the Family Sculpting that we did last week?*
Carlos:	*It was a surprise for me when Sarah, Casey, and Lisa all sculpted me with my back to Sarah. It helped me realize that I have been too strict with the family and that I need to involve the family more in making decisions.*
Sarah:	*After our session last week Carlos said to me: "Do you really feel like my back is to you?" And I said yes, you are always making decisions for us and I don't like it. We talked at home for 2 hours and I felt hopeful we can have a better marriage.*

This is only a brief exchange, but is meant to illustrate how Family Sculpting can safely open up an area of difficulty in a family because of the "play" quality of Family Sculpting. In this example, Carlos becomes more aware of his need to be more flexible (Perceiving) and less rigid (Judging) with his family.

Additional Strategies: See Box 11.2 for five additional strategies for strengthening Perceiving.

Box 11.2 Five Additional Ways to Strengthen Perceiving

Approach	Example
Narrative Therapy	Ask the client for an example of when they were once successful in being flexible, then explore this incident in depth.
Cognitive Restructuring	Teach the client to dispute dysfunctional thoughts that block flexible behavior (e.g. "There is only one correct way to do anything." "If I don't make all the decisions nothing will get done.").
Ordeal Therapy	Arrange with the client a positive ordeal the client must undergo each day the client acts in a rigid or authoritarian manner.
Unbalancing	Use the Talking Stick exercise to encourage family members to Share their feelings about the client acting rigid and authoritarian.
Caring Days	Have the client's partner place in their Caring days list items like "asks my opinion", "is open to alternatives."

Resources

Satir, V. (1988). *The new Peoplemaking*. Science & Behavior Books.

This is the classic Satir text with many examples of Family Sculpting, her signature technique. Satir's approach to Family Sculpting relied on her intuition to develop her picture of the family's inner dynamics. Because Satir's intuition was highly developed she was a genius at uncovering the "heart of the matter" in family relationships.

12 Strategies for Using Type Development With Children and Adolescents

INTRODUCTION

Even when children are young, examining how children interact with the world is indicative of how they will be later in life. Observing the growth of how personality traits evolve from the time of birth through adulthood is magical. Signs of personality trait dominance appear quite early and will develop continually until early teen years. Everyone has their own gifts that can be developed in a positive manner for who they want to be. Stretching is a term used which describes building the skills of an opposing personality trait and putting it to use frequently. The nondominant type is referred to as an auxiliary type (secondary). Developing auxiliary functions (the less preferred functions) through play and practice will help support and balance the dominant function.

Children, from birth on, will have different temperament styles and personality traits that will be obvious to the parent in how children are physically and verbally expressive and how they respond to their environment. Does a child cry when being held by strangers? Do they gravitate towards their parents? How do they take in information? Are they social at the playground? How do they use their imagination? Are they thought-based or do they approach things based on feelings? Do they appear content or involved with alone time? It is exciting to know that the children in this world are so different from each other and develop into unique individuals. Even if two children have the same personality type, their behavior, experience, and environment will create their individuality. There is joy in observing how a child takes in information and expresses themselves. Different aspects of their uniqueness can be nurtured and strengthened while helping them to build a well-rounded life. Figuring out how to relate to children in a way that inspires rather than is criticizing is key to their growth and development.

Assessment of Children's and Adolescents' Type

While the most common and widely used instruments for assessing psychological type in adults is the MBTI, it is important to note that, developmentally, adults are at a much different stage than children and adolescents, therefore, the type indicator for adolescents must be different. The Murphy-Meisgeier Type Indicator for Children (MMTIC) is a comprehensive tool for children and adolescents to discover their personality type and provides valuable insights into differences in how they learn and engage in healthy social interactions (Murphy & Meisgeier, 2008). Questions in the MMTIC are geared towards children and their capacity of intellectual, social and experiential understanding. For therapists, play and artwork are also a useful tool for insights into psychological type. Puppet interviews have been used with children as young as four to assess self-views of traits and could be used to measure a wide range of traits early in childhood (Measelle et al., 1998).

There is a certain importance in understanding personality type while raising and guiding children. According to Murphy & Meisgeier 2008, when adults understand psychological types, they can increase their awareness of more effective ways to reach children and help them develop their unique talents and skills. Teachable exercises like retaining thoughts and ideas until a child is called on in school, attentive listening, and ability to work independently are just a few of the necessary behavioral skills children must learn to develop their personality type.

Personality traits develop very early in life, and these differences shape how individuals experience, interpret, and respond to developmental tasks throughout their lives (Caspi et al., 2005). It is important to note functionality of personalities develop over time but the initial preference is pretty steady. Understanding the key elements of a child's psychological type is elemental to understanding *who they are*. Using positive affirmations, acceptance, stretching and reframing will help breed confidence and give them the tools to manage and cope with positive and negative life experiences. As a pioneer in Humanistic psychology, Virginia Satir stated that 'the greatest gift I can receive of having from anyone is to be seen by them, heard by them, to be understood and touched by them." It is important that parents and adults value the innate beginning of a child's personality traits that Katharine Briggs and Isabel Briggs Myers (MBTI) aptly described as gifts.

Extraversion – Introversion in Children

The way a child interacts with the world and how they are energized and regain their energy is a personality trait that has an unchangeable dominance, but there is an ability to develop different aspects of the trait to give more depth. This is called building the auxiliary type. The extraversion and introversion traits are apparent from an early age, though common behaviors associated with each type are not always evident. A child who is dominant in extraversion may have auxiliary behaviors of introversion and vice versa. Characteristics of each type may be evident, though one will hold dominance.

The Introverted Child

With introverted children, it is important to show them that their ideas are valued to give them the confidence they need to speak up. Introverted children may not be the first to speak up, raise their hand in school, or immediately voice their opinion, but that is indicative of their nature. Growing their confidence, teaching them to work in team settings, and developing their interpersonal skills are important for their personal growth. Allocating personal time for them, giving them space, providing attentive listening, and being patient is key to their growth and confidence.

Introverts prefer to have the space to fully formulate their ideas and observations before interacting with others. According to Murphy (2013), it is important to allow them the space to do so to develop their confidence and communication. There is a distinct importance with introverted children to give them time to fully formulate thoughts before expressing them.

> Introverted children prefer to observe before interacting… children may not share their ideas until they finish thinking them through… some of the conflicts between parent and child or teacher and student can be attributed to differences in this attitude. The conflict centers on how the child interacts more than on the content of the child's thinking… conflicts may develop when the child's natural preference differs from the expectations of the parent or teacher (Murphy, 2013, p. 27).

The Extraverted Child

When interacting and experiencing the world, extraverts tend to enjoy communicating, adventuring and discussing. If you ask an extraverted child a question, they may answer immediately and confidently- but they will change their answer later when their thoughts are fully formulated. They tend to have an external form of thought process where what they say is not exactly what they mean. They vocalize immediate thoughts in order to process. This is exactly where regulating behavior can be beneficial. Imagine the consequences of an extraverted child saying something inappropriate. To avoid this type of situation, an importance must be placed on the consideration of others, selective word choice, and active reflection of the things they vocalize.

> The Extraverted child is drawn to interact with the world and may touch things first and think to ask for permission later. Extraverts want to experience activities and enjoy telling about these experiences. In school, these children understand information better if given frequent opportunities to discuss it (Murphy, 2013, p. 27).

Box 12.1 compares the characteristics of extraverted and introverted children.

Box 12.1 Characteristics of Extraversion and Introversion in Children and Adolescents

Characteristics of Extraversion	Characteristics of Introversion
• Very Social • Prefers to play in groups • Makes friends with ease • Outspoken and speaks before thinking • Prefers interactive social media • Energized by social interaction	• Cautious when meeting new people • Reserved and internally focused • Prefers one on one interactions • Fully formulates thoughts before speaking • Territorial over their space and alone time • Energized by their alone time

Sensing – Intuition in Children

These categorical types of classifying children's nature are the ways that children mentally perceive information in the world. As with adults, children who are dominant in Sensing (S) collect information using vision, hearing, smell, touch and taste and examine this information in detail. They see the specifics of things that are tangible utilizing the five senses. An intuitive child also uses the five senses, but their process of information involves looking at the bigger picture. When given assignments, a Sensing child may follow along in great detail, while an Intuitive (N) child will utilize their sixth sense and take the same assignment in a different direction by following what many call the sixth sense.

Intuitive children see things in the bigger picture and therefore need guidance to implement their vision. Teaching them how to take smaller steps to lead to their bigger picture is a key tool for their success. When given a broad topic with less direction, sensing children have a difficult time starting because they gravitate to defined direction and detailed tasks. Showing them how to define broad tasks into steps utilizing their five senses will give them a clearer mindset on how to begin. Box 12.2 compares Sensing and Intuition in children.

Box 12.2 Characteristics of Sensing and Intuition in Children and Adolescents

Characteristics of Intuitive Children	*Characteristics of Sensing Children*
• Imaginative • Love spontaneity • Draw conclusions quickly • Insightful	• Prefer facts and detailed approach • Thrive in routine • Reach conclusions by following detailed instructions

Thinking – Feeling in Children

This personality type refers to the way judgments and decisions are made using the information gathered using the perceiving functions. Note that all children have a range of feelings and experience emotions. This section just refers to the dominant type of the decision making process. According to Murphy (2013), the judgment system (the decision-making system) develops after the perceiving functions of Sensing and Intuition. If a child gravitates toward Thinking, they base their decisions on the facts presented to them and rationality. Because Thinking types focus on facts, they are often logical, analytical, rational and practical which leads to difficulty when dealing with other people's feelings. Children who are Feeling types base their decisions on their own feelings and the consideration of others. They are often sensitive and eager to please others. It is important to establish a strong bond with both Thinking and Feeling children before offering criticisms. Feeling children will take criticism personally and thinking children will take it as a deduction of their achievement if clear roles, responsibilities and expectations have not been established. Providing specific, constructive feedback in a complimentary way is a helpful tool for both Thinkers and Feelers.

Understanding the perceptions of children is also a key tool when analyzing conflict in the classroom. Feelers can be devastated by any sort of ridicule and because they are concerned with the feelings of others they avoid conflict and confrontation as a means of harmony. They take comments personally and thrive on praise and feeling valued amongst their peers. Children who perceive things in a thinking manner are analytic and deal in facts and the truths of what is before them. In conflict

Box 12.3 Characteristics of Thinking and Feeling in Children and Adolescents

Characteristics of Thinking Children	Characteristics of Feeling Children
• Leads their decision making with logic • Wants to make sure the rules are followed • Analytical and direct • Values independence and competence	• Sensitive and empathetic • Feeds off of validation and praise • Values relationships • Very considerate of the feelings of others

resolution, if the feelings of others are presented in a logistical manner it makes the matter easier for a thinker to digest. According to Murphy (2013) "children with a Thinking preference are able to evaluate their skills, while children with a Feeling preference depend on the opinion of others"(p. 49). Box 12.3 compares Thinking and Feeling in children.

Judging-Perceiving in Children

Judging and Perceiving functions are the way children prefer to live their outer life. Children who prefer Judging thrive in structured routines because they like when things have been predetermined. Lists, tasks, organization, and goals are positive elements of judging type. Making room for spontaneity and gathering last minute information can be quite stressful for them. Children who prefer perception remain open to new information, work in bursts of energy and delay decision making and plans. These children may appear to be casual and flexible – and it is not because they don't care – they are open to possibility and spontaneity. These functions can cause the most conflict between children and adults because the outer world draws attention to disorganization, time management and structure. It is important to teach children strengths in both categories of this function and allow space to fluctuate between each type.

A structured set of rules is important to both judging and perceiving children. Both types may test boundaries for different reasons; Judgment types want to see what is acceptable and Perceiving types are spontaneous and may forget the rules. Box 12.4 compared Judging and Perceiving in children.

Box 12.4 Characteristics of Judging and Perceiving in Children and Adolescents

Characteristics of Judging Children	Characteristics of Perceiving Children
• Thrives under structure, routine and plans • Completes tasks and projects on time • Prompt and values time…theirs and others • Decisive • Organized	• Spontaneous, flexible, playful • Comfortable with change of plans and events • Gathers information before making a decision on their own time schedule

The Importance of Adult Type in Relating to Children

Recognizing the personality traits of adults is a key consideration when dealing with children. The adult's knowing how to relate through type preference of their own and the child will improve interactions, develop understanding, decrease conflicts/frustration, and facilitate a connected relationship.

Parents leading by having a good understanding of type will naturally create an environment where children are aware of type differences as well. It is important for adults to model openness to experience with children in the process of personal growth and self-actualization because after young adulthood, data shows that people exhibit declines on traits related to openness (Small et al. 2003).

Understanding a child's personality type brings insight into their thought process and actions. Creating a meaningful relationship with children and teaching children to communicate based on their understanding of personality differences is a great way to bridge the differences in types in a positive way. Naturally, there are conflicts between parental figures, authority figures and children Conflicts arise from differences in type. Authority figures tend to impose their own personality type onto children.

Murphy's (2013) research supports this idea of type difference causing conflict. Murphy asserts the following:

> Some parent-child conflict occurs naturally as children strive to find independence and become adults. Some conflict exists because parents and children do not understand and acknowledge the normal, healthy personality differences that exist between them…

194 *Type Development*

An awareness of type differences can help to explain why some parents discipline behaviors that other parents encourage (p. 62).

As a therapist it is important to emphasize the individuating process between parents, children and their educators. Adults valuing developing unique individuals will help children form positive feelings towards themselves and facilitate development of a healthy self-identity. This will help children navigate through life with whatever unfolds for them. Strong, positive associations with unique personality identities will act as a filter for life experiences and lead individuals to experience new events in a way that is true to themselves (Caspi, Roberts, & Shiner, 2005).

Recognizing Psychological Type in Children

Figure 12.1 provides brief portraits of the most typical behaviors characteristic of children and adolescents for the 16 psychological types.

Utilizing Personality Type in Clinical Practice With Children and Adolescents

Type in Therapist-Client Bonding

As a therapist, it is imperative to consider personality type when bonding with children, adolescents and parents in order to strengthen parent/child connection. When differences occur, knowing the personality type of the therapist, parent, child and other people involved will bring an understanding on how to treat the family. Understanding the strengths and weaknesses of each personality type of both the parent and child can help the therapist strengthen parenting and family relationships. It is critical to create a bond with each member of the family. This is facilitated by the therapist being able to recognize the different personality types in the family and being able to speak to each family members type.

Teaching Parents to Talk in Type

As a therapist it is important to know young children look to adults for guidance because they play the role of caretaker and hold the power of experience and authority. Positive reframing, positive reinforcement, and effective communication may help children see their dominant type as an asset while also strengthening characteristics of the auxiliary type. Knowing the difference between type attributes is a key tool in mastering effective communication. Authority figures and adults who recognize their own dominant type and the dominant type of the child are attuned to perceiving the wants and needs for the child.

Type Development   195

ESTJ Outgoing Realistic Logical Organized	**ISTJ** Contemplative Realistic Personal Flexible	**ENTJ** Outgoing Imaginative Logical Organized	**INTJ** Contemplative Imaginative Logical Organized
ESTJ children are usually hard workers who seek respect and faith in their capabilities. These children thrive on consistency, trust and freedom.	It is important for ISTJs to have consistently dependable parents. It is important to build a relationship with them based on honesty, loyalty and trust.	ENTJ children are very independent and can often seem older than they are. They are logical, level headed and very creative. They yearn to be respected and trusted and have great creative vision.	INTJ children want to feel that they are listened to, respected, and that their ideas are valued. They are deeply insightful, and when a parent asks their opinion and thoughts it is a meaningful connection for them. Authenticity, respect, and open-mindedness are essential for them.
ESTP Outgoing Realistic Logical Flexible	**ISTP** Contemplative Realistic Logical Flexible	**ENTP** Outgoing Imaginative Logical Flexible	**INTP** Contemplative Imaginative Logical Flexible
ESTP children are competent, capable, and independent. They like freedom and enjoy facing and overcoming challenges. They take risks, seeking adventure and thrills. They thrive with love, admiration, words of affirmation, respect and attention.	ISTP children aren't particularly verbal or expressive of their feelings. They enjoy their alone time, have great imaginations and enjoy their privacy. Respect, trust, and making space for quiet quality time together are important factors.	ENTP children tend to ask a lot of questions because seeing different sides to things comes naturally to their inquisitive mind. They may also argue in situations because they see things from different angles. Praise for their open-mindedness and creativity is essential	It is important to show INTP children that you value their intellect, thoughts, and ideas. They enjoy time spent alone, reading, studying and researching things that they are passionate about. They are highly intellectual and respond well to attentive listening and problem solving.

Figure 12.1 Profiles of the 16 Psychological Types for Children and Adolescents.

196 Type Development

ESFJ Outgoing Realistic Personal Organized	**ISFJ** Contemplative Realistic Personal Organized	**ENFJ** Outgoing Imaginative Personal Organized	**INFJ** Contemplative Imaginative Personal Organized
ESFJ children desire affirmation, a sense of belonging and closeness. Their tendency to exceed expectations can leave them feeling depleted or overwhelmed.	ISFJ children do not outwardly seek attention for themselves, but they need a sense of belonging and need to feel appreciated and loved. They recognize the details and feelings of others.	ENFJ children are passionate, friendly and filled with imagination. They are very giving children whose feelings need to be heard and understood.	INFJ children search for meaning, insights, and abstract connections and possibilities. They search for validation of their ideas and need to feel understood of questions, insights and mysteries that play through their minds. Valuing their curiosity is important.
ESFP Outgoing Realistic Personal Flexible	**ISFP** Contemplative Realistic Personal Flexible	**ENFP** Outgoing Imaginative Personal Flexible	**INFP** Contemplative Imaginative Personal Flexible
ESFP children are enthusiastic, lively and like to make people laugh. They are affectionate and like to spread joy. They have a sense of adventure and are sincere.	ISFP children are sensitive, individualistic, and practical. They tend to feel misunderstood, but they also enjoy feeling unique. They want to be appreciated for what makes them stand apart. Sincerity, affection, and gentleness are key when relating to an ISFP child.	ENFPs have creative thoughts, ideas, and are in tune with possibility. They need guidance in taking small steps to lead to the bigger picture and need reassurance that they are capable of achieving great things.	INFP children at times may be overly-sensitive. While they are in tune with their own feelings as well as those around them and are acutely aware of morality. They are deeply affected by the good and bad in the world and are very aware of the moral value of things. Affirm to your child that their imagination, sensitivity and compassion are positive attributes to see them thrive.

Figure 12.1 Continued.

Type Development 197

Catering to the assets of the child and encouraging their natural type is a key component to building their self-esteem. Building positive awareness to who they are requires an acceptance of differences. Box 12.5 lists suggestions for parents in how to communicate with their child in a way

---

Box 12.5   Suggestions for Parents for Talking in Type

When the Parent's Preference is:	*and the Child's Preference is:*	*Consider Talking in Type By:*
Extraversion	Introversion	Ask your child thought provoking questions and allow them uninterrupted time to answer fully.
		Read books together. Allow time for thoughts to process when responding to important matters.
		Know that if the child does not respond right away, it is likely that they are still formulating their answer.
Introversion	Extraversion	Apply good listening skills and ask relevant questions. Allow them to tell you stories and be patient for their answers.
		Know that when they voice their opinion it may change with time after they fully process the information.
		Allot time to give them undivided attention.
Sensing	Intuition	These children have a great gut instinct and can have a natural moral compass.
		Allow them to be imaginative and encourage their creativity.
Intuition	Sensing	Give your child detailed information when you want them to do something
		Ask your child what they feel needs to get done immediately and expand with the details
		Explain why what you want to do has a practical value.
Thinking	Feeling	This child needs reassurance that they are loved and they react strongly when their feelings are hurt.
		When disciplining them, first let them know they are loved, then explain the situation and ask them how it would make them feel.
		When making a decision that affects them, think about how their feelings would be affected
Feeling	Thinking	These children may be rational, thoughtful and logistic.
		They respond well to explanations and reasoning.
Judging	Perceiving	Have a routine in place with additional options that can fluctuate.
		Allow them time to make decisions, they will want to consider all options
Perceiving	Judging	These children thrive on routine.
		They are decisive, so have them look at multiple outcomes of their decisions.

that "speaks" to the child's personality type. This approach is called "talking in type".

Strategies for Strengthening the Type Characteristics

While the preferred function of personality type will remain dominant, it is possible to strengthen the second type called the auxiliary preference. While this can provide a certain amount of balance in function, it does not change the dominance of personality type. It is important that adults working with children understand that personality growth and development will occur only when children have had ample opportunities to explore all the functions until they naturally become more comfortable with the one they prefer. Practice using the different functions will help differentiation to occur (Murphy, 2013). Being able to utilize opposing type characteristics sets children up for success by giving them multiple tools. Murphy (2013) notes the following

> The attitudes – EJ, EP, IJ, and IP – seem to be stable from birth and do not seem to change as people age. For example, people who prefer to relate to the world in an extraverted way continue to prefer Extraversion throughout their lives. People are simply more comfortable using their preferred attitude throughout their lifetimes. This preference for attitude becomes apparent from an early age and does not appear to fluctuate (p. 20).

Stretching Personality Types in Children

The act of stretching refers to utilizing type characteristics and tools of the opposing type in order to build auxiliary type. Once parents and counselors are aware of a child's dominant and auxiliary types, it helps knowing how much the child must stretch to meet task expectations (Murphy, 2013). Psychological Type approach and stretching types can positively reframe negative viewpoints of the opposing type.

Building life experience by practicing the non-preferred Type characteristics will help children and adolescents see things from more than one angle. Stretching types will not change the dominance of the preferred type. Children and adolescents learn from experience, so providing encouragement and opportunity to explore the different facets of each type is key to their development. Once the tools of both sides have been explored fully, this will help differentiation to occur where one type will take dominance over the opposing type (Murphy, 2013).

From an early age, Anna (E) seemed to be a born entertainer. She was consistently the center of attention and loved to make up dances to show to her friends and family. She thrived on attention and was crestfallen anytime she wasn't paid undivided attention. Through the use of positive reframing and restructuring routines, Anna was allotted reading/independent play time to explore her (I) side. She was encouraged to take "peace time" and her mother created a reading nook in her room. By encouraging "peace time," Anna's mother positively reframed the idea of spending time alone.

Research shows we can stretch beyond our inherited characteristics, but only to a point; our temperaments continue to influence us throughout our lives and change as we grow (Walsh, 2012). Developing the opposing preference does not mean that it will overtake the dominant preference, rather, it will balance any changes when an intervention is put in place and assess the outcome.

Experience dictates what dominant and auxiliary type characteristics are preferred. Fluctuations happen in early childhood because until the dominant function becomes differentiated by experience and practice a child may appear Sensing one day and Intuitive the next or may present as Feeling one day and Thinking the next (Murphy, 2008). A child who complains that a family member is hurtful and mean may be guided to look at the relationship differently by a therapist who explains that they (the child) are a Feeling type and the family member they feel challenged by is a Thinking type. It is in the nature of Thinking types to be direct and sometimes blunt in speech and Feeling types often take the bluntness as rejection which is not the intent of the Thinking type family member. Type language is well suited to reframe negative or pejorative labels which often arise in work and family relationships.

Below are a series of exercises that therapists can encourage parents and educators to use to help children develop their auxilliary functions.

Exercises to Build Extraversion:

1. Utilize play to build their social skills. Staring contests can help children hold eye contact.
2. Group projects. Working together as a team to complete projects will teach children to be team players.
3. Enrollment in expressive extracurricular activities (acting, dance, singing).
4. Charades.
5. Karaoke.

Exercises to Build Introversion:

1. Independent reading time.
2. Individual playtime to explore their imagination.
3. Enrollment in individualized extracurricular activities (swimming, track and field, golf, snowboarding) to build intrinsic motivation.

4. Writing poetry or journaling.
5. Microscope for focus and concentration.

Exercises to Build Intuition:

1. Have the sensing child list out the detailed steps and logic of an experiment, then have them look at those details and draw out different theories. Provoke them to imagine as many abstract ideas as possible.
2. Give them vague directions in a creative writing project and have them write their own story and create their own art to go along with it.
3. Have them keep a daily journal or write letters to an imaginary friend.
4. Incorporate the joy of spontaneity into their routine by taking a break to do something exciting (go for a walk, give them time to play, listen to music, visit the zoo- something interactive).

Exercises to Build Sensing:

1. Have the intuitive child look at their answers and have them write out the step by step approach on how they reached it; especially important to draw conclusions from facts based on gathered evidence from the five senses.
2. Help them build their knowledge on how to do things step by step. Practice following directions and help them see the details.
3. Work on attention and concentration by giving them a set amount of time to complete a task with full focus.
4. Give them a regular routine that they are held accountable for.

Exercises to Build Feeling Type:

1. Kindness cards. Brainstorm to come up with different ways of showing kindness to others. Write each down on its own piece of paper. Each day, have the children select a kindness task to complete.
2. Use puppets and enact conflict scenarios and have the child create dialog from the other person's perspective.
3. Take a piece of literature where there is a clear villain and make up a story from the villain's perspective. This was done in the book "The True Story of the Three Little Pigs" by Jon Sciezka who wrote from the Wolf's perspective that he was suffering from terrible allergies and sneezed.
4. Feeling Charades. Without using words, use different facial expressions and have children guess what feeling is being expressed by using body language and facial expressions.

Exercises to Build Thinking Type:

1. Mystery analysis. Read a story, and before reaching the conclusion have children list out the evidence gathered throughout the text to see if they can guess what the conclusion will be.
2. In conflicts, list out the facts of the situation and hold children accountable to the rules and regulations.
3. It's OK to say "Why."
4. Engage in an intellectual debate using rhetoric and challenge the child.

Exercises to Build Perceiving Type

1. Explore and document new possibilities and prioritize options.
2. Include time for breaks in between work.
3. Limit project and take responsibility for time management.
4. Give them a task and then ask the child what they think needs to be added. Praise them for their ideas.

Exercises to Build Judging Type

1. Have a daily chores calendar with a small reward for completed tasks.
2. Share plans with others and be accountable for punctuality.
3. Reward them with higher levels of responsibility and independence; utilize positive affirmations and praise when they act on good judgment.
4. Look at new experiences with a structure and design in mind.

Stretching the 16 Types

Figure 12.2 contains useful suggestions of ways to develop children's opposing type. Box 12.6 contains additional suggestions that parents and educators can use to help children develop their non-preferred Type characteristics. Box 12.7 is a brief guide for parents on the importance of valuing their children's psychological type.

How to Help Educators Use Psychological Type With Students

If the therapist knows the type function of the teacher and the type preference of the student it will facilitate an understanding of how to resolve conflict, tailor learning experiences and strengthen rapport with parents/guardians. Students who are Extraverts and who exhibit "bad behavior" may talk over others, be perceived as obnoxious and not respect the boundaries of others. Students who are Introverts may purposely avoid

Type Development

ISTJ Interpersonal skills Creativity Social engagement Spontaneity	**ISFJ** Imagination Ability to influence others Logic and attention to detail Spontaneity and flexibility	**INFJ** Take action Risk taking Improvisation Interpersonal Skills	**INTJ** Enthusiasm Interpersonal skills Improvisation Creativity
ISTP Imagination and new ideas Expressive communication Creativity Flexibility	**ISFP** Leadership qualities Interpersonal Skills Organization Problem Solving	**INFP** Communication skills Organization Methodology Structure	**INTP** Perception of feelings of others Communication skills Attention to detail Emotional connection
ESTP Compassion and intuition Listening skills Imagination Completing projects and follow through	**ESFP** Strategic thinking Follow through and completion of projects Future focus Practical thinking	**ENFP** Organization Strategic planning Methodology Perseverance	**ENTP** Organization Strategic Planning Perception of feelings of others Perseverance
ESTJ Imagination and new ideas Compassion and intuition Spontaneity Empathy	**ESFJ** Explore concepts and new ideas Compassion and intuition Spontaneity Logic and strategy	**ENFJ** Self directed learning Exploration of new concepts and ideas Independence and objective analysis	**ENTJ** Independence Attention to detail Empathy Acting on instinct

Figure 12.2 Strategies for Developing Children's Opposing Type.

Box 12.6 Suggestions for Stretching Type to Opposites

Preference:	Needs to develop:	Interventions:
Extraversion	Introversion	Encourage them to express themselves through journaling, creative writing and art. Give the child quiet time to read. Teach them how to meditate.
Introversion	Extraversion	Encourage the child to spontaneously share personal information and connect with others. Give them space and platform to discuss and share.
Sensing	Intuition	Encourage imaginative play. Teach them to listen to both their head and their heart when making decisions. Rather than giving them assignments and clear steps, give them a basic construct allowing them to use their instincts with permission and safety. Lead by example.
Intuition	Sensing	Teach them to follow clear directions and listen to directions. Show them how to look for details by using their 5 senses.
Thinking	Feeling	Work on helping them describe and talk about emotions they feel. Teach them how to read emotions and practice empathy. In conflicts, listen carefully to their views and have them actively listen and place themselves in other perspectives.
Feeling	Thinking	Practice objective analysis by sticking to situational facts. Encourage them to make fact based decisions.
Judging	Perceiving	Incorporate spontaneity into their lives and encourage out of the box thinking.
Perceiving	Judging	Have them adhere to a set schedule and remain focused on completing the task without veering off course. Have set chores or tasks for them to complete each week with no variances. Introduce the daily planner book for goal setting and everyday scheduling.

Box 12.7 Personality Type Reminders for Parents

POCKET GUIDE FOR PERSONALITY TYPE REMINDERS

Are U Balanced?

Acceptance	Developing a child with acceptance to who they are.
Respect differences	Allow your child to evolve. Take your time and let your child develop without force.
Experience and explore	"Unlocking their magic requires a focus on their skills and attributes, not their problems" – Elsie Jones Smith.
Utilize Strengths	The interesting thing about kids is that they have a future, and it is in their future that lies the potential for them to stretch and learn their personality types.
Balanced	Balance your type by strengthening your auxiliary type to give you the tools you need in life.

Box 12.8 Common Educator Temperaments and How It Affects Their Teaching

SP Projects, spontaneous and open for expressive communication from students, incorporates games or competitive challenges in class to stimulate energize and motivate class,* Educator specialty: Arts, Physical Education, Music and Drama

SJ Places high value on responsibility and utility of work assignments and frequent tests to keep up with a lesson plan in a timely manner. Prepares class material with organized precision which includes logistical outlines and charts. Checks in frequently with students to evaluate their comprehension of studies presented and gives detailed feedback.* Educator specialty: History, Political Science and Business

NF Self-discovery activities and value- oriented open discussions welcomed in class and includes Narrative style writing and reading aloud with expressive and dramatic flair. Presents visual and creative designs in demonstrating material. Encourages after-school activities and volunteerism* Educator specialty: Social Science, Humanities. Foreign Languages, Religious Studies

NT Skills building activities, emphasis on retaining the knowledge from course work Lecture format* Educator Specialty: Technology/ STEM, Communication

social interaction, block out their feelings and other people, and avoid responsibilities that involve others. Having a clear set of rules to abide by and having children adhere to those rules with clear consequences may help behavioral change. Children need to know what is expected of them and that they will be held accountable.

Personality type plays a significant role in the classroom. It affects social interaction, how a student responds to rules, how they complete assignments and tasks and how they absorb information. Box 12.8 describes four common type temperaments of educators and how this influences their teaching.

An extraverted child may need social interaction before settling in to get school work done whereas an introverted child has the ability to work quietly. An extraverted child has a tendency to blurt out answers before fully formulating thoughts. When asked to take time to reflect on that thought, their answer is likely to change and be more informed. By contrast, an introverted child will wait until their thoughts are fully formulated before speaking up, and they value hearing what other people have to say before voicing themselves. Extraverts work well in group settings and will build on information provided by their peers; Introverts may find it draining to work amongst extraverts and tend to work more productively by themselves. As an educator, it is interesting to recognize how one's own personality type influences how one chooses the curriculum and plans classroom activities with students.

Box 12.9 illustrates how educators can teach more effectively when working with children whose personality type is opposite to their own.

Box 12.9 Suggestions for Teachers for Educating by Type

When the Educator's Preference is	*and the Student's Preference is:*	*Consider Educating in Type By:*
Extraversion	Introversion	Allow them time to formulate answers fully before calling on them. Teach your students two different hand signals: (1) I'm still thinking (2) I'm ready to answer and allow them space to formulate thoughts.

		Ask your student thought provoking questions and allow them uninterrupted time to answer fully. Give them a comfortable environment for solitude and a space to work in groups. Having a separate space to recharge is important.
Introversion	Extraversion	These students may need time to socialize prior to sitting down and getting to work. Apply good listening skills and ask relevant questions to what they are saying and allow their ideas to formulate in the process. Know that when they voice their opinion it may change with time after they fully process the information. Group collaborations are ideal for their best work.
Sensing	Intuition	These children have a great gut instinct and can have a natural moral compass. Their process doesn't always follow a formula, but they will instinctually find the answer. Allow them to be imaginative and encourage their creativity.
Intuition	Sensing	This student relies on detailed information and step by step process. This student gathers information through the five senses and will do great with science projects. Explain the practical value of projects and how it relates to what they are learning.
Thinking	Feeling	Create a strong connection with this student before criticizing them. When correcting this student, do so in a positive manner. When making a decision that affects them, think about how their feelings would be affected.
Feeling	Thinking	These students tend to be rational, thoughtful and logistic. They respond well to explanations and reasoning. These students like to make sure that rules are followed and abided by. Encourage them to think of the feelings of other classmates when conflicts occur.

Judging	Perceiving	Have a classroom routine in place with additional options that can fluctuate. Allow them time to make decisions, they will want to consider all options. These students will delay until the last minute when working on projects because they will wait for last minute information.
Perceiving	Judging	These students thrive on routine and do well when organizing and planning. They are decisive, so have them look at multiple outcomes of their answers in class.

Resources

Belsky J. & Barends, N. (2005). *Personality and parenting*. In M. H. Bornstein (Ed.) *Handbook of parenting: Volume I: Children and parenting*. Psychology Press.

Caspi, A., Moffitt, T. E., & Roberts, B. W. (2001). The kids are alright: Growth and stability in personality development from adolescence to adulthood. *Journal of Personality and Social Psychology*, 81(4):670–683. doi: 10.1037/0022-3514.81.4.670

de Haan, A. D., Deković, M., & Prinzie, P. (2012). Longitudinal impact of parental and adolescent personality on parenting. *Journal of Personality and Social Psychology*, 102(1), 189–199. 10.1037/a0025254

Harkey, N. & Jourgensen, T. (2012). *Parenting by temperament*. Createspace.

Dunning, D. (2008). *Introduction to type and learning*. CPP.

Jones-Smith, E. (2019). *Theories of counseling and psychotherapy: An integrative approach*. SAGE Publications.

Komsi, N., Räikkönen, K., Heinonen, K., Pesonen, A.-K., Keskivaara, P., Järvenpää, A.-L. and Strandberg, T. E. (2008). Transactional development of parent personality and child temperament. *European Journal of Personality*, 22: 553–573. 10.1002/per.690

Lawrence, G. & Sommer, E. (2009). *People types and tiger stripes: Using psychological type to help students discover their unique potential*. CAPT.

Lee, S. J., Cloninger, C. R., Park, S. H., & Chae, H. (2015). The association of parental temperament and character on their children's behavior problems. *Peer Journal*, 3, e1464. 10.7717/peerj.1464

Murphy, E. (2013). *The developing child. Using Jungian type to understand children*. CAPT.

Tieger, P. D., & Barron-Tieger, B. (2001). *Nurture by nature: Understand your child's personality type - and become a better parent*. Little, Brown.

References

Caspi, A., Roberts, B. W., Shiner, R. L. (2005). Personality development: Stability and change. *Annual Review of Psychology*, 56, 453–484.

Murphy, E. (2013). *The developing child. Using Jungian type to understand children*. CAPT.

Murphy, E. (2008). *Verifying type with students: A teacher's guide*. CAPT.

Murphy, E. & Meisgeier, C. (2008). *MMTIC Manual: A guide to the development and use of the Murphy-Meisgeier Type Indicator for Children*. CAPT.

Measelle, J. R., Ablow, J. C., Cowan, P. A., & Cowan, C. P. (1998). Assessing young children's views of their academic, social, and emotional lives: An evaluation of the self-perception scales of the Berkeley Puppet Interview (1998). *Child Development*, 69 (6), 1556–1576.

Small, B. J., Hertzog, C., Hultsch, D. F., & Dixon, R. A. (2003). Stability and change in adult personality over 6 years: Findings from the victoria longitudinal study. *The Journals of Gerontology Series B: Psychological Sciences and Social Sciences*, 58(3), 166–176.

Walsh, F. (2012). Family resilience: strengths forged through adversity. In F. Walsh (Ed.) *Normal family processes*. Guildford Press, 399–427.

13 Detailed Case Studies in Psychological Type Development

THE BOY IN THE MIDDLE TRYING TO GROW UP

Background

Charlie, a 12-year-old boy, is having difficulty communicating with his teachers in middle-school and struggles to answer quickly when called on in class. Charlie's parents, Lily and Will, describe their son as a bright and loving child who withdraws from conversations when exposed to larger crowds and new people. Charlie has always enjoyed smaller group settings and one on one friendships, like his strong friendship with his best buddy Ron who he has known since first grade. Charlie's mom is aware of his reserved nature and tries to communicate with an open and uplifting dialog when Charlie comes home from school. However, Charlie chooses not to express his thoughts and feelings with his mom, even though she greets him with love and acceptance.

Lily thinks Charlie is pushing her away and feels helpless because she wants so desperately to help her son thrive. Lily misses the times when he was younger and they had a very close relationship. She felt needed and in control, but now feels lost because she cannot find the ways to get his attention and have meaningful conversations. She worries about Charlie's future and well-being if he continues on the path of not expressing his feelings. Lily tries to lean on her husband Will, but is not supported by him since he believes boys do not need to talk about their emotions. Instead, Will is adamant that his son Charlie would be "healed" if he joined a sports team. Will is withdrawn from the fact that Charlie's grades are slipping and is completely oblivious to Charlie's struggle to open up about what he is going through. Charlie feels the tension building between his parents' disagreements on how to raise him which leads to him shutting them both out even more.

Assessment

The initial therapy phase included joining and observing how the family interacted during the session. Lily described, with both verbal and copious

DOI: 10.4324/9781003097167-13

pre-written notes, her impressions of Charlie's problems and her goals for therapy. Will described therapy for his son as "not needed," but said he would attend sessions anyway. At first, Charlie had limited verbal interaction, but after a time he added his opinions and discussed his need for more independence, less questions and concerns from his mom, and more understanding and acceptance from his father. He also voiced that he wished his father would be more available. Charlie added the school environment had changed and larger enrollment had been a difficult adjustment this year. He felt unnoticed and had not yet connected with anyone in his current class.

During the family assessment phase, a therapist gains a comprehensive sense of how the family functions and interprets their version of the presenting issues. I (JS) observed their conflicting personality types and formulated a treatment plan to include assessment of personality preference type: Myers-Briggs Type Indicator (MBTI) for the parents and the Murphy-Meisgeier Type Indicator for Children (MMTIC) for Charlie. I stressed that this was a completely positive and non-pathological survey and would make our sessions more productive because we can see each other's strengths versus limitations. A more detailed description followed to familiarize the family on how this information gained would facilitate a common language and focus in our sessions.

Lily: MBTI	identified as an ENFJ
Will: MBTI	identified as an ESTJ
Charlie: MMTIC	presented as an ISFP

Seeing the entire family together as a system has been the mainstay model of family therapy. It also directs planning and delivery of care. I saw the family as a unit, first alternating separate sessions with parents followed by sessions with their child and rejoining intermittently. Structuring sessions like this are helpful during the assessment phase especially if evenly dispersed.

Observations

In our first family session, I observed Lily (ENFJ) did the majority of the talking for the family as she described the worrisome issues in great detail. She described feeling "so sad that my child could be left out of friendships" and didn't want him to feel "invisible." I could see that between the three of them Lily had the dominant voice, and although Will was also prone to strong statements, he stated that it had been decided long ago to leave school matters up entirely to his wife. This role was clearly defined and both parents agreed it worked most of the time - until now. Will is efficient, practical, organized and related how the division of parenting roles was ideal for many years. He was direct with the fact that he did not like change. Charlie's (ISFP) type exhibited the hallmarks of an Introverted Feeling personality type: he values alone-time and harmony, thinks before speaking and finds acceptance important.

In addition to type, I introduced the psychosocial stages of growth and development to his parents noting that this is a normative progression for Charlie's age group. His developmental stage is described by Erikson's Eight Stages of development as identity vs. confusion. It is a time of searching for self and personal identity; a time when one becomes more aware of their values, goals and beliefs. This stage is usually the beginning of family conflicts and battle of the wills. They responded with how reassuring it was to normalize this particular time of their son's life.

The next few sessions I met with Charlie alone. As an ENFP therapist, I knew that in order to bond effectively, I needed to give him space to open up and talk in his own time and formulate his responses. I would limit the natural tendency to explore our conversation with an overly expressive tone and allow him time to fill in his answers. When he returned to my office the following week, I adapted to his style by mirroring and started speaking quietly in a non-inquisitive manner. I observed that a significant increase in his comfort level had been reached which signaled an opening to address some deeper concerns about family and school environment. Charlie was ready but still needed reassurance of trust and how much of his dialog would be quoted in family sessions. I explained the exceptions and he understood the significance of my obligation. Charlie stated that things at home had been uncomfortable for him being the center of his parent's discord and staying out of the fray seemed a good choice. I took this opportunity to explore with Charlie the options to respond differently to his dilemma. His natural Introvert trait was to wait before responding and to formulate the best course of action to handle his parents' complaints. He was upset that for the first time his mother was unhappy with him and his father was, to his surprise, interested in him. These were two very conflicting messages that were a new experience for him and he needed guidance. This was a good opening to explain individual differences and how they can be understood and used to learn ways to cope, adjust, tolerate and change.

I explained that his type (F) preference related to his "unhappy" feelings because his natural tendencies prioritized feelings of others as something very important to him. Seeing (S) his Mom cry and worry about him was described as confusing because he knew he was fine, but felt unable to convey that message to her. I appealed to his sense of curiosity to explore some ways to manage this intense concern. We talked about his need for more independence and fear of having that discussion with his Mom because he didn't want to hurt her feelings. I gave him an opportunity to practice using role-play to rehearse dialog he could use to express himself.

I gave Charlie the opportunity to voice his discomfort about being seen as the problem in connection to his parent's own issues and the way they interpret his choices as unacceptable and unhealthy. He was open to first role-play the possible reactions from his parents when he ventured into this new experience of sharing what he was experiencing. He was concerned they might see him as defiant and not a good son anymore. I was hoping this could be an opportunity for Charlie to reassess his current thoughts and have a more realistic view of his natural traits and increase his self-worth and confidence by speaking to them directly.

Working with Charlie at a slower pace was an essential factor in understanding his issues and allowing him to grow in his ability to see his strengths. Using strength-based therapy techniques, we looked at the benefits of his type. He began to get excited that this would be considered a project to research, design and implement.

A separate couple session was advantageous as Lily's and Will's conflicts had centered around Charlie's need for space and his choice of communicating more with his friends virtually rather than with them. In the assessment it was noted that Charlie was not exhibiting any depressive or anxiety symptoms. Lily described her role as the "ideal mother" and sole caregiver as diminishing. She lamented that their plan to strictly delineate marriage roles was one that she had originally not fully accepted. She now recognized that a boy needed his father's continual input from the beginning. Will's reaction to his son's distancing was one of blaming Lily for years of over-mothering and he described Charlie as a "Mama's boy." Will described his attempts to bond over the years with Charlie as unsuccessful because Charlie was "not like me" or "not showing interest in partaking in the same activities I wanted to do." He admitted this may not have been the right attitude. He had sensed (S) that Charlie looked more comfortable around Lily than with him. I introduced the aspect of how their ways of interpreting the past may be the first step going forward for change to occur.

The sessions that only included Lily and Will were a significant opportunity to recognize their struggle to change the status quo of their current marital state and come to a mutual agreement on how things could be improved. It is not uncommon at this stage of their marriage to re-evaluate and assess what is no longer satisfying, functional or acceptable. The catalyst was most likely their son's need for change that included his independence and desire to manage his own life. Normalizing their process diminished blaming and held both of them accountable to discover new ways of communicating while adjusting to their new roles. They were comfortable with the suggestion of couples counseling to help them collaborate and balance their relationship, communicate clearly, and address current issues with their son. I reinforced that as the family system changed, the changes would affect all of them and they could see these changes as an opportunity for positive growth.

Lily (ENFJ) was relieved to have another opportunity to her marriage by redefining the rigid design of their roles to a more collaborative partnership. Will (ESTJ) was more concerned about the choice of therapist, financial aspects and predicted timeline of couple counseling. My explanation was that it was worth the effort to experience it first and then evaluate its potential. It was more of a challenge for Will to visualize how he could begin a new relationship connection with Charlie. I introduced the idea that children are more flexible than adults and that it could be seen as a benefit to them. I presented counseling as an interesting experience rather than a forced directive. Again, Charlie (ISFJ) would appreciate a structured therapy plan that would be collaborative, thereby taking him off the family problem list. It would include activities that would describe likes, dislikes, differences and similarities. Ways to bond, communicate and understand type would be included in its design with encouragement to be open to discuss feelings. Charlie would be given the opportunity to voice his discomfort about being seen as the problem in connection to their own issues and his parents interpreting his choices as unacceptable and unhealthy. He was open to first role-play the possible reactions from his parents when he ventured into this new experience of sharing what he felt. He was concerned they might see him as defiant and not a good son anymore. By using a Type preference, approach, I was hoping this could be an opportunity for Charlie to reassess his current thoughts and have a more realistic view of his natural traits and increase his self-worth and confidence.

Family therapy would continue to foster an improved relationship for all. I used workable interventions based on seeing natural preferences for understanding, accepting and tolerating each other's similarities and differences. I gave them new bonding ideas and stretching suggestions to see things from the other's perspective. Instilling hope for positive change is embedded in a therapeutic relationship with the family. Hope needs a plan.

Figure 13.1 shows a Psychological Type Map for Charlie's family and illustrates the type development ("stretching type") direction for each family member.

Specific Interventions

In counseling sessions, adolescents dislike questions but relate that silence can be even more excruciating. A useful technique is to give up to a minute of being silent which allows them to think and experience that time without interruption. The therapist can observe the non-verbal communication and any change in body-language, then be open to change direction with new techniques or topics. Flexibility, creativity and patience on the part of the therapist may allow for trust and bonding to occur instead of increasing pressure on the student. It is a different way of

214 *Psychological Type Development*

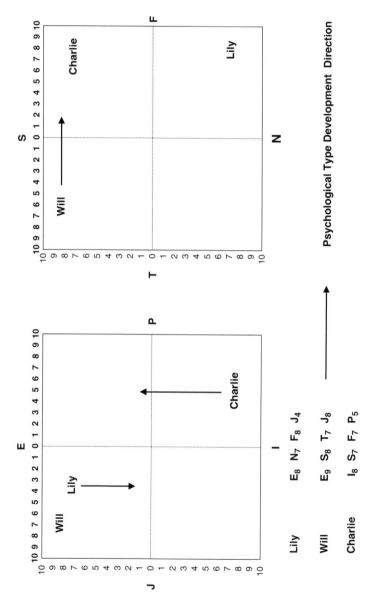

Figure 13.1 Psychological Type Map for Charlie's Family.

using positive and respectful interventions instead of describing the child as shut down, unmotivated, non-compliant, or disrespectful. This suggestion is significantly applicable to introverts.

My plan was to monitor any changes when I put an intervention in place and then observe what the outcome is. Microscopic changes can make all the difference and have room to be expanded. My goal was to affirm the positive changes and validate the family members' efforts to be open to change. My approach is to encourage and challenge children to experiment with stretching to their opposing types and at the same time strengthen and validate their natural preferences.

Lily: I suggested to Lily that when Charlie comes home from school for the next few weeks, she greet him and say how lovely it was to see him, and allow him time to recharge before asking him questions. I suggested that she change the topic to something different than be Charlie centered. For instance, she could relate her own days' events in a positive fashion. This intervention was meant to moderate Lily's Extravert tendency to move too swiftly into Charlie's private space. In addition, it was focused on teaching Lily to respect Charlie's need for alone time.

Will: I invited Charlie to have a father-son discussion to a) see what activities would be seen as enjoyable for both and being flexible in trying each other's preferred activity. My goal was to have Will (ESTJ) be more flexible (P) with doing activities with Charlie (ISFP).

Charlie: My goal with Charlie was to stretch Charlie to expand into his more extraverted side in which his classroom could be seen as the training ground for the experiment. I suggested to Charlie that he observe his classmates' and teacher's reaction to his more extraverted behaviors and evaluate the responses of his actions by scaling them along the way from 1 to 10. I felt this intervention would appeal to Charlie's Sensing side.

Teacher Consultation

I was able to meet with Charlie's teacher, Mrs. Kelly, and she described that it was difficult to get Charlie to speak in front of his classmates, but all of his written work was precise and exquisitely detailed. After describing differing personality types, Mrs. Kelly was interested in integrating suggestions regarding personality traits into her classroom. I gave her different methods she could implement to help the introverts gain confidence, like hand signals to signify when Introverts need more time to process their thoughts and when they have fully formulated their thoughts. I also suggested adding a reading nook to give introverts time to recharge from the action of the classroom. As an aside, she reported that in her college years, her MBTI report was ENFJ and teaching was a good fit. I later learned from Charlie that Mrs. Kelly utilized the techniques I shared with her and Charlie was pleased that he felt seen and appreciated. He felt like there was less pressure on him and now he actually volunteered answers. Mrs. Kelly had even taken the time to bond with Charlie one-on-one.

Conclusion

The final outcome of therapy for this family was the ability to see the benefits of utilizing the Personality Type lens to discover the value of their own strengths and relate more effectively as a family. The attention given to create a positive atmosphere of acceptance and the possibility of renewal and change was a driving force in their work. Each person was given special attention to self-discover their identifiable gifts by nature and appreciate and recognize each other's traits. They were able to see how understanding personality types could diffuse conflicts, increase compatibility and have various positive outcomes. They were able to establish better connections and learned new ways to relate to each other without losing their own unique personality. Structure, plans, emotional release, open communication style, time management and a chance to dream out loud were just a sample of topics discussed. Lily (F) remarked that couples therapy was very helpful as it gave more opportunities to express her own needs for emotional intimacy with her husband. Working with Will's resistance to change was challenging, but after time, he softened.

A significant moment in the relationship between Will and Charlie was when Will voiced that he was proud of Charlie and respected his work ethic. Charlie spoke about Will's efforts to relate to him in session and he agreed to make time to spend time with his father. Will added that he would be patient and let him choose the time, day and place. The family showed resilience and courage in diligently following the stretching exercises in the treatment plan. They described having the reassurance of a normalizing therapeutic experience as comforting. They were excited for new beginnings and felt a renewed confidence. Although the family had arrived in therapy for Charlie in a challenging time of conflict, they positively reframed it as "a blessing in disguise" for their family unit with the new found understanding of Type. On our last visit Charlie gave me the news about a new addition to the family... a long unfulfilled family request was finally granted. His father brought home a rescue dog - type unknown at this time.

Use of Psychological Type With a Cancer Patient

This case study describes an intervention I (BG) did with my family in 1993 when I discovered that my younger sister, Patty, had colon cancer.

Over a 5 month period she had made repeated visits to her family physician who misdiagnosed her symptoms as benign. After she insisted the family physician refer her to an internist, it was then that Patty learned that she had advanced colon cancer.

Because another family member died of cancer a year earlier, I was familiar with different forms of cancer treatment, both, traditional and non-traditional. I learned that frequently when modern medicine had nothing more to offer cancer patients, there were other alternatives available, such as psychological and dietary approaches to cancer treatment. Many cancer patients embraced both traditional and non-traditional healing approaches. I was particularly interested in the literature on psychological approaches to cancer healing. For example, the Carl Simonton approach, which emphasizes the use of visualization, is described in his book: *Getting Well Again: A Step-by-Step Self Help Guide to Overcoming Cancer for Patients and their Families*. I learned a lot about this approach from a close colleague who survived breast cancer. She had attended several workshops based on the Simonton approach. In addition, I was familiar with the macrobiotic dietary approach to cancer as described in Michio Kushi's book: *The Cancer Prevention Diet*.

Most of my communication with my sister was by letter and telephone as I was a faculty member in the Counseling Psychology department at the University of San Francisco. She lived in Edmonton, Canada where our parents also lived. However, I made more frequent trips back home so that I could check on her and my parents.

Initially, Patty's cancer physician treated her surgically. I remember visiting Patty when she was in ICU recovering from the first of several surgeries. I recall at one point that she described in a humorous way her surgical scars making her abdomen look like a "map of Texas." During this visit I was disturbed to learn that Patty's diet consisted of foods not considered to be desirable if you have colon cancer: greasy fast food hamburgers, soda drinks and licorice. I decided that I would make an intervention to try and help her. Over several weeks I sent Patty books on psychological healing and macrobiotic diet. When I visited her a month later, I was sitting in her living room and she went to another room and returned with the six books that I had sent her and handed them to me saying: "You know I just have too many books so I would like to give these back to you, so maybe you could use them with someone else." I realized at that point that my intervention to change her dietary habits had completely failed.

After I returned to San Francisco, I consulted with my friend and colleague Dr. Emily Girault. She had introduced me to psychological type. With her help, we analyzed the psychological type of Patty and my family. Here is what we decided:

Patty ESFP

Brian INFJ

Mother ENFJ

Father ISTJ

The difference in the psychological types of my family members is more clearly shown in a Psychological Type Map (see Figure 13.2).

Although Patty and I were both Feeling types, we were very opposite on the other dimensions. Patty was very outgoing, loved talking to strangers, and was generally talkative. I was very introverted, often preferring to communicate with others in writing or by email. Patty was a strong Sensing type, very accomplished at paying attention to detail. I was an Intuitive type, often not good at detail. Patty was a Perceiving type continually seeking other ways of doing things and not wanting to make quick decisions. I was a Judging type, preferring an organized lifestyle and quick decision-making. In David Keirsey's approach to temperament, Patty was an SP, what he called an Artisan. This is the personality type that particularly loves freedom and does not like to be constrained by rules or directives. I had always known that Patty and I had different personalities. I was the older brother who excelled at school and went to college and then entered an academic career. Patty graduated from high school, obtained a clerical job and rented a house in a rural area of Edmonton where she bought two horses and pursued her passion of riding and living a country lifestyle.

It was suddenly clear to me why my intervention with Patty had failed. I had used an Introvert approach (sending letters and books) with an Extravert who liked to talk directly with people. In addition, I recommended a specific remedy to an Artisan who did not like direction from her older brother. I described my sister's terrible diet to Dr. Girault since I believed it was impairing her health. I had also recently learned from Patty that her physicians had told her that the cancer had spread to her liver and that there was no further treatment they could offer. When I researched the mortality rate associated with liver cancer, I learned that many patients only lived approximately 4 months after diagnosis. I struggled with how I could be of more assistance to her.

Dr. Girault suggested that I return to Edmonton and spend time with Patty to have meals together in which I model eating healthy food but make no comments about diet, mine or hers. Dr. Girault's assessment was that because Patty was an Artisan (SP) she would feel controlled by an older brother who was a psychology professor giving her what appeared to be psychological advice. I did as she advised and returned to Edmonton. Over four weeks, I regularly had lunch and dinner with Patty. I began to eat a macrobiotic diet. It was very challenging for me to give up so many foods that I loved. I avoided any comment on our diets. On

Psychological Type Development 219

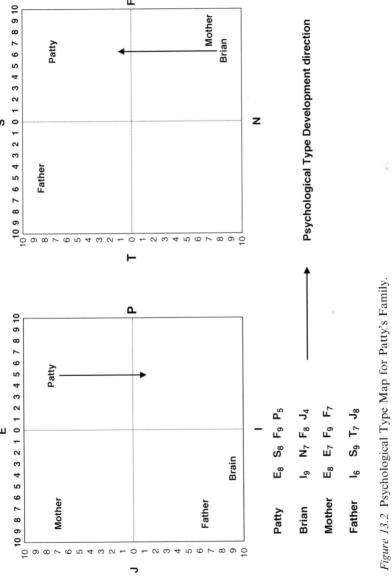

Figure 13.2 Psychological Type Map for Patty's Family.

one occasion she asked me to drive her to the grocery to buy her a case of soda. I honored her request and made no critical comment that I believed that type of drink was very bad for colon cancer. While I was in Edmonton, I also made an effort to encourage our parents to support Patty if she decided to change her diet. Because our mother was an Intuitive Feeling type, I gave her Dr. Anthony Sattilaro's book *Recalled by Life,* a very heartfelt personal account of how he was diagnosed with stage 4 bone cancer and cured himself by adopting a macrobiotic diet. Because our father was a Thinking type, I gave him a book titled *Doctors Look at Macrobiotics,* which presents medical research on the macrobiotic approach. Obviously, I was using an Introvert intervention approach (giving books), but I was selecting them now based on the reader's psychological type. I returned to San Francisco and refrained from sending Patty more books.

When I returned to Edmonton two months later, not only had Patty changed her diet along more macrobiotic lines, but also during my stay, she treated the family to a dinner at a vegetarian restaurant. I learned that Patty had begun seeing a therapist in order to maximize her psychological healing. And she began sending me books on psychological healing. I particularly remember when she sent me Louise Hay's book: *You Can Heal Your Life* which describes how Hay overcame cancer using positive thinking strategies. I was completely taken aback by these dramatic changes in Patty's behavior. What seems clear to me was that Patty had strengthened her Introversion side in pursuing reading about psychological healing and pursuing an introspective therapy approach. She survived 1 ½ years beyond her diagnosis of liver cancer after her physicians could not offer further medical treatment. I cannot say for certain whether Patty's living longer was due to her using macrobiotic and psychological healing approaches; nor was it clear whether my psychological type intervention was the critical factor, but when there was no other alternative, it was worth the try.

The next case study is a reprint of an article I (BG) published in the *Journal of Psychological Type (JPT).* The article describes a psychological type intervention I conducted to help a student deal with the discriminatory behaviors of a professor. Although the student and I were in a consultation relationship rather than a therapy relationship, the psychological type intervention principles described in this book apply. The article received the JPT's 2009 Award for Best Application of Psychological Type.

A Case Study Suggesting the Use of Psychological Type to Reduce Discrimination in Organizations*

This article examines how psychological type might aid administrators in reducing discrimination in organizations.

Abstract

This article presents a theoretical analysis of how the Myers-Briggs Type Indicator® (MBTI®) measure of psychological type may be used to reduce discrimination in organizations. A great strength of the type literature has been its emphasis on the positive contributions of all of the personality types. This article examines more closely the negative type characteristics that may challenge administrators and employees in dealing with discrimination and suggests some ways that the MBTI instrument can be used to overcome these challenges. A model emphasizing both the positive and negative aspects of each type characteristic is presented and applied to a case study.

In order for antidiscrimination legislation to be useful, it must be implemented at the organizational level. However, in order for that implementation to be effective, human relations skills are required. The administrative injunction, "Don't discriminate or you will be fired," delivered in subtle and not so subtle ways, may be effective in eliminating some of the more blatant forms of discrimination, but something more is needed to help organizations make the transition into environments in which all employees feel they belong. The central idea presented here is that an understanding of personality, as represented by psychological type, may be useful in promoting compliance with antidiscrimination legislation and in developing workplace environments in which everyone has a "voice."

---

*Reprinted with permission: Gerrard, B. (2007). A case study suggesting the use of psychological type to reduce discrimination in organizations. *Journal of Psychological type*, 68 (3), 19-27.

Note: For the Myers-Briggs Type Indicator® (MBTI®) instrument, the eight preference categories are the following: Extraversion (E) versus Introversion (I), Sensing (S) versus Intuition (N), Thinking (T) versus Feeling (F), Judging (J) versus Perceiving (P).

The Concept of Challenge in Psychological Type

In Gifts Differing, Myers and Myers (1995) discussed how each of the 16 psychological types is a "gift" and advocated the value of personality differences. Myers' positive, nonpejorative approach to personality accounts for much of the popularity of the psychological type model. In the MBTI measure of psychological type, personality is comprised of four pairs of opposite scales: Extraversion–Introversion, Sensing–Intuition,

Table 13.1 The Psychological Type Preferences with Examples of Strengths and Challenges

Psychological Type Preference	Strength	Challenge
Extraversion	E+ Socializing	E− Monopolizing
Introversion	I+ Contemplating	I− Withdrawing
Sensing	S+ Being realistic	S− Being overly focused on detail
Intuition	N+ Being visionary	N− Being absent-minded
Thinking	T+ Being tough-minded	T− Being overly critical
Feeling	F+ Harmonizing	F− Abdicating
Judging	J+ Organizing	J− Being rigid
Perceiving	P+ Being flexible	P− Being indecisive

Thinking–Feeling, and Judging–Perceiving. Each of these scales describes 8 mental functions or attitudes that can be expressed positively, as strengths, or negatively, as challenges. (See Table 13.1.) Inclusion of negative aspects of psychological type, uncommon in the MBTI literature, does have a tradition going back to Carl Jung, who made the following comments about the shadow side of personality:

> The shadow is a moral problem that challenges the whole ego-personality, for no one can become conscious of the shadow without considerable moral effort. To become conscious of it involves recognizing the dark aspects of the personality as present and real. This act is the essential condition for any kind of self-knowledge. (Jung, 1979, p. 872)

> Unfortunately, there can be no doubt that man is, on the whole, less good than he imagines himself or wants to be. Everyone carries a shadow, and the less it is embodied in the individual's conscious life, the blacker and denser it is. If an inferiority is conscious, one always has a chance to correct it. Furthermore, it is constantly in contact with other interests, so that it is continually subjected to modifications. But if it is repressed and isolated from consciousness, it never gets corrected. (Jung, 1970, p. 14)

More recently, Quenk (1993) has emphasized the value of examining the ways an individual's psychological type may be negatively expressed as she extensively describes the hidden or unfamiliar aspects of personality, also known as the inferior function. Hirsch and Kummerow (1989) discussed how each of the 16 types can "lose out" through negative behaviors. The purpose of identifying these negative behaviors or challenges that may arise from our unconscious is to link them to type characteristics that are less developed, bringing awareness of them to our conscious mind, and thereby facilitate personal type development.

Psychological Type and Discrimination

An assumption made in this paper is that some of the behaviors associated with discrimination represent psychological type challenges that may be converted to strengths. For example, a supervisor whose preference clarity index is clear or very clear for Sensing and Thinking would be expected to lack skills that reflect good type development related to Feeling and Intuition. This person may not be aware that his or her blunt language with an employee whose dominant function may be Feeling or Intuition could be experienced by the employee as discriminatory. Some of the traditional antidiscrimination interventions, such as being reprimanded, or sent for multicultural sensitivity training, may not work because those are not tailored to fit to the psychological type of the supervisor. This is where an MBTI-based approach may be particularly useful. The supervisor described above might be encouraged to develop his or her dominant and auxiliary function skills to assist with recognizing how to approach someone with a dominant Feeling preference. This might be done by coaching the supervisor about how to first point out something positive to an employee with a Feeling preference before criticizing that employee's work.

The supervisor might also be coached about how to distinguish between an employee's emotional expression or reaction (which may be conciliatory) from the employee's nonverbal behavior (e.g., folding of arms across chest). This would be an example of strengthening the supervisor's type development skills in relating to people with a dominant preference for Feeling or Intuition through instructions that emphasize use of the supervisor's dominant or auxiliary Sensing and Thinking functions. This type of intervention is focused on building strength, but it is used as a strength intended to remedy a weakness (i.e., bringing to consciousness his or her underdeveloped function).

Examples of ways in which the MBTI instrument might be used to understand discrimination and promote type development that reduces discrimination are shown in Tables 13.2 and 13.3. Table 13.2 gives examples of how the psychological types of administrators and employees may affect discrimination. Table 13.3 lists examples of type-based interventions an administrator might make with employees who engage in discrimination. The role of psychological type in discrimination and in the prevention of discrimination will be examined by focusing on three organizational roles: (1) the individual discriminated against; (2) the employee who discriminates; and (3) the administrator who is in a position to prevent discrimination.

Table 13.2 Examples of Psychological Type Strengths and Challenges Experienced by Administrators and Employees in Dealing with Discrimination

Type Preference	The Employee Being Discriminated Against	The Administrator
Extraversion		
Strength E+	Speaking out	Openly discussing discrimination
Challenge E−	Acting out	Patronizing those discriminated against
Introversion		
Strength I+	Reflecting on personal strengths	Reflecting on the negative impact
Challenge I−	Remaining silent about the discrimination	Failing to solicit feedback about the employee morale/discrimination
Sensing		
Strength S+	Recognizing a discriminatory act	Giving employees concrete guidelines; Documenting discriminatory acts
Challenge S−	Focusing on irrelevant details	Focusing on irrelevant details
Intuition		
Strength N+	Discerning a discriminatory attitude	Having a vision of the organization Empowering employees; discerning Subtle forms of discrimination
Challenge N−	Failing to notice a discriminatory act	Failing to notice a discriminatory act
Thinking		
Strength T+	Confronting someone who acts in a discriminatory manner	Confronting someone who acts in a discriminatory manner
Challenge T−	Persecuting those who act in a Discriminatory manner	Criticizing those who complain; modeling oppression by oppressing those who act discriminatory
Feeling		
Strength F+	Seeking personal support when discriminated against	Modeling caring, respectful behavior towards all employees; providing support to those discriminated against
Challenge F−	Avoiding confrontation	Being afraid to deal with an aggressive discriminatory employee
Judging		
Strength J+	Deciding to act swiftly to deal with discrimination	Implementing a plan to prevent discrimination
Challenge J−	Lacking the flexibility to change an ineffective response	Lacking the flexibility to change an ineffective plan

(*Continued*)

Table 13.2 (Continued)

Type Preference	The Employee Being Discriminated Against	The Administrator
Perceiving		
Strength P+	Problem-solving different solutions to prevent the discrimination	Problem-solving different solutions to prevent the discrimination
Challenge P−	Being paralyzed by uncertainty about how to address the discrimination	Giving others the impression that discrimination is tolerated because of indecisiveness about how to respond

Psychological Type and the Individual Discriminated Against

Table 13.2 illustrates some of the ways an individual's psychological type preferences may be a strength or a challenge in dealing with the effects of discrimination. It is my hypothesis that the two personality types most susceptible, and least susceptible, to being discriminated against are probably INFP and ESTJ, respectively.

The psychological type probably at the greatest risk in dealing with discrimination is INFP:

I− Remaining silent in the face of discrimination

N− Not noticing discriminating acts

F− Avoiding confrontation with the oppressor

P− Paralyzed by uncertainty

The psychological type that probably will deal with discrimination most effectively is ESTJ:

E+ Speaking out about the discrimination

S+ Recognizing a discriminatory act

T+ Confronting an oppressor

J+ Deciding to act swiftly

Personal growth in the type literature involves developing the non-preferred, or weaker, psychological type characteristics after the preferred

Table 13.3 Examples of Type-Based Interventions by Administrators with Employees Who Discriminate

Type Preference	Challenge for Employee Who Discriminates	Example of Type-Based Intervention by Administrator
Extraversion	E− Acting patronizing; dominating conversations	E+ Confronting Extraverts in a personal meeting (not through memo)
Introversion	I− Being unavailable to others; avoiding direct communication	I+ Giving Introverts time to reflect on the confrontation; encouraging Introverts to talk about their behavior
Sensing	S− Focusing on irrelevant details	S+ Presenting concrete examples of the discriminatory behavior
Intuition	N− Forgetting to do important things for others	N+ Helping Intuitives to see the connection between their attitude and their behavior
Thinking	T− Constantly criticizing; being Insensitive to other's feelings	T+ Coming straight to the point; focusing on negative organizational Impact instead of feelings
Feeling	F− Failing to stand up for others	F+ Letting Feeling types know they are valued; being aware the Feeling types may become defensive if criticized
Judging	J− Rigidly enforcing arbitrary decisions; never allowing exceptions	J+ Scheduling an appointment to discuss the discrimination; being organized in listing concerns and expectations; having a systematic approach for preventing discrimination
Perceiving	P− Being indecisive about how to help someone; failing to follow-through with a commitment	P+ Giving the employee alternate ways to improve his or her behavior

functions are strengthened. INFPs experiencing discrimination can empower themselves through four possible routes:

1. by being aware of their psychological type and how being challenged by an oppressor can cause them to "lose voice" and fail to access the sides of their personality (the E, S, T, J characteristics) best suited for dealing with "battle."

2. by consciously building on the positive sides of their preferred psychological type characteristics:

   I+ Reflecting on personal strengths
   N+ Intuiting a discriminatory act
   F+ Seeking personal support
   P+ Problem-solving different solutions

3. by working to strengthen their underdeveloped ESTJ sides (e.g., becoming more tough-minded).

4. by forming an alliance with advocates who can act on their behalf to perform ESTJ functions (e.g., T+, confronting an oppressor).

Psychological Type and the Individual Who Discriminates

One focus of the psychological type literature is on the importance of "talking to someone's type" (reference: Judy Allen FlexTalk and others) That is, if you want someone to see your point of view, you will have greater success if you present your ideas in a way that is consistent with that person's psychological type. For example, if you want to motivate Thinking types to do something, they will be more likely to do what you want if you appeal to logic rather than talk about how others will feel happier. Conversely, people with a Feeling preference are more likely to be open to your point of view if they believe you care about them (and they will be less likely to be moved by logical arguments).

Table 13.3 lists some ways that employees of different psychological types might be expected to engage in discrimination. Table 13.3 also illustrates how an administrator might use psychological type to deal with an employee who has acted in a discriminatory manner.

The goal of using a psychological type approach with persons who have engaged in discrimination is: (a) to motivate them to stop; and (b) to motivate them to develop a positive (rather than negative) relationship with persons they formerly discriminated against. This is in line with Freire's (1998) belief that in order to liberate persons and organizations, it is essential that the oppressors, as well as the oppressed, be liberated.

Psychological Type and the Administrator's Role in Preventing Discrimination

Table 13.2 describes how the administrator's psychological type might help or hinder the prevention of discrimination. Because of the importance of leaders in shaping organizational climate and group norms, the administrator's role in the prevention of discrimination is critical.

Two psychological types that are at greater risk for discriminatory behavior are the Thinking type (T−, might have a tendency to become overly critical) and the Judging type (J−, might have a tendency to become overly rigid). When people who have these psychological types discriminate, they do so openly and actively and perhaps with a sense of (misdirected) righteousness. However, the administrator who encourages discrimination through inaction, as may occur with an Introvert (I−, who might have a tendency to remain silent), the Feeling type.

(F−), who might have a tendency to avoid confrontation), or the Perceiving type (P−, who might have a tendency to be indecisive), can have an equally destructive effect on employees who are being discriminated against. A sin of omission is sometimes as destructive as a sin of commission. Fortunately, as shown in Tables 13.2 and 13.3, administrators of every psychological type may strengthen the positive aspects of their type to terminate discrimination and promote empowerment within their organizations.

Case Study: The Professor Who Would Not See

In the case study that follows, names and selected aspects of the case have been altered to provide confidentiality.

Beth (INFP) was a visually impaired graduate student in a social science course taught by Nathan (ESFJ). Nathan had taught this course several times and generally received good ratings from students. During the first class, Nathan acknowledged Beth's presence and said, "I'm really happy you are here. I once had a blind student in another class, and I wasn't sure if she was going to do well, but she did just great!" Beth reported that on hearing Nathan say this, she wanted to disappear.

During the second class, the class representative, Julie, told Beth that Nathan had said to her during the class break, "Beth's being here is making it difficult for me to teach the way I usually do. It is too time consuming and stressful to send materials for her Braille typing to the Disability Office." Julie stated that Beth had said she did not want to talk to Nathan about this, even with Julie present. Following this incident, Beth contacted the Disability Office at the University and complained about Nathan.

Beth began to feel that the class was perceiving her differently because of Nathan's behavior. Beth thought that she was becoming alienated from the class. To remedy this, she organized a pizza take-out dinner for the final class. When Nathan said in front of the class, "Beth, how are you keeping track of who paid for the take-out food?" Beth felt crushed. During that same class, Nathan also said he was thinking about changing the format for the final exam because it was "too expensive and too time consuming to use the usual exam format with Beth."

Following this class, Beth complained again to the Disability Office, which then contacted the faculty advisor/administrator (myself: INFJ).

I interviewed Beth, who told me she had experienced an unpleasant incident in every class so far with Nathan. With Beth's permission, I also interviewed the class representative as well as Nathan. I encouraged Beth to speak directly to Nathan about her concerns, as she had not yet done so. It was University policy that students first discuss their concerns with the individual professor and attempt to resolve the problem at that level. Because Beth was an Introverted Feeling type, she was especially reluctant to confront Nathan (because confrontation involves the use of Extraverted Thinking). I coached Beth about how to talk to someone with Nathan's psychological type preferences (ESFJ) by first pointing out something positive about the course, then giving concrete examples of what he had done that had upset her.

Beth called me a week later (following the last class) and reported that the class had gone well and that there were no further negative incidents with Nathan. She also reported that during her phone call to him he had listened to her complaints, but he had not apologized, and he spent a lot of time talking to Beth about how her childhood experiences were perhaps making her shy. Beth's conclusion was that "He just doesn't get it." She said that she felt "really bad" after talking to him. Nathan also called me following the last class and left me a message stating that he had had a conversation with Beth and that he thought it went "really well."

A psychological type analysis of this situation suggests the following: In the relationship with Beth, Nathan was exhibiting some typical negative characteristics of ESFJs.

> E— Nathan's attitude toward Beth was reported by the class representative as "benevolent." However, Nathan's statement in the first class reveals a clearly patronizing attitude toward Beth. A weakness of Extraverts is that they sometimes talk without listening, neglecting to use Introversion, and as a result not "hearing" what the other person is saying. This is what happened during the phone call with Beth.
>
> S— Nathan lacked the skills of those who have a preference for Intuition, and thus was unable to see that he was making Beth uncomfortable. When Beth showed typical Introverted Feeling behavior (i.e., to focus on the other person's point of view), Nathan didn't pick up on the cues that Beth was actually quite angry towards him.
>
> F— Another interpretation is that Nathan did pick up on some of Beth's "frustration" cues but chose not to focus on them. This can be typical of Feeling types who abhor conflict and will often go to great lengths to avoid confrontation.

J− Nathan found it difficult to change the way he taught his course (e.g., his exam format) to accommodate a visually challenged student. This type of behavior can be typical of Judging types who may lack the skills or experience with using their nonpreferred Perceiving attitude to use flexibility to adapt to change.

Beth's initial responses to Nathan showed some of typical characteristics of INFPs:

I− Beth was silent with Nathan about her frustration until encouraged to confront Nathan by her faculty advisor.

N+ Beth quickly discerned that Nathan "didn't get it."

F− Beth showed the typical Feeling type's aversion to confrontation by her statements to Julie that she did not want to tell Nathan she was unhappy with his treatment of her.

F+ Beth sought personal support from the Disability Office. She also built a greater connection with her classmates by organizing dinner for the final class. She began her telephone confrontation with Nathan with some positive statements about his course.

P− When I first spoke to Beth, she was feeling stuck and unable to come up with a plan of action to deal with Nathan. She wavered back and forth between "letting it go" and filing a formal complaint.

P+ One month after her class ended, Beth called me with several different ideas about how to raise the consciousness of faculty dealing with disabled students. Later that spring, I incorporated one of her ideas that involved having guest speakers give a seminar to faculty on disability culture.

T+ Being tough-minded is a quality that Beth prefers not to use in her relationships. However, the fact that she did call and complain to Nathan indicated that Beth had initiated type development. The fact that she had difficulty sustaining her confrontation when Nathan shifted the topic of conversation to Beth's childhood is a sign there is room for Beth to develop this quality further.

The faculty advisor/administrator also exhibited some typical qualities (strengths and challenges) of INFJs.

F− I found myself feeling reluctant to confront Nathan, and I delayed calling him for several days. When I did confront him, I softened the confrontation by referring to concerns the Disability Office (not I) had about liability.

T+ Although my own confrontation of Nathan was gentle, it was nevertheless a confrontation.

As is typical of Feeling types, I am better at confronting someone when doing so represents my supporting (i.e., using Feeling function) another person.

J+ When I reviewed with Beth how to confront Nathan, I emphasized the importance of her being organized and using a series of steps:

1. Leave a phone message to set up a telephone appointment.
2. Have the confrontation on a phone to create a "level playing field."
3. Begin with some positives to build support with Nathan as a Feeling type.
4. Keep the confrontation short (to avoid overloading both Feeling types–Nathan and Beth).
5. Give detailed examples of discriminatory incidents (as Nathan as a Sensing type needs specifics).

Three months later, Beth was doing well in her classes and reported she was getting along well with her classmates. Although further discrimination of Beth by Nathan appears to have been eliminated, there are type development issues that remain for Nathan, Beth, and me. All three of us are Feeling types with an inclination to avoid confrontation. I need to develop my tough-minded (T+) side further so I can be more direct and forceful in confronting insensitive instructors with the areas where they need to grow. Nathan needs to "see" that he hurt someone through being overly rigid (J−) and patronizing (E−). And, of the three of us, Beth, I think, showed the most type development in her courage to do something she had never done before—to use her tough-minded (T+) side and empower herself by speaking the truth to someone who had difficulty "hearing."

Discussion

The advantage of the psychological type model described above (focusing on both positive and negative characteristics) is that it suggests that we need to use "different strokes for different folks." Everyone is not the same, and this also applies to personality. By understanding how personality differences contribute to discrimination, and how these differences affect persons in different roles within an organization, we are more likely to be able to motivate ourselves and others to strengthen our skills and minimize our challenges in the pursuit of our "best selves."

The psychological type model applied to discriminatory behavior has a number of weaknesses. First, despite the popularity of the MBTI instrument, the model is complex and can take a long time to learn. Second,

232 *Psychological Type Development*

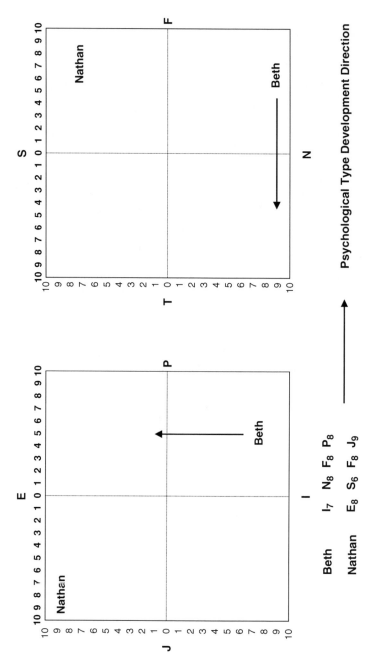

Figure 13.3 Psychological Type Map for Beth and Nathan.

this model has not yet been studied for its effectiveness in eliminating discrimination. Evidence to support its use is strictly anecdotal. Third, MBTI purists might argue that the above analysis is "reductionist", because psychological type mental functions or attitudes should not be considered in isolation from each other. That is, the combination of the four pairs of type characteristics has a synergistic effect, and this is being overlooked by an analysis that is too simplistic (Mitchell, 2001). Fourth, there are other psychological models that may be equally or more effective in reducing or eliminating discrimination, e.g., modeling, operant conditioning, multicultural counseling for empowerment, and family systems therapy that describes the formation of scapegoats.

References

Freire, P. (1998). *Pedagogy of the oppressed.* New York: Continuum.
Hirsch, S. K., & Kummerow, J. M. (1989). *Lifetypes.* New York: Warner Books.
Jung, C. G. (1970). *Psychology and religion: West and east. Volume 11 of Collected works of C. G.* Jung. Princeton, NJ: Princeton University Press.
Jung, C. G. (1979). *Aion: Researches into the phenomenology of the self. Volume 9, Part 2 of Collected works of C. G.* Jung. Princeton, NJ: Princeton University Press.
Mitchell, W. D. (2001). A full dynamic model of type. *Journal of Psychological Type,* 59, 12–28.
Quenk, N. L. (1993). *Beside ourselves: Our hidden personality in everyday life.* Palo Alto, CA: Davies-Black.

Postscript: It was some years later that the Psychological Type Map was developed. Figure 13.3 shows a Psychological Type Map for Beth and Nathan which more clearly reveals the differences in their type and the type development direction.

14 The Importance of Therapist Type Development

EVIDENCE-BASED SUPPORT FOR THERAPIST PSYCHOLOGICAL TYPE

Although mental health therapists are represented among all the 16 psychological types, there is evidence that the most frequent mental health practitioner types are Intuitive and Feeling types based on a wide variety of mental health professionals (see Box 14.1).

Myers, McCaulley, Quenk, and Hammer (2003) summarized this research as follows:

> Across all these studies, Intuition and Feeling tended to predominate. Occupations that require practitioners to deal with large numbers of people tended to have more Extraverts, and there were relatively more Sensing types in the occupations in which counseling is accompanied by more paperwork. Given that the majority of the population prefers Sensing, the fact that most counselors prefer Intuition creates a responsibility for counselors to learn methods for communicating with and treating Sensing type clients.
>
> ...Differences on other dichotomies also provide potentially useful information for therapists in understanding their own styles of doing therapy and insight into ways they can modify their style to better accommodate clients of different types. (p. 247)

The point made in the above quote cannot be emphasized enough. At some point every therapist will have a client whose personality will differ from that of the therapist. Given research that suggests that the theoretical orientation and techniques preferred by therapists are affected by the therapists' personality (Levin, 1978; Quenk & Quenk, 1996), it seems reasonable to ask therapists to consider whether some of their clients might benefit from a therapy approach that is more congruent with the clients' personality. For example, Jinkerson, Masilla, & Hawkins II (2015) found that clients who preferred the Thinking function showed greater benefit from cognitive therapy than clients who preferred Feeling.

DOI: 10.4324/9781003097167-14

Box 14.1 Research on Mental Health Practitioner Psychological Type

Beck, F. (1973). Affective sensitivity of counselor supervisors as a dimension of growth in their trainee groups (Doctoral dissertation, University of Southern California), *Dissertation Abstracts International*, 33, 3277A.

Braus, J. (1971). The empathic ability of psychotherapists as related to therapist perceptual flexibility and professional experience, patient insight, and therapist-patient similarity (Doctoral dissertation, Fordham University). *Dissertation Abstracts International*, 32, 2391B.

Casas, E. & Hamlet, J. (1984). *Les Types psychologiques des clients, des etudiants-conseillers et des superviseurs dans un Centre d'entrainement clinique: Etude sur la compatibility client-conseiller et l'apprentissage de la therapie.* Interim Report, CRSHC, Sunvention No. 410 834 0428, University of Ottawa, Canada.

Coan, R. (1979). *Psychologists: Personal and theoretical pathways.* Irvington.

Elliott, G. (1975). A descriptive study of characteristics and personality types of counselors of runaway youth. (Doctoral dissertation, University of Maryland). *Dissertation Abstracts International*, 36, 3119B–3120B.

Frederick, A. (1975). Self-actualization and personality type: A comparative study of doctoral majors in educational administration and the helping relations. (Doctoral dissertation, University of Alabama). *Dissertation Abstracts International*, 35, 7055A–7056A.

Galvin, M. (1976). Facilitative conditions and psychological type in intake interviews by professionals and paraprofessionals. (Doctoral dissertation, University of Florida). *Dissertation Abstracts International*, 36, 6378B.

Levell, J. (1965). Secondary school counselors: A study of differentiating characteristics (Doctoral dissertation, University of Oregon). *Dissertation Abstracts International*, 26, 4452.

Levin, L. (1978). Jungian personality variables of psychotherapists of five different theoretical orientations (Doctoral dissertation, Georgia State University), *Dissertation Abstracts International*, 39, 4042B–4043b.

McCaulley, M. H. (1977). *Application of the Myers-Briggs type indicator to medicine and other health professions. Prepared for the division of medicine, bureau of health manpower, health resources administration, U.S. Dept. of health, education and welfare.*

McCaulley, M. H. (1977). *The Myers longitudinal medical study. Monograph II. Final report.* Center for Applications of Psychological Type.

Newman, L. (1975). Counselor characteristics and training as related to the process of empathy and its manifestation (Doctoral dissertation, University of Florida). *Dissertation Abstracts International,* 37, 4138A–4139A.

Perry, H. (1975). Interrelationships among selected personality variables of psychologists and their professional orientation (Doctoral dissertation, Ohio State University). *Dissertation Abstracts International,* 44, (06), 1974B.

Quenk, N. & Quenk, A. (1996). Counseling and psychotherapy. In A.L. Hammer (Ed.), *MBTI applications: A decade of research on the Myers-Briggs Type Indicator* (pp 105–122). CPP, Inc.

Terrill, J. (1970). Correlates of counselor role perception (Doctoral dissertation, University of Colorado). *Dissertation Abstracts International,* 31, 166A.

Witzig, J. (1978). Jung's typology and classification of psychotherapies. *Journal of Analytical Psychology,* 23 (4), 315–331.

Consequences of Therapists Not Demonstrating Type Development

Successful therapist type development implies that while the therapist may have a preference for a type characteristic (e.g., Feeling) they also have developed their less preferred type characteristic (e.g., Thinking) to the point that they can use it effectively to help clients. The Dreyfus model of skill acquisition (Dreyfus & Dreyfus, 1988) describes five levels of competence:

Beginner

Advanced Beginner

Competent

Proficient

Expert

Therapists in training function typically at the Beginner and Advanced Beginner levels. However, when they graduate from university professional training programs, they are expected to function at a Competent level in a particular therapy approach (such as Cognitive Behavioral Therapy, Humanistic Therapy, or Family Therapy). As they gain professional experience under supervision and then go on to become licensed therapists, they ideally move to the higher levels of competence: Proficient and Expert.

A Personal Example: A few years into my (BG) career, when I considered myself Competent in Client-Centered Therapy, a Feeling approach to therapy that was very congruent with my psychological type (INFJ), I was doing a workshop demonstration of Active Listening with a volunteer from the audience. The volunteer was a medical resident who described an incident involving a mistake with a patient. My active listening response to them was: "You felt frightened because you thought you had harmed the patient." The medical resident denied they were frightened and then said very little else. I realized that my reflection of their underlying feeling was probably accurate, though premature and that I had erred in identifying that the medical resident was likely a Sensing Thinking type for whom my Intuitive Feeling response did not connect. In short, I had failed to take into account the medical resident's personality type and I was using a "one size fits all" approach to empathic listening. In retrospect, I realized that an empathy response that would probably have been better received would have been: "You were concerned that you had made a mistake with the patient." That is, I should have focused more on content rather than on emotion during this rapport building phase. About 1 year later, while doing a similar workshop on Active Listening, this time with correctional officers, my volunteer said: "Well, I was driving in my truck 2 weeks ago and it skidded off the road and ended upside down in the ditch." After this very short statement the officer stopped talking. Using my Intuition I visualized being upside down in my car in a ditch and I made my Active Listening response: "You thought you were about to die." "That's right" the officer said and I knew I had connected with someone who was a Thinking type.

You will see in this example my progression from Advanced Beginner to Competent because I took the volunteer's personality type into account. To do this I had to develop my Thinking side and use it to develop a deeper understanding of how Thinking types "feel" about what happens to them. The Dreyfus model implication for type development is this: it is natural for a therapist who is (say) a Feeling type to learn and become competent in a Feeling approach to therapy (such as Client-Centered Therapy). However, if that therapist is presented with a client who is a Thinking type and who might benefit more from a Thinking therapy approach (such as CBT), the therapist who has not developed their Thinking side will be likely to be functioning at a Beginner level in using a Thinking type therapy.

Ideally, then a therapist who has engaged in type development will be competent in using their less preferred functions to assist clients. Early in my career, I developed an INFJ approach to doing therapy because it "felt right." I studiously avoided doing group therapy because I (as a strong Introvert) did not feel comfortable in groups, particularly where several very talkative Extraverts were present. I had not developed my Extraversion to a level that would permit me to facilitate a group therapy session effectively. Over a 10 year period when I began doing family therapy with initially small, then larger families, I gradually became comfortable working with a group (family therapy may be viewed as a type of group therapy). Then when I finally did get around to doing group counseling with persons who had lost a loved one to cancer, I was surprised to learn that I was competent at it. With the passage of time I had developed my Extravert side and was now at ease managing group sessions even with many Extraverts present. I had become competent at doing an Extravert therapy approach (group counseling) through developing my Extravert side doing family counseling with small, then larger, families.

Particularly when doing family therapy, therapists are likely to encounter family members with very different personality types. To make friends with one member, you may have to talk a lot and reflect feelings; with another you may have to listen and ask questions. Being good at talking (Extraversion) and at listening (Introversion) requires one to have done type development involving both Extraversion and Introversion. Therapists who cannot do this may become Competent, Proficient or Expert in their "favorite" approach to therapy. The risk is that they will remain a Beginner should the client need a different therapy approach.

The Therapist Type Inventory

The Therapist Type Inventory is an educational tool for stimulating your thinking about how your psychological type affects how you prefer to work with clients. It has not been assessed for reliability or validity. We recommend you use it as a stimulus to help you reflect on your "favorite" approaches to therapy as well as reflect on the therapy approaches that would require you to undergo type development.

Therapist Type Inventory

Name:_____ Date:_____

Instructions: For each set of items listed below, circle the letter of the response (A or B) that most closely indicates the way you prefer to work as a therapist. Record all your responses on the Answer Sheet provided.

Do you prefer to:

1. A) Go with the "flow" of whatever comes up in the session, or
   B) Follow a treatment plan

2. A) Wait for clients who are vague to be more specific, or
   B) Encourage clients who are vague to be more specific

3. A) Work with clients who are friendly, or
   B) Work with clients who are intelligent

4. A) Listen passively for important themes, or
   B) Ask clients questions to determine the facts

5. A) Ask about what the client specifically did and said with others, or
   B) Reflect the client's underlying feeling involving others

6. A) Focus on what clients think about things, or
   B) Focus on what clients feel about things

7. A) Ask questions, or
   B) Listen passively

8. A) Let the client do most of the talking, or
   B) Talk as much, or almost as much, as the client

9. A) Form hypotheses about what the client is experiencing, or
   B) Have no preconceptions whatsoever about what the client is experiencing

10. A) Not use personality tests with clients, or
    B) Use personality tests with clients

11. A) Work in a therapist-centered fashion, or
    B) Work in a client-centered fashion

12. A) Identify clients' irrational beliefs, or
    B) Reflect clients' feelings

13. A) Help the client to be more creative, or
    B) Help the client to be more practical

14. A) Show a lot of warmth for clients, or
    B) Maintain a professional distance from clients

15. A) Diagnose clients' problems only after carefully gathering data over several sessions, or
    b) Tentatively diagnose client's problems swiftly

16. A) Use just a few techniques consistent with a particular theoretical approach, or
    B) Use a wide variety of techniques that come from different theoretical approaches

17. A) Not touch your clients, or
    B) Occasionally (appropriately) touch your clients

18. A) Work with clients in a spontaneous, unplanned fashion, or
    B) Work with clients in a systematic, step-by-step fashion

19. A) Focus your attention on specific emotions and experiences your client is clearly aware of, or
    B) Focus your attention on underlying feelings and experiences your client is only dimly aware of.

20. A) Introduce issues that you want your client to explore, or
    B) Let the client introduce issues to explore

21. A) Share personal things about yourself with clients, or
    B) Not share personal things about yourself with clients

22. A) Select a therapy technique because it feels right, or
    B) Select a therapy technique because there is a logical rationale for it

23. A) Carefully plan for your next session, or
    B) Not have any expectations for what should happen in a session

24. A) Promote client change as quickly as possible, or
    B) Take your time to thoroughly understand all aspects of your client's situation

25. A) Show the client that you understand his/her feelings, or
    B) Help the client to view his/her problem differently

26. A) Help clients be more aware of their feelings, or
    B) Help clients be more aware of their thoughts

27. A) Help clients to make effective decisions, or
    B) Help clients to become more flexible

28. A) Work at eliminating the client's symptom, or
    B) Work on underlying issues that seem to maintain the symptom

29. A) Not assign clients homework, or
    B) Assign clients homework

30. A) Make a tentative decision fairly quickly about the client's problem and try out an intervention, or
    B) Get as much information as you can about the problem even though this means waiting a while before making an intervention

31. A) Confront immediately clients who seem manipulative, or
    B) Wait a while before confronting clients who seem manipulative

32. A) Try a particular intervention because there is research support for it, or
    B) Try a particular intervention because it feels right

33. A) Reflect surface feelings that the client is aware of, or
    B) Reflect underlying feelings that you think the client needs to be aware of.

34. A) Confront clients who fail to complete homework assignments, or
    B) Work harder at building trust with clients who fail to complete homework assignments

35. A) Reflect back to your client what you think your client is feeling, or
    B) Just ask your client what the client is feeling

36. A) Help clients control their angry feelings, or
    B) Help clients express their angry feelings

37. A) Help clients to take action, or
    B) Help clients to consider alternatives

38. Do you sometimes get a mental image of your client that reveals something important to you about your client (e.g., image of your client as a "puppet").
    A) Often, or
    B) Rarely

39. Do you sometimes have trouble telling what your client is feeling?
    A) Yes, or
    B) No

40. Do you frequently get "gut feelings" about what your client is experiencing?
    A) Yes, or
    B) No

Answer Sheet for Therapist Type Inventory

Name:_____   Date:_____

1.	A	B	21.	A	B
2.	A	B	22.	A	B
3.	A	B	23.	A	B
4.	A	B	24.	A	B
5.	A	B	25.	A	B
6.	A	B	26.	A	B
7.	A	B	27.	A	B
8.	A	B	28.	A	B
9.	A	B	29.	A	B
10.	A	B	30.	A	B
11.	A	B	31.	A	B
12.	A	B	32.	A	B
13.	A	B	33.	A	B
14.	A	B	34.	A	B
15.	A	B	35.	A	B
16.	A	B	36.	A	B
17.	A	B	37.	A	B
18.	A	B	38.	A	B
19.	A	B	39.	A	B
20.	A	B	40.	A	B

242 *Therapist Type Development*

Scoring Key for Therapist Type Inventory

Instructions: Circle on this sheet the same items you circled on the Answer Sheet. Next, add up the total number of circled items for each Psychological Type dimension.

										Total
EXTRAVERSION										
2B	7A	8B	11A	20B	24A	25B	31A	33B	36B	E = ____
INTROVERSION										
2A	7B	8A	11B	20A	24B	25A	31B	33A	36A	I = ____
SENSING										
4B	5A	13B	15A	19A	28A	35B	38B	39B	40B	S = ____
INTUITION										
4A	5B	13A	15B	19B	28B	35A	38A	39A	40A	N = ____
THINKING										
3B	6A	12A	14B	17A	21B	22B	26B	32A	34A	T = ____
FEELING										
3A	6B	12B	14A	17B	21A	22A	26A	33B	34B	F = ____
JUDGING										
1B	9A	10B	16A	18B	23A	27A	29B	30A	37A	J = ____
PERCEIVING										
1A	9B	10A	16B	18A	24B	27B	29A	30B	37B	P = ____

Summary: Therapist Type: ___ ___ ___ ___

Opposite Therapist Type: ___ ___ ___ ___

Strategies for Promoting Therapist Type Development

- Are you an Introverted therapist who would like to be able to use more Extraverted therapy approaches like Family Therapy or Group Therapy?
- Are you an Extraverted therapist who would like to be able to listen more effectively or ask questions that stimulate clients to be more deeply introspective?
- Are you an Intuitive therapist who would like to learn to use detailed CBT techniques or to help clients develop more practical skills?
- Are you a Sensing therapist who would like to develop your intuition so that you can more accurately discern your client's underlying concerns?

- Are you a Feeling therapist who would like to learn how to confront clients when they act irresponsibly, or how to gently but firmly block family members who interrupt each other?
- Are you a Thinking therapist who would like to learn how to develop a stronger rapport with your clients?
- Are you a Judging therapist who would like to learn how to make spontaneous interventions during a session?
- Are you a Perceiving therapist who would like to learn how to give your client sessions more direction?

If you answered Yes to any of the above questions, you are a good candidate for therapist type development.
How do you do it?

Step 1 A starting point we recommend is for you to first be aware of (a) where your type strengths are as a therapist and (b) where your type challenges are. The combination of your type strengths and challenges will mean that you are likely to be more effective with certain clients (with psychological type "x"). There will be clients with a particular psychological type "y" that you would prefer to not work with. These may be persons whose psychological type is opposite to your own. Taking stock of all this is an excellent first step.

Step 2 If you are Competent, Proficient, or Expert in a particular therapy approach, we want you to keep doing that. However, if there is a therapy approach or technique that you believe would expand your ability to help your clients, but require you to "stretch" and develop an underdeveloped side of yourself, this deserves attention. We have written earlier of the Type Demand that therapy approaches and techniques have. For example, to use systematic desensitization, a behavior therapy technique that has very strong evidence-based support with over 60 years of research, the therapist needs to use Extraversion, Sensing, Thinking and Judging. Therapists who are Introverted, Intuitive, Feeling, Perceiving types and have not developed their ESTJ sides, will find this technique challenging to use, and yet it is a technique that can be particularly helpful to clients who are very anxious. Alternatively, Solution-Focused Therapy is a strength-based approach that may be very appealing to clients who do not want to be given a DSM label. However, the Solution-Focused approach requires the therapist to use an Introverted Sensing Feeling Perceiving approach. Therapists who are Extraverted Intuitive Thinking Judging types and have not developed their ISFP side, will find this approach challenging to use.

Step 3   This step requires that you conduct some research into the therapy approach that is "type opposite" for you, but which you believe could help you become a better, more versatile therapist.

Step 4   This involves learning the type opposite therapy approach keeping in mind the Dreyfus model. That is, when a therapist engages in type development, the therapist will typically move from Beginner, to Advanced Beginner, and then on to Competent, Proficient, and Expert. When developing your underdeveloped type function and the therapy techniques that connect to it, you may not reach Expert or Proficient (which you are more likely to do with your preferred type). However, if you reach Competent your clients will benefit when you use the "new" approach. Many of the therapy strategies described in this book can be used to promote therapist type development. For example, you could reward (i.e., reinforce) behavior that moves you one step at a time towards strengthening your underdeveloped type characteristic.

References

Dreyfus, H. & Dreyfus, S. (1988). *Mind Over Machine (Second Edition)*. Free Press.

Jinkerson, J., Masilla, A., Hawkins, R. C. II. (2015). Can Myers-Briggs dimensions predict therapy outcome? Differences in the thinking-feeling function pair in cognitive therapy for depression/anxiety. *Research in Psychotherapy: Psychopathology, Process and Outcome*, 18(1), 21–31.

Levin, L.S. (1978). Jungian personality variables of psychotherapists of five different theoretical orientations.(Doctoral dissertation, Georgia State University). Dissertation Abstracts International, 39, 4042B–4043B.

Myers, I., McCaulley, M., Quenk, N. and Hammer, A. (2003). *MBTI manual: A guide to the development and use of the Myers-Briggs type indicator*. CPP, Inc.

Quenk, N. L. & Quenk, A. T. (1996). Counseling and psychotherapy. In A. L. Hammer (Ed.) *MBTI applications: A decade of research on the Myers-Briggs Type Indicator*, CPP, Inc., 105–122.

Appendix 1: Psychological Type Sorter

Psychological Type Sorter

Instructions:

Step 1   Cut out the Psychological Type Sorter Headings shown as Table 15.1.

Table 15.1 Psychological Type Sorter Headings

VERY UNLIKE ME -3
MODERATELY UNLIKE ME -2
SLIGHTLY UNLIKE ME -1
SLIGHTLY LIKE ME +1
MODERATELY LIKE ME +2
VERY LIKE ME +3

Step 2 Cut out the Psychological Type Sorter Words shown as Table 15.2.

Table 15.2 Psychological Type Sorter Words

OUTGOING	E+	ENTHUSIASTIC	E+	TALKATIVE	E+
MONOPOLIZING	E -	IMPULSIVE	E -	OVER-TALKATIVE	E -
REFLECTIVE	I+	INTROSPECTIVE	I+	CONTEMPLATIVE	I+
RECLUSIVE	I -	SHY	I -	DETACHED	I -
PRACTICAL	S+	CONVENTIONAL	S+	FOCUSED ON DETAILS	S+
UNCREATIVE	S -	OVERLY CAUTIOUS	S -	NITPICKING	S -
ABSTRACT	N+	IMAGINATIVE	N+	SEES FUTURE POSSIBILITIES	N+
VAGUE	N -	UNREALISTIC	N -	FAILS TO DEAL WITH PRESENT REALITY	N -
LOGICAL	T+	RATIONAL	T+	TOUGH-MINDED	T+
UNFEELING	T -	ARGUMENTATIVE	T -	HARD-HEARTED	T -
TENDER-HEARTED	F+	SENSITIVE	F+	FORGIVING	F+
OVERLY SOFT-HEARTED	F -	OVERSENSITIVE	F -	AVOIDING CONFRONTATION	F -
ORGANIZED	J+	DECISIVE	J+	METHODICAL	J+
INFLEXIBLE	J-	CLOSED TO ALTERNATIVES	J-	UNCOMPROMISING	J-
FLEXIBLE	P+	SPONTANEOUS	P+	ADAPTABLE	P+
DISORGANIZED	P -	UNFOCUSED	P-	HESITANT	P-

Step 3 Arrange the Headings like this on a table:

Very Unlike Me	Moderately UnLike Me	Slightly Unlike Me	Slightly Like Me	Moderately Like Me	Very Like Me
-3	-2	-1	+1	+2	+3

Step 4 Take each PR Sorter word and place it under the heading that you feel best describes you. For example, if the word describes a characteristic that you believe is very like you, place it under Very Like Me. If the word describes a characteristic that is moderately unlike you, place it under Moderately Unlike Me. Place the words under whatever headings seem appropriate. Be sure to use all the words.

Step 5 Scoring
   To score the PT Sorter use the PT Sorter Scoresheet.

Psychological Type Sorter Scoresheet

Name:_____ Date:_____

Type Category	Slightly Like Me +1 N	Score	Moderately Like Me +2 N	Score	Very Like Me +3 N	Score	Total Score
Extraversion E							
Introversion I							
Sensing S							
Intuition N							
Thinking T							
Feeling F							
Judging J							
Perceiving P							

N = The total number of words for a specific type category listed unde the heading

Score = the weighted score calculated by multiplying the N (Number) of words x the +1, +2, or +3 "weight" listed in the Heading.

Example:

Type Category	Slightly Like Me +1 N	Score	Moderately Like Me +2 N	Score	Very Like Me +3 N	Score	Total Score
Extraversion E	2	2	1	2	2	6	10
Introversion I	0	0	2	4	0	0	4

A complete example is shown on the following page

Detailed Psychological Type Sorter Example

Very Unlike Me -3	Moderately UnLike Me -2	Slightly Unlike Me -1	Slightly Like Me +1	Moderately Like Me +2	Very Like Me +3
Outgoing E	Talkative E	Stubborn S	Detailed S	Objective T	Friendly F
Loud E	Rigid J		Concrete S	Rational T	Listening I
Nitpicking S	Inflexible J		Organized J	Shy I	Compassionate F
Blunt T	Indecisive P		Spontaneous P	Withdrawn I	Visionary N
Critical T				Forgetful N	Intuitive N
Monopolizing E				Decisive J	Contemplative I
Disorganized P				Easily Hurt F	Flexible P
					Absent-minded N
					Avoids conflict F

Type Category	Slightly Like Me +1 N	Score	Moderately Like Me +2 N	Score	Very Like Me +3 N	Score	Total Score
Extraversion E	0	0	0	0	0	0	0
Introversion I	0	0	1	2	2	6	8
Sensing S	2	2	0	0	0	0	2
Intuition N	0	0	2	4	2	6	10
Thinking T	0	0	2	4	0	0	4
Feeling F	0	0	1	2	3	9	11
Judging J	1	1	2	4	0	0	5
Perceiving P	1	1	0	0	1	3	4

N = The total number of words for a specific type category listed under the heading

Summary:
I8 N10 F11 J5

Note: The Psychological Type Sorter has not yet been evaluated for reliability and validity. It is included here for educational purposes. It's utility seems to lie in the fact that one's responses are all laid out and visible at one time. For instance, in the example shown above, which is for myself (BG), the "like me" words clearly are consistent with my MBTI scores as an INFJ. However, the challenge side of my personality is also evident (I-, N-, F-). In the "Most unlike me" sector are the psychological type characteristics I normally find challenging to deal with in others (E-, S-, T-, P-).

Appendix 2: The Psychological Type Dictionary: A Computer Content Analysis Approach to Measuring Psychological Type Themes in Text

Content Analysis

Content analysis is a quantitative reseach approach for analyzing the frequency with which particluar themes occur in text. A concise definition is offered by Wikipedia:

> Content analysis is a research method for studying communication artifacts. Social scientists use content analysis to quantify patterns in communication. Practices and philosophies of content analysis vary between scholarly communities. They all involve systematic reading or observation of texts or artifacts which are assigned labels (sometimes called codes) to indicate the presence of interesting, meaningful patterns [1] [2]. After labeling a large set of texts, a researcher is able to statistically estimate the proportions of patterns in the texts, as well as correlations between patterns. (https://en.wikipedia.org/wiki/Content_analysis)

Content analysis involves the counting of words and phrases that indicate the presence of larger themes. Table 16.1 illustrates this for the eight Psychological type characteristics.

As can be seen in this table, there are three words/phrases listed for each Psychological Type theme (or characteristic). These words/phrases are designed to reveal the presence of a particular Psychological Type theme withing a text.

Example:

The text: She was a very reflective person who was always quiet in groups. However, if someone needed help she was supportive and showed caring behavior. For anyone who had a problem she was good at coming up with a flexible alternative.

The content analysed text:

She was a very **reflective** person who was always **quiet** in groups. However, if someone needed help she was supportive and showed caring behavior. For anyone who had a problem she was good at coming up with a *flexible alternative*.

250 *Appendix 2*

Table 16.1 Words and Phrases that Indicate Psychological Type Themes

Psychological Type Theme	Sample Words and Phrases
INTROVERSION	reflective, quiet, withdrawn
EXTRAVERSION	outgoing, talkative, venturesome
SENSING	detailed, concrete, down to earth
INTUITION	visionary, ideal, imaginative
THINKING	rational, tough-minded, blunt
FEELING	harmonious, caring, supportive
JUDGING	organized, decided, scheduled
PERCEIVING	possibilities, flexible, alternatives

Content analysis score:

	n
INTROVERSION (I)	2
FEELING (F)	2
PERCEIVING (P)	2
Psychological Type theme:	IFP

Computer Content Analysis

Computer content analysis (CCA) uses a computer to conduct the analysis of words (themes) in text.

Figure 16.1 Illustrates how this is done.

Computer content analysis (CCA) has several advantages:

1. When it is not possible to administer a standardized psychological test like the Myers-Briggs Type Indicator (MBTI) or the Murphy-Meisgeier Type Indicator for Children (MMTIC), a text description of a person can be analyzed by using CCA.
2. Large amounts of text that would take hours to code manually can be coded in less than a second.
3. Because CCA coding on the same text is always the same, the reliability is perfect (r = 1.00). From a methodological point of view this is an important strength. There is no need to train coders to test inter-rater or intra-rater reliability.
4. CCA software programs (such as QDA Miner and Wordstat) allow the formation of complex rules that facilitate sophisticated text analysis (for example, the handling of negations: "He is friendly" is very different from "He is not friendly.").

Appendix 2 251

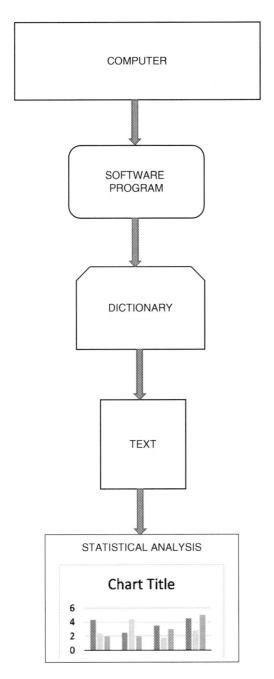

Figure 16.1 Computer Content Analysis Flow Chart.

	FREQUENCY	% SHOWN	% PROCESSED	% TOTAL	NO. CASES	% CASES	TF • IDF
FEELING	22	18.33%	2.33%	2.33%	1	100.00%	0.0
NF_IDEALIST_WORDS	21	17.50%	2.23%	2.23%	1	100.00%	0.0
INTUITION	17	14.17%	1.80%	1.80%	1	100.00%	0.0
INTROVERSION	11	9.17%	1.17%	1.17%	1	100.00%	0.0
THINKING	11	9.17%	1.17%	1.17%	1	100.00%	0.0
PERCEIVING	9	7.50%	0.95%	0.95%	1	100.00%	0.0
NT_RATIONAL_WORDS	7	5.83%	0.74%	0.74%	1	100.00%	0.0
SENSING	7	5.83%	0.74%	0.74%	1	100.00%	0.0
JUDGING	6	5.00%	0.64%	0.64%	1	100.00%	0.0
SJ_GUARDIAN_WORDS	4	3.33%	0.42%	0.42%	1	100.00%	0.0
SP_ARTISAN_WORDS	3	2.50%	0.32%	0.32%	1	100.00%	0.0
EXTRAVERSION	2	1.67%	0.21%	0.21%	1	100.00%	0.0

Figure 16.2 Psychological Type Dictionary Analysis of an INFP Profile.

The Psychological Type Dictionary

The Psychological Type Dictionary (PTD) is a 2000+ word dictionary containing words and phrases that measure the presence of themes related to the eight psychological type characteristics: Introversion, Extraversion, Sensing, Intuition, Thinking, Feeling, Judging, Perceiving. The PTD was constructed using the following steps:

1. A manual content analysis was conducted of psychological type profiles in the books *Gifts Differing* (Myers & Myers, 2010) and *Please Understand Me: Character and Temperament Types* (Keirsey & Bates, 1984). This produced lists of basic words and phrases that seemed unique to each psychological type category.
2. This basic list was expanded using an online thesaurus to 2177 words/phrases.
3. A validity panel of three experts in psychological type rated the words and phrases on a scale measuring the likelihood that a particular word or phrase described someone who was Introverted, Extraverted, etc. Ratings were made using the scale: Very Likely, Moderately Likely, Slightly Likely, Not At All Likely. Words/phrases rated Not At All Likely were removed if at least two persons

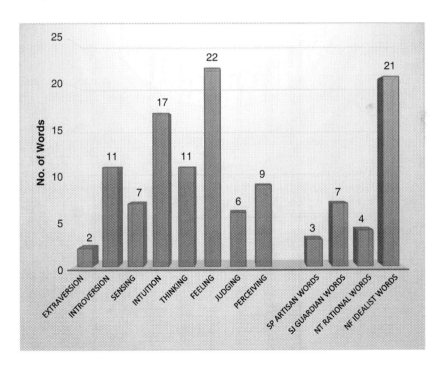

Figure 16.3 Bar Chart for INFP Scores in Figure 16.2.

made that rating. Because of considerable variation of raters within the "likely" categories, all words/phrases that received any likely rating were retained.
4. The PTD is currently in a disambiguation phase. Dictionary refinement is currently occurring through the application of the PTD to psychological type profiles in books and internet sites. A keyword in context analysis is conducted to identify and correct words/phrases that are miscoded.
5. When the PTD disambiguation phase is complete, a validity study will be conducted to determine the accuracy of the PTD in classifying psychological type profiles.

A sample print out for the PTD when applied to the Please Understand Me profile of an INFP is shown as Figures 16.2 and 16.3.

Resources

Babbie, E. R. (2020). *The practice of social research.* Cengage AU.
The chapter on Unobtrusive Measures provides concrete examples of how to use content analysis as a research tool.
Stone, P. J., Dunphy, D. C., Smith, M. S., & Ogilvie, D. M. (1966). *General inquirer: A computer approach to content analysis.* M.I.T. Press.
This is the classic text on computer content analysis and essential reading for anyone interested in developing and using content analysis dictionaries.
https://provalisresearch.com
Provalis Research is a content analysis and text mining software company that provides Wordstat and QDA Miner. WordStat is used for quantitative analysis of text in conjunction with the qualitative data analysis software QDA Miner. The Psychological Type Dictionary (PTD) was developed using these easy to use content analysis software programs.

References

Keirsey, D., & Bates, M. M. (1984). *Please understand me: Character & temperament types.* B & D Books.
Myers, I., & Myers, P. (2010). *Gifts differing: Understanding personality type.* Nicholas Brealey.

Appendix 3: PTRI Case Example

Psychological Type Relationship Inventory

Name of Rater (Self): ____*Alexis*____

Name of the Other Person: __*Blair*____

Date: ____*Jan 5*____

Instructions: This inventory is designed to collect information on how you perceive your relationship with a specific person. On the next two pages are lists of adjectives/phrases that describe different ways a person can behave in a relationship.

In Part 1 you rate your behavior towards the Other Person in the relationship.

In Part 2 you rate the Other Person's behavior towards you in the relationship.

Part 1 and Part 2 together provide a picture of how you perceive the Other Person and yourself behaving towards each other in the relationship. This information can be used to get a better idea of the areas of strength in your relationship and any areas in which you would like to see an improvement.

Part 1: As you read down the lists, check any adjectives/phrases that describe how **you** typically behave towards the Other Person.

Part 2: As you read down the lists, check any adjectives/phrases that describe how the **Other Person** typically behaves towards you.

PTRI Case Example

PART 1. SELF RATING: Rate **yourself** as you currently behave with _____Blair_____ (Other Person).   2A

A	B	C	D
___ intruding	___ initiating	_X_ receptive	___ withdrawn
___ monopolizing	___ outgoing	_X_ reflective	___ reclusive
___ domineering	___ assertive	___ observing	_X_ submissive
___ overinvolved	___ company-seeking	_X_ privacy-seeking	___ uninvolved
___ over-talkative	___ talkative	_X_ quiet	___ close-mouthed
___ over-expressive	___ expressive	_X_ reserved	___ inhibited
___ impetuous	_X_ passionate	_X_ tranquil	___ unresponsive
___ excitable	___ enthusiastic	_X_ calm	___ detached
___ overbold	___ bold	___ contemplative	_X_ timid
___ impulsive	___ venturesome	_X_ introspective	_X_ shy
0 Total	**1** Total	**8** Total	**3** Total

E	F	G	H
___ unimaginative	_X_ realistic	_X_ imaginative	___ unrealistic
___ trite	___ practical	___ inventive	___ impractical
___ obsessive	___ precise	_X_ abstract	___ vague
___ nitpicking	___ focused on details	_X_ focused on ideas	_X_ absent-minded
___ hairsplitting	___ factual	_X_ creative	_X_ forgetful
___ unoriginal	___ traditional	___ original	___ eccentric
___ banal	___ conventional	_X_ ingenious	___ odd
___ trite	___ conservative	_X_ novel	___ peculiar
___ fails to see future possibilities	_X_ deals with present reality	_X_ sees future possibilities	___ fails to deal with present reality
0 Total	**2** Total	**7** Total	**2** Total

PTRI Case Example   257

PART 1. SELF RATING: Rate **yourself** as you currently behave with ___Blair___ (Other Person). 2B

I	J	K	L
___ impersonal	___ logical	_X_ personal	___ illogical
___ deciding without compassion	___ deciding with objectivity	_X_ deciding with compassion	___ deciding without objectivity
___ unfeeling	___ rational	_X_ emotional	___ irrational
___ indifferent	___ objective	_X_ sympathetic	___ unreasonable
___ insensitive	___ tough	_X_ sensitive	_X_ oversensitive
___ hard-hearted	___ tough-minded	_X_ tender-hearted	_X_ overly soft-hearted
___ argumentative	___ disagreeing	_X_ agreeing	_X_ placating
___ intolerant	___ critical	_X_ tolerant	___ glossing over
___ rebuking	___ criticizing	_X_ praising	___ whitewashing
___ punishing	___ confronting	_X_ forgiving	_X_ avoiding
_0_ Total	_0_ Total	_10_ Total	_4_ Total

M	N	O	P
___ inflexible	___ organized	_X_ flexible	_X_ disorganized
___ rigid	___ focused	_X_ spontaneous	_X_ unfocused
___ unbending	___ systematic	_X_ improvising	___ unsystematic
___ has difficulty modifying plans	___ sticks to plans	_X_ open to changing plans	_X_ has difficulty sticking to plans
___ unmovable	___ prepared	___ impromptu	___ unprepared
___ closed to alternatives	___ decisive	_X_ open to alternatives	_X_ indecisive
___ unchangeable	___ certain	___ changeable	_X_ uncertain
___ stubborn	___ determined	_X_ adaptable	_X_ hesitant
___ unmodifiable	___ decided	_X_ searching	_X_ unsure
___ uncompromising	___ methodical	___ seeking	_X_ wavering
_0_ Total	_0_ Total	_7_ Total	_8_ Total

258   PTRI Case Example

PART 2. OTHER RATING: Rate __Blair__ (the Other Person) as she/he currently behaves with you.   3A

A	B	C	D
___ intruding	_X_ initiating	___ receptive	___ withdrawn
_X_ monopolizing	_X_ outgoing	___ reflective	___ reclusive
_X_ domineering	_X_ assertive	___ observing	___ submissive
___ overinvolved	_X_ company-seeking	___ privacy-seeking	___ uninvolved
___ over-talkative	_X_ talkative	___ quiet	___ close-mouthed
___ over-expressive	_X_ expressive	___ reserved	___ inhibited
___ impetuous	___ passionate	___ tranquil	___ unresponsive
___ excitable	_X_ enthusiastic	___ calm	___ detached
___ overbold	_X_ bold	___ contemplative	___ timid
___ impulsive	_X_ venturesome	___ introspective	___ shy
2 Total	**9** Total	**0** Total	**0** Total

E	F	G	H
___ unimaginative	_X_ realistic	___ imaginative	___ unrealistic
___ trite	_X_ practical	___ inventive	___ impractical
___ obsessive	_X_ precise	___ abstract	___ vague
_X_ nitpicking	_X_ focused on details	___ focused on ideas	___ absent-minded
_X_ hairsplitting	_X_ factual	___ creative	___ forgetful
___ unoriginal	___ traditional	___ original	___ eccentric
___ banal	_X_ conventional	___ ingenious	___ odd
___ trite	_X_ conservative	___ novel	___ peculiar
_X_ fails to see future possibilities	_X_ deals with present reality	___ sees future possibilities	___ fails to deal with present reality
3 Total	**9** Total	**0** Total	**0** Total

PTRI Case Example   259

PART 2. OTHER RATING: Rate _Blair_____ (the Other Person) as she/he currently behaves with you.   3B

I	J	K	L
_X_ impersonal	_X_ logical	___ personal	___ illogical
_X_ deciding without compassion	_X_ deciding with objectivity	___ deciding with compassion	___ deciding without objectivity
_X_ unfeeling	_X_ rational	___ emotional	___ irrational
___ indifferent	_X_ objective	___ sympathetic	___ unreasonable
_X_ insensitive	___ tough	___ sensitive	___ oversensitive
___ hard-hearted	_X_ tough-minded	___ tender-hearted	___ overly soft-hearted
_X_ argumentative	_X_ disagreeing	___ agreeing	___ placating
_X_ intolerant	_X_ critical	___ tolerant	___ glossing over
_X_ rebuking	_X_ criticizing	___ praising	___ whitewashing
___ punishing	_X_ confronting	___ forgiving	___ avoiding
_6_ Total	_9_ Total	_0_ Total	_0_ Total

M	N	O	P
___ inflexible	_X_ organized	___ flexible	___ disorganized
___ rigid	_X_ focused	___ spontaneous	___ unfocused
___ unbending	_X_ systematic	___ improvising	___ unsystematic
_X_ has difficulty modifying plans	_X_ sticks to plans	___ open to changing plans	___ has difficulty sticking to plans
___ unmovable	___ prepared	___ impromptu	___ unprepared
___ closed to alternatives	_X_ decisive	___ open to alternatives	___ indecisive
___ unchangeable	_X_ certain	___ changeable	___ uncertain
_X_ stubborn	_X_ determined	___ adaptable	___ hesitant
___ unmodifiable	_X_ decided	___ searching	___ unsure
___ uncompromising	_X_ methodical	___ seeking	___ wavering
_2_ Total	_9_ Total	_0_ Total	_0_ Total

Scoring Sheet for Psychological Type Relationship Inventory

Scoring Instructions Part 1:
Step 1: On pages 2A, 2B, 3A and 3B total up the number of words/phrases you checked in each column.

Step 2: Transfer these totals to the sheet below.

Score Category	Score for: Self	Score for: Other	Type Symbol	Type Category	Colloquial Name
A	0	2	E-	Extraversion Challenge	Monopolizing
B	1	9	E+	Extraversion Strength	Socializing
C	8	0	I+	Introversion Strength	Contemplating
D	3	0	I-	Introversion Challenge	Withdrawing
E	0	3	S-	Sensing Challenge	Nitpicking
F	2	8	S+	Sensing Strength	Being Realistic
G	7	0	N+	Intuition Strength	Being Visionary
H	2	0	N-	Intuition Challenge	Being Absent-Minded
I	0	6	T-	Thinking Challenge	Being Critical
J	0	9	T+	Thinking Strength	Being Objective
K	10	0	F+	Feeling Strength	Being Harmonious
L	4	0	F-	Feeling Challenge	Abdicating
M	0	2	J-	Judging Challenge	Being Autocratic
N	0	9	J+	Judging Strength	Organizing
O	7	0	P+	Perceiving Strength	Being Flexible
P	8	0	P-	Perceiving Challenge	Hesitating

PTRI Case Example

Scoring Instructions Part 2: Transfer the scores from Part 1 to this page. To calculate overall E/I, S/N, T/F, and J/P scores within each pair making up a type continuum subtract the smaller score from the larger. For example, if Total Extraversion = 8 and Total Introversion = 2, the E/I score is 8 – 2 = 6 (on Extraversion). If Total Extraversion = 2 and Total Introversion = 8, then the E/I score is 8 – 2 = 6 (on Introversion). * Note preference direction (e.g., E or I).

Score Category	Score for: Self	Other	Type Symbol	Type Category
A + B	1	11	E	Total Extraversion
C + D	11	0	I	Total Introversion
Subtract	11 *I**	11 *E**	E/I	**Extraversion/Introversion score**
E + F	2	11	S	Total Sensing
G + H	9	0	N	Total Intuition
Subtract	7 *N**	11 *S**	S/N	**Sensing/Intuition score**
I + J	0	15	T	Total Thinking
K + L	14	0	F	Total Feeling
Subtract	14 *F**	15 *T**	T/F	**Thinking/Feeling score**
M + N	0	11	J	Total Judging
O + P	15	0	P	Total Perceiving
Subtract	15 *P**	11 *J**	J/P	**Judging/Perceiving score**

Summary: Psychological Type expressed in this relationship

Self: _I_ _N_ _F_ _P_

Other: _E_ _S_ _T_ _J_

PSYCHOLOGICAL TYPE RELATIONSHIP INVENTORY: SUMMARY SCALE

Names:
SELF (S): __Alexis__   OTHER (O): __Blair__

Instructions: Using the scores from Part 2 and **S** for Self and **O** for Other Person, label where each of you is on the scale below.

EXTRAVERSION ———O————————S———— INTROVERSION
20 18 16 14 12 10 8 6 4 2 0 2 4 6 8 10 12 14 16 18 20

SENSING ———O————————S———— INTUITION
20 18 16 14 12 10 8 6 4 2 0 2 4 6 8 10 12 14 16 18 20

THINKING ———O———————————S——— FEELING
20 18 16 14 12 10 8 6 4 2 0 2 4 6 8 10 12 14 16 18 20

JUDGING ———O——————————————S—— PERCEIVING
20 18 16 14 12 10 8 6 4 2 0 2 4 6 8 10 12 14 16 18 20

Psychological Type: * SELF __I__ __N__ __F__ __P__

** Score: __10__ __7__ __14__ __15__

* OTHER __E__ __S__ __T__ __J__

**Score: __11__ __11__ __15__ __11__

*Show letters here, e.g. E, I, etc.
** Show actual score here.

PTRI Case Example 263

PTRI Bar Graphs for Strengths and Challenges 7

Instructions: Use this page to develop bar graphs for comparing strengths and challenges.

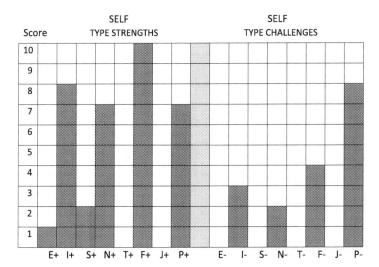

Self Strengths: _I_ _N_ _F_ _P_   Self Challenges: __ __ _F_ _P_

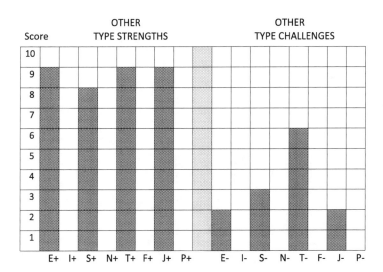

Other Strengths: _E_ _S_ _T_ _J_   Other Challenges: __ _S_ _T_ __

Appendix 4: Psychological Type Map

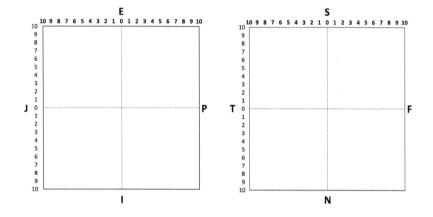

Index

Active Listening 23, 77–81, 103, 120, 181, 237
Assertion Training 122

Behavior Rehearsal 122–129
Big Five 14
Blocking Directives 68, 70–73, 81–83, 134–135

Caring Days 85, 100–103, 153, 186
Charting 87–91, 120
Cognitive Restructuring 13, 51, 72, 104, 109, 112, 137, 153, 162, 169, 186
Computer Content Analysis 249–251, 254; Reliability 250
Contracting 164

Decision Grid 85, 154–161, 170–175
Doubling 143, 145–147
DSM 8–10, 20–21, 243; Reliability 20

Educators 115, 194, 199, 201, 205
Empty Chair Technique 72, 103, 130–133, 169

Family Sculpting 51, 85, 153, 179–186

Group Social Skills Training 73–74
Guided Visualization 112–115, 137

Humanmetrics Jung Typology Test 16, 41

Ignoring 164–168
Imagery Meditation 112–116
Intentional Dialog 143–147
In Vivo Desensitization 43, 45, 61

Jung 1–8, 14–16, 19–20, 23–25, 35–39, 222, 235

Keirsey Temperament Sorter II 16, 19, 25, 41; Validity 16, 20

Method III Problem Solving 103, 116, 118
Miracle Question 51, 72, 103, 121, 175–179
Multimodal Assessment 93, 120
Murphy-Meisgeier Type Indicator for Children (MMTIC) 15–16, 188, 208, 210, 250
Myers-Briggs Type Indicator (MBTI) 1, 4, 7, 10–16, 19, 25–38, 41, 187–188, 210, 216, 221–223, 244, 248, 250; Reliability 7, 11, 14, 20; Validity 7, 12, 14

Narrative Therapy 62–63, 65, 67–68, 72, 137, 186

Ordeal Therapy 85, 103, 139, 143, 169, 186

Paradoxical Intention 120, 161–164
Positive Reinforcement 50, 72, 76, 85, 87–88, 126, 137, 139, 164–167, 194
Psychological Type Dictionary 19, 249–254; Validity 19, 253–254
Psychological Type Relationship Inventory 25–26, 35, 41, 255; Reliability 25
Psychological Type Relationship Scale (PTRS) 16–17, 25, 41, 44–45; Reliability 18

Staging an Enactment 68, 70–72
Systematic Desensitization 13, 20, 51, 53–57, 61, 137, 243

Talking Stick Exercise 81–86, 186
Temperaments 7, 8

Two Question Rule 73–74, 76, 80
Type Development 1, 4, 18, 22, 23–25, 38–40, 46, 183, 187, 209, 213, 223, 230–233, 236–238, 242–244

Unbalancing 81–85, 134–137, 186

Printed in the United States
by Baker & Taylor Publisher Services